THE LOVERS' GUIDE ILLUSTRATED ENCYCLOPEDIA

THE DEFINITIVE GUIDE TO SEX AND YOU

Consultant Editor
DOREEN E MASSEY, MA

Editor 2nd Edition
DR CHRIS F FARIELLO, PhD MA LMFT

Contributing Editor
ROBERT PAGE, MA

LIFETIME PUBLISHING

THE LOVERS' GUIDE ILLUSTRATED ENCYCLOPEDIA

First published as The Lovers' Guide Encyclopedia 1996 by
Bloomsbury Publishing Plc, 38 Soho Square, London W1V 5DF

Consultant Editor: Doreen E. Massey MA
Editor 2nd Edition: Dr. Chris Fariello PhD MA LMFT
Contributing Editor and Project Director: Robert Page MA
Original Writer and Researcher: Olivia Preston
Author of 'Sex and You': Elizabeth Fenwick
Author of 'Sex Through the Ages': Reay Tannahill
Picture Editor and Researcher: Liz Boggis
Original Art Direction: Simon Jennings
Photo work, graphics and illustrations 2nd Edition: Christopher Page

Edited, designed and typeset by Bookshaker

The Lovers' Guide is a trademark of Lifetime Vision Limited

For copyright © in individual illustrations and photographs see picture credits

ISBN: 978 1 78133 004 3

A CIP catalogue record for this book is available from the British Library

Dr. Chris Fariello PhD MA LMFT
*This book is dedicated to my mother, Marge Fariello. I can't imagine a
better role model for all of life's wonderful pleasures. Your passion and
dedication has been a continuous driving force in my life.*

*I would like to give special thanks to my girlfriend Renata and my kids
Julianna, Luca and Selina who continue to be my inspiration in everything
I do. I would also like to extend heartfelt gratitude to Robert Page for his
dedication, fortitude and passion to this project.*

Doreen E. Massey MA
*I dedicate this work to my family: husband Les, and children Lizzie,
Owen and Ben. They are my constant inspiration and support.*

*I want to thank Robert Page for his courage and vision in presenting
sexuality as a vital part of human existence.*

CONTENTS

Advisory Committee

Professor Milton Diamond, Professor of Anatomy and Reproductive Biology, sex educator and researcher, University of Hawaii, John A Burns School of Medicine, Pacific Centre for Sex and Society; author of *Sexwatching* (Consulted on 'Sex and Culture').

Hazel Slavin, Principal lecturer in Health Studies, South Bank University, London: sex therapist ('Sexual Attraction', 'Making Love', 'Sexual Practices' and 'Sexuality').

Professor Michael Adler, Professor of Genitourinary Medicine (Sexually Transmitted Diseases), University College London Medical School, and author of *The ABC of Sexually Transmitted Diseases* and over 200 papers and articles on STDs and AIDS ('Health and Hygiene').

Dr. Lars-Gosta Dahlof, Associate Professor in Psychology and Sexology, Goteborg University, Sweden; main author of *Sexology for Swedish National Encyclopedia* ('Sexual Attraction' and 'Sexual Practices').

Harriett Gilbert, writer and broadcaster; author of *A Woman's History of Sex* and editor of *The Sexual Imagination* ('Sex and Culture').

Tricia Kreitman, psychosexual counsellor, advice columnist for *MIZZ* and *Chat* magazines, director of Brook Advisory Centres ('Growth and Change' and 'Sexual Learning').

Dr. Diana Mansour, Medical Adviser/Lecturer, Margaret Pyke Family Planning Centre, London. ('Conception to Childbirth', 'Contraception' and the Dictionary).

Dr. Tuppy Owens, author of *Planet Sex* and *The Sex Maniac's Diary*, and Administrator for the Outsiders Group for the disabled ('Sex and Disability', 'Sexual Practices' and 'Sex and Culture').

Dr. Fran Reader, Consultant in Reproductive and Sexual Health Care, Ipswich Hospital ('Anatomy of Sex', 'Growth and Change', 'Sexual Intercourse' and the Dictionary).

Ryo Tanaka, Director of Human Sexuality, Centre for Education and Culture, Gifu City, Japan ('Sexuality').

Kaye Wellings, AIDS, Public Health in Europe, London School of Hygiene and Tropical Medicine ('Making Love').

Simon Wilson, Tate Gallery, London, author of books on modern art and on Aubrey Beardsley and Egon Schiele ('Sex and Culture').

Support also came from:

Vivienne Evans, Prof. Dr. Erwin J Haberle, Dr. Dinant Haslinghius, Dr. Merra Kishen, Dr. Prakash Kothari, Dr. Nathaniel Mc Conaghy, Ellen Visser, Morgan Williams, Dr. Kenneth Zucker.

The Editor of the first edition wishes to thank the above (cited as they were in the original) for their invaluable help, advice and support in the writing of this book. However, the opinions expressed here are those of the Editors or those of the credited authors.

Sexuality is an important force in our lives. Sexual expression at its best, whatever form it takes, encourages and enhances strong, loving relationships; it should be enjoyable, respectful and safe for both partners.

Everyone needs the information and skills to find fulfilment in sex for themselves and their partner(s) – and to equip them to reject negative aspects of sex. This encyclopedia, for adults, is full of reliable information about sex, presented in a clear, non-judgmental and comprehensive way.

It has six sections, designed to help the reader to identify his or her own interests easily:

- Part 1 offers factual information
- Part 2 discusses sexual attitudes and feelings
- Part 3 examines sexual practices
- Part 4 encourages the reader to explore his or her sexuality, offering advice and challenges
- Part 5 discusses sex and its relationship with society, recognising that sexual attitudes and behaviour are closely linked to, and influenced by, their social context
- Part 6 is a comprehensive dictionary of sexual terminology.

Some people feel shy and inadequate about sex. Some have sexual problems such as erectile and ejaculation problems for men and painful intercourse or inability to reach orgasm for women. The Lovers' Guide Illustrated Encyclopedia gives guidance on sexual anxieties and difficulties.

The Lovers' Guide productions have had an enormous impact on social history, virtually worldwide, because of their honesty, accuracy and frankness.

They have helped many millions to have a better, more fulfilling sex life and worked to break down many taboos about sexual matters, thereby removing much of the guilt many have misguidedly associated with sex. The responses of the general public and experts to The Lovers' Guide videos and books have been overwhelmingly positive.

People have appreciated the encouragement The Lovers' Guide offers to explore sexuality and sexual techniques. Many were reassured that their own desires and practices were shared by others and were, at long last, being discussed openly.

Many people have little knowledge of sex, and are often misinformed about it. This lack of information and confusion may lead to risk-taking and exploitation which can result in unhappy relationships and consequences such as unplanned pregnancy and sexually-transmitted infections.

The media often uses sex to sensationalise and exploit. Myths and taboos can be reinforced, and have powerful effects, especially on young people, who say they receive little advice from parents or schools. No-one should be subjected to sexual harassment or abuse. Young people must be protected from grooming and pornography.

This encyclopedia supplements all The Lovers Guide material that has gone before it, and is written to explain all aspects of sexual experience, to debunk myths and inaccuracy, and give its readers clear information on which to base their own sexual practice. Sex is a wonderful natural activity which should be enjoyed without fear or danger and we hope this book will contribute further to a safe and happy sex life for everyone.

Doreen Massey MA, Consultant Editor of the original edition
Dr. Chris Fariello, Editor of the new, fully updated, 2nd edition

SEXUAL FACTS

S.J. XII 83   RECREATION   #3

The breasts are a powerful expression of femaleness in three ways: as a sexual signal, as an erogenous zone and as the source of nourishment for a newborn baby.

FEMALE ANATOMY

The Female Body

The **nipple** ❶ is the tip of the breast, and the most sensitive part of the breast for many women. It typically becomes erect during sexual arousal.

The **areola** ❷ is the dark area surrounding the nipple, which swells slightly during sexual arousal and may become larger and darker during pregnancy.

The **vulva** or **pudendum** ❸ is the collective term for the external female genitalia. It includes the labia majora, mons pubis, labia minora, clitoris, bulb of vestibule, vulval vestibule and the opening of the vagina.

The **mons pubis** or **mons veneris** ❹ is the hair-covered fatty tissue which covers the upper part of the pubic bone.

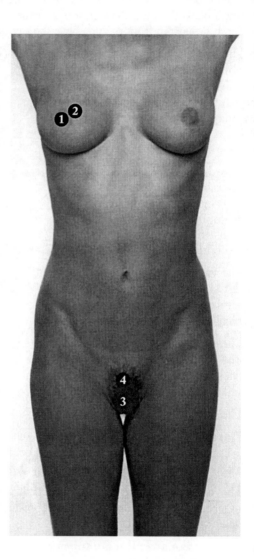

Female Reproductive System

❶ The **vestibule** is the term sometimes used to refer to the area between the labia minora in which the vaginal opening and the urethral opening are situated.

❷ The **clitoris** is a larger organ than first thought; its legs (crura) wrap around the **urethra**. This is the tube through which urine is passed out of the body from the bladder. It lies just in front of and above the vaginal opening.

❸ The **fourchette** is the point where the labia minora join at the bottom of the vulva (the delicate area of skin beneath the vaginal opening, which may may be cut, a procedure known as an episiotomy, or may tear in childbirth).

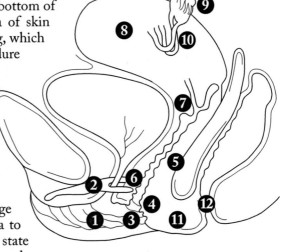

❹ The **hymen** is the thin membrane that partially covers the opening to the vagina. This membrane typically remains in tact in childhood.

❺ The **vagina** is the passage that leads in from the vulva to the cervix and in its resting state is typically around four inches deep.

❻ The **G-spot** is the name given to a small area of highly sensitive tissue situated inside the front of the vagina behind the pubic bone. Some scientists believe it to be the female equivalent of the prostate in the male; some believe it is related to the back of the clitoris, while others dispute its very existence.

❼ The **cervix** is the neck of the uterus.

❽ The **uterus** or **womb** is the organ in which a fertilised ovum can develop into a baby. It is about the size of a small pear (upside down), and lies between the bladder and the rectum where it is held in place by various ligaments.

❾ The **ovaries** are the organs that produce the female sexual hormones oestrogen and progesterone and the reproductive gametes, the ova. They are equivalent to the testes in the male.

❿ The **ovarian** or **Fallopian tubes** are the tubes that connect the ovaries to the uterus, in which fertilisation occurs.

⓫ The **perineum** is the area of skin and underlying fibrous and muscle tissue between the vagina and the anus.

⓬ The **rectum** is the last section of the intestine, or lower bowel, leading to the anus.

The Vulva

The **clitoris** is the female equivalent of the tip of the penis, and often the most sensitive and erotic part of the female genitalia. It is unique in being the only human organ dedicated entirely to pleasurable sexual feelings.

The **labia majora** or **outer labia** are the two lips that surround the vaginal opening, usually lying close together to protect it. Anatomically they are equivalent to the scrotum in the male. At the front they join near the top of the mons pubis; at the back they join at the perineum. They engorge during sexual arousal and become plump enough to act as a cushion during intercourse. They contain sweat and odour-producing glands, which keep the smooth inner part moistened and give the vulva its highly sexual odour (or cassolette).

The **labia minora** or **inner labia** are the smaller, hairless lips or folds of skin within the outer labia, immediately around the vaginal opening. At the top they join to form the hood of the clitoris and at the base they join together to form the fourchette. Anatomically they are equivalent to the penile shaft. They contain sebaceous glands on their outer side and sweat glands on the inner parts that help with lubrication. During sexual arousal they become engorged with blood (in a similar manner to the penis), which makes them darken in colour and swell to about two or three times their normal size. Again, they act as a cushion during intercourse.

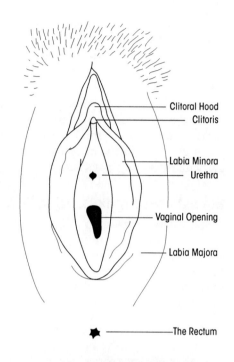

- Clitoral Hood
- Clitoris
- Labia Minora
- Urethra
- Vaginal Opening
- Labia Majora

——————The Rectum

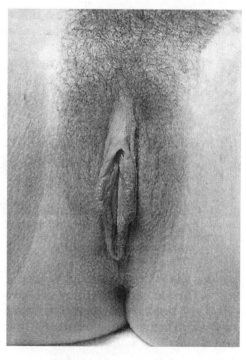

Breasts

In most societies the breasts are seen as a powerful expression of femaleness. Humans are unique among mammals in that the breasts seem to serve not one but several purposes: as well as producing the milk for the newborn offspring, they have taken on secondary roles as major symbols of feminity and as a major erogenous zone in sexual activity, particularly in Western society.

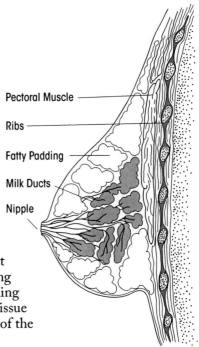

Pectoral Muscle

Ribs

Fatty Padding

Milk Ducts

Nipple

Breasts and milk production

The breasts are made up of fatty tissue that contains thousands of tiny milk-producing glands known as alveoli, with ducts leading to the nipple. A network of connective tissue that also maintains the shape and firmness of the breasts support these structures.

The changes in hormone production in the course of pregnancy cause a number of changes in the breasts. Within the first three weeks of pregnancy the woman may notice some increased sensitivity, but it is not until the fifth month that the first milk is produced. At this stage a difference in size becomes noticeable and the areola grow darker and more prominent.

Bras are designed and worn for more than their functional qualities – they emphasise the sexual attraction of the breasts, as this advertisement shows

The breasts as a sexual signal

No other mammal has such large rounded (as opposed to flat) breasts constantly throughout adult life. In every other mammal the breasts remain flat except during pregnancy. The best-known explanation for this is that proposed by the anthropologist and zoologist, Dr. Desmond Morris. He suggests that the breasts developed in this way as part of the evolutionary process, when humans started to have sexual intercourse face-to-face. In this way, the breasts mimic the shape of the buttocks, which were the primary sexual signal in a man's distant ancestors, the apes. This role is emphasised by the sex flush which occurs during intercourse in some women, and which appears on the breasts and chest; a colour signalling fertility in animals.

The breasts as erogenous zones

The sex flush – together with the swelling of the areolae and the hardening of the nipples during sexual arousal – also draw attention to the breasts as powerful erogenous zones. This varies greatly from one woman to another. Indeed, in research carried out by Masters and Johnson (1966), and Paget (2001), some women stated that they can experience orgasms from breast or nipple stimulation alone, and others claimed to have come to orgasm during breast-feeding.

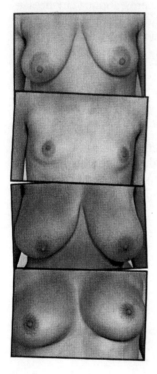

Breast shape and size

The initial growth of the breasts and their ultimate size are determined to some extent by genetic factors but primarily by hormone production; if a male is injected with a female hormone oestrogen he will develop breasts in the same way. It may be because of this hormonal factor that large breasts are sometimes seen as a symbol of fecundity. However, size is no indication of a woman's milk-producing capacity or her fertility. The variety in the size and shape of women's breasts is

> A curved line is the loveliest distance between two points.
> **MAE WEST**

almost infinite, as is the range of people's notions of what size and shape is most attractive. In addition, it is fairly common for women to have breasts that are different shapes and sizes from each other.

Slang terms for the breasts: Boobs, boobage, cans, chabooms, chest, fun bags, gazongas, hooters, tatas, rack, twins, knockers, tits, Bristols, Manchesters, norks, zards, melons, brown eyes, headlights, trapfruits, hammocks, muffins, Vaticans, lungs, jugs, udders, wabs.

Breast Self-Examination (BSE)

Breast self-examination (BSE) involves checking your breasts to help detect breast problems, such as a lump or change in appearance, that may indicate breast cancer or other breast conditions that may require medical intervention. Breast lumps can be noncancerous (benign) or cancerous (malignant).

Breast cancer can occur at any age, though it is most common in women older than 50. When breast cancer is detected in its early stages, your chances for surviving the disease are greatly improved.

Breast exams, once thought essential for early breast cancer detection, are now considered optional, though mammograms have been proven to save lives and you should consult your doctor if you have any concerns about your breasts. Though there is less evidence to suggest that self-breast exams are as effective, doctors stress the importance of breast awareness. Being familiar with the normal consistency of your breasts and the underlying tissue could help you be the first to notice any potential breast problems.

The breast self-exam is a way that you can check your breasts for changes (such as lumps or thickenings). It includes looking at and feeling your breasts. Any unusual changes should be reported to your doctor.

It can take practice to perform a thorough breast self-examination. The best time to examine your breasts is usually seven to 10 days after your menstrual period begins, when your breast tissue is least likely to be swollen or tender. In order to carry out a self-breast exam, follow these steps:

Step 1: In Front of a Mirror

Stand with your arms relaxed at your sides. Check for changes in the look and or shape of your breasts, including changes in size, shape, or position, or any changes to the skin of the breasts. Look for any skin puckering, dimpling, sores, or discoloration. Inspect your nipples and look for any sores, peeling, or change in the direction of the nipples. Continue to look closely at your breasts as you:

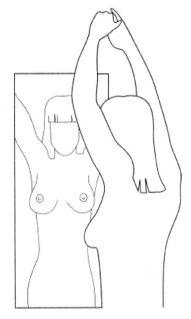

1. Raise your arms overhead.
2. Place your hands on your hips and flex your chest muscles firmly.
3. Bend forward. Roll your shoulders and elbows forward to tighten your chest muscles. Look for any changes in the shape or contour of your breasts. Don't be alarmed if they do not look equal in size or shape. Most women's breasts aren't.

4. Clasp your hands behind your head and press your hands forward. Turn from side to side to inspect your breasts' outer portions.

5. Lift each of your breasts with your hand to inspect the border underneath your breasts.

Step 2: In The Shower

Wet, soapy hands make it easier to slide your fingers over your skin to feel what's beneath the surface. Use your right hand to examine your left breast, and your left hand to examine your right breast:

1. Holding your fingers flat, move the pads of the fingers with gentle pressure over every part of each breast. Move fingers in small circles in an up-and-down pattern over the breast.

2. Check above and below the collarbone and under each armpit for any lump, hard knot, or thickening. Check both sides as breast tissue extends up into the armpits, around the side and towards the collarbone.

Step 3: Lying Down

1. Place a pillow under your right shoulder, and fold your right arm behind your head.

2. With the pads of your fingers of the left hand, press your right breast gently in small circular motions, moving in an up-and-down pattern across your whole breast. Use a combination of light and firm pressure.

3. Gently check your nipple for lumps. Do not squeeze your nipples as a discharge is a perfectly normal response to nipple massage.

4. Repeat these steps for your left breast, beginning by placing the pillow under your left shoulder.

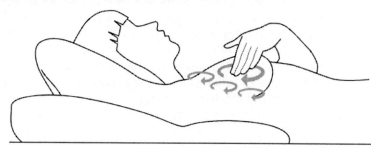

Vagina

The vagina is a primary female sexual organ. The term derives from the Latin word meaning sheath, which serves only as a limited, male-oriented description of its function in simply sheathing the penis in sexual intercourse. In reality the vagina's functions are considerably more complex than this description would suggest.

Physiology of the vagina

The vagina is the passage which leads in from the vulva and vestibule (the outer parts of the female genitalia) to the cervix (the neck of the uterus) and is usually around four inches deep in its resting state. Apart from its role in sexual pleasure, the vagina has other major functions: to enable the male's sperm to pass up through the cervix and womb and travel along the Fallopian tubes to an ovary, where it can fertilise an egg; to provide the conduit for menstrual fluids to exit the body and also the birth canal for a developed foetus to be born.

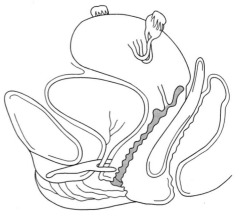

The vagina is the term for the passage which leads from the vulva to the cervix. It is marked in grey on this cross-section diagram.

The vagina is a fibro-muscular structure, covered with a thin mucus membrane. The various layers of muscle, together with the numerous folds of skin by which they are covered, give the vagina great capacity for expansion and contraction. This means that most vaginas can accommodate an object of almost any size such as a penis (at least in girth), up to, potentially, the head of a developed foetus. The length of a vagina differs from woman to woman, though in its resting state is usually around four inches and, again, is very stretchable to accomodate the length of most penises.

There are two main types of muscles in the vagina. The smooth muscle within the vaginal wall is not under voluntary control and will relax and stretch during sexual arousal and penile penetration without conscious effort. The muscle fibres surrounding the outer third of the vagina are under voluntary control, enabling the woman to grip the penis by tensing the pelvic floor muscles. It is these muscles which may go into involuntary spasm in the condition known as vaginismus, closing up and making it difficult or even impossible for penetration to occur. These muscles may also be damaged during childbirth.

Facts and fictions about the vagina

- It is widely believed that the size of both a woman's vagina, and a man's penis, is partly determined by race. There is, however, no conclusive medical evidence for this.

- It is often thought that smaller (tighter) vaginas give greater pleasure to the partner in penetrative sex. While this may be true in some cases, it is a fact that in the latter stages of arousal the inner recesses of all vaginas distend and balloon, reducing friction for both partners.

- In a virgin the vagina may be partially covered by a thin membrane known as the hymen. Traditionally taken as evidence of virginity, the hymen can in fact be broken quite easily, through bicycle- or horse-riding or gymnastics, or when using a tampon, as well as by first intercourse. When broken it may bleed a little, but this is rarely painful. In some women, the hymen is retained and may need surgical attention to allow penile penetration.

- In 1950 Dr. Ernst Grafenberg wrote of *'an erotic zone ... on the anterior wall of the vagina.'* The term G-spot was later coined (see *The G Spot* by US sexologists Ladas, Whipple and Perry, 1982), referring to the small area of tissue containing

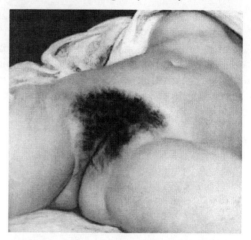

L'origine du monde (The Origin of the World) by Gustave Courbet (1866) is a celebration of female sexuality – emphasising both sensuality and fecundity

nerve endings situated inside the front of the vagina, behind the pubic bone which responds to stimulation by hand, in a *come hither* motion, or a penis in certain sexual positions.

- Controversy about the nature of the female G-spot and indeed its very existence continues today. Some have suggested that its swelling and pleasurable sensations arise from this being the other end of the clitoris, discovered to be a much larger organ than previously thought.

- Other research has suggested that it is the female equivalent of the male prostate gland and as such, produces pleasure when aroused. Unfortunately, in some cases, this may cause the woman to feel as if she needs to urinate and thus, many women shut down the potentially pleasurable experience.

- Further, stimulation of the G-Spot may lead to the production of an ejaculate of clear fluid at orgasm which appears largely not to be urine. This may cause embarrassment for some women as well.

The Vagina's Self-Care System

The vagina has a unique system which, if not interfered with in any way, ensures that it remains healthy and functions correctly.

One kind of fluid is constantly present. It is formed through the fermentation of the vagina's natural bacteria on its walls, creating a slightly acidic environment which maintains the vagina's healthy state and its natural bacterial balance. The vagina is self-cleansing and therefore usually needs no special treatment. Doctors generally discourage the practice of douching and using other feminine products to clean or deodorise the vagina.

Another fluid is produced during sexual arousal to provide lubrication and to aid the passage of the sperm in to the cervix when the woman is at her most fertile. This was originally thought to come from the cervix or the Bartholin's glands on the inner side of the inner labia. It is in fact produced as droplets, like sweat, on the walls of the vaginal barrel, the quantity of which may vary according to the individual, her age, and her state of arousal.

Slang terms for the vagina: Pee-hole, hole, coozy, pussy, twat, bearded clam, fanny, quim, cunt, slit, crack, box, doughnut, snatch, beard, beaver, badger, brownie, camel foot/toe, cherry pie, cooch, cooter, fern, fur-burger/pie/sandwich, gash, fish taco, muff, tail, nook, nooky, happy valley, trench, snapping turtle, Y, minge, money box, mousetrap, jelly roll, garden, hatch, promised land, rattle, snake canyon, poonani, poontang, love tunnel, vertical smile, vajayjay.

Clitoris

The clitoris has long been believed to be the key to women's sexual pleasure: in fact the very word comes from the ancient Greek kleitoris, meaning key. It is fundamental in that, for the vast majority of women, direct or indirect stimulation of the clitoris is a very important part of sexual arousal and, for many, essential to reaching orgasm. It is the most sensitive of human erogenous zones and is unique in that its sole function seems to be as receptor and transmitter of sensual pleasure.

Female and male development

The clitoris is anatomically the female equivalent to the head of the penis. It contains a very high concentration of nerve endings and is therefore very sensitive. In the development of embryos of both sexes a small bud of tissue forms between the legs. This then develops into a penis in the male and a clitoris in the female. Other physiological equivalences include the nipples in both sexes, the ovaries and the testes, the labia majora and the scrotum, and the G-spot and the male prostate gland.

Parallels Between Clitoris and Penis

- they develop from the same lump of tissue in the embryo
- the head of the clitoris and the penis is made up of sensory tissue
- the shafts of both contain erectile or spongiosum tissue that engorges with arousal
- they are surrounded by soft tissue
- the small head of the clitoris and the glans of the penis contain a high concentration of nerve endings
- their size and shape are no indication of their capacity to give or receive sensuous pleasure

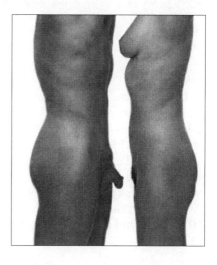

The main difference between the clitoris and the penis is that the penis has other, non-sensual functions, such as carrying the urethra. While a man's erection is one of the first and most visible signs of arousal, the changes in the clitoris are more subtle and may be slower. The clitoris, though containing erectile tissue, may respond to sexual arousal much more gradually than the penis, although some surveys suggest that it can be just as quickly responsive as the penis in masturbation.

Location of the clitoris

The pea-shaped tip of the clitoris is about 1.5 to 2.5 cm above the vaginal opening, where the inner labia meet. The whole organ is generally about seven centimetres long, although all but the tip or glans, located at the head of the shaft and only 0.3 to 1.3 cm in diameter, lies within the body. Even then the tip can be hidden by a hood or prepuce formed by the meeting of the inner labia. There appears to be some variety of size and shape.

The clitoris is marked by the grey shaded area and sits under the clitoral hood

Self-exploration

Unlike the male sexual organs, those of the female are not immediately visible and some parts are not visible at all. However, a healthy and fulfilling sex life can be helped by both partners understanding as much as possible about their own and each other's sexual organs and how they look and feel.

This is particularly important with regard to the clitoris, probably the most mysterious of all the sexual organs – even now, it is not known exactly what happens to the clitoris at orgasm. However, knowing where it is and how to stimulate it can, in most women, be the major key to female sexual satisfaction.

The clitoris and sexual arousal

When a woman becomes aroused, the shaft of the clitoris thickens and grows longer as it becomes engorged with blood. The tip or glans also swells considerably, sometimes up to as much as twice its normal size, making it more exposed and sensitive. However, during the plateau stage of sexual arousal, just before orgasm, the glans withdraws completely beneath its hood, making it difficult to understand fully what happens to the clitoris during orgasm. Clearly, though, maintaining stimulation of the clitoral area continues to arouse the woman. After orgasm the glans quickly goes back to its usual position, normally within 10 seconds, and returns to its unstimulated size within five or 10 minutes.

FACT
The word clitoris comes from the ancient Greek kleitoris, meaning key.

Clitoral and vaginal orgasms

The long-standing debate about the nature of the female orgasm has led to two main points of view.

Medically, there is no difference between clitoral and vaginal orgasms. The main muscle involved in the muscular contractions associated with the female orgasm encircles the vagina and contains fibres that are also attached to the tip of the clitoris and the associated spongiosum tissue swells with blood and surround the vaginal neck like a collar.

While it is known that the clitoris develops from the same tissue as the penis in the male, the existence of a female G-spot, like the male's prostate, has not been conclusively proven.

Most women can have an orgasm without vaginal penetration (or a partner). For most (but not all) women sexual arousal seems to be focused on the clitoris, and for the vast majority direct stimulation of the clitoris alone is necessary for them to achieve orgasm. However, the clitoris can be stimulated indirectly and some women can reach orgasm through stimulation of the vagina, the breasts and other erogenous zones. Some women are even capable of achieving orgasm through fantasy alone.

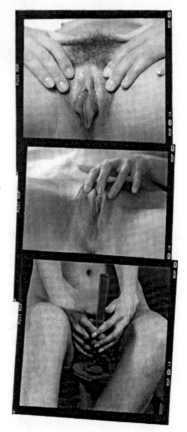

Vaginal Self-Examination

For a woman to examine herself, she can squat down over a small mirror, or sit in front of one, with her legs apart (bottom). By opening the labia majora, the various parts of the vulva can be identified.

The head of the clitoris can be seen when the labia minora are gently pulled apart (top); it is fairly firm and can be felt by drawing a finger upwards from the vagina (centre).

Throughout time and in almost all cultures the penis has been a powerful symbol – of male sexuality, of potency, of the force of life, and of virility. No other organ of the human body has been surrounded by as many myths and misconceptions as this, the primary male sex organ.

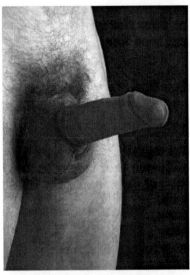

Man has proportionately the largest penis
of all primates. As Dr. Desmond Morris put it,
"Men are apes with oversized penises"

Physiology of the penis

The penis is made up of erectile and muscular tissue along with many sensory nerves. The erectile tissue lies in three columns, two on the back forming the corpora cavernosa, and one on the front forming the corpus spongiosum and extending to form the glans (head). Internally, this tissue is arranged in the form of honeycomb-like structures. When the penis is flaccid the muscle fibres which form this honeycomb are contracted. During sexual arousal, the muscles actually relax to allow more blood to flow into the tissue in these three columns. The many blood vessels and spaces in these structures become engorged with blood, causing the penis to become erect and stiff.

The urethra is the tube through which urine is passed out of the body from the bladder and semen is passed on ejaculation. It passes from the bladder, through the prostate gland, along the length of the penis through the corpus spongiosum, to its opening in the tip of the head or glans.

The penis is covered with loosely-attached, fatless skin, which folds back on itself at the tip to make up the prepuce or foreskin. This covers the glans of the flaccid penis in an uncircumcised male. Part or all of this section of skin may be removed in the practice of circumcision. The prepuce is attached to the inner side of the glans by an extremely sensitive bridge of skin termed the frenum or frenulum. When the penis becomes erect, the prepuce is pulled back and the glans is revealed.

Slang terms for the penis:
Bishop, boner, canary, cock, cockchoad, chub, cong, dick, dingus, dong, hammer, Hampton Wick, hot dog, John Thomas, Johnny, joy stick, love muscle, machine gun, main vein, meat, member, Mickey, nob, old man, one-eyed monster, one-eyed trouser snake, organ, pecker, Percy, Peter, pistol, plonker, poker pole, prick, prong, pud, putz, rod, shaft, skin flute, stick, sweet meat, tool, wand, wanger, wee-wee, wiener, willie, winkle

Male Reproductive System

❶ The **epididymis** is the duct that leads from each testis, in which the sperm are matured and stored until being passed into the vas deferens when needed. Each one is six to seven metres long and tightly coiled to fit into the testes.

❷ The **vas deferens** is the duct that connects the left and right epididymis to the ejaculatory ducts in order to expel the sperm. Each tube is 30 centimetres long.

❸ The **prostate gland** is the organ in which the two vas deferens meet each other before joining the urethra. It produces secretions that form part of the seminal fluid. It is also the site of the most common male cancer.

❹ The **urethra** is the tube through which urine is passed out of the body from the bladder and semen is ejaculated at orgasm.

❺ The **Cowper's glands** join the urethra below the prostate. They produce a mucus substance whose purpose is to neutralise the acidity of any urine left in the urethra which could kill the sperm before it even leaves the penis. This substance also helps to lubricate the tip of the penis prior to ejaculation and forms part of the seminal fluid.

❻ The **perineum** is the area of skin and underlying fibrous and muscle tissue between the scrotum and the anus. It includes a central ridge called the median raphe. It is colloquially known as the taint.

❼ The **rectum** is the last part of the intestine, or lower bowel, leading to the anus.

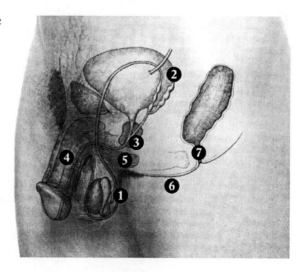

The Erect Penis

The **penis** is the most prominent male sex organ. Its function is to pass urine, which it mainly does in its limp, flaccid, state, and to carry semen out of the body in its erect state. The erect state also allows it to penetrate the vagina (or other orifices) and deposit its sperm deeply into it. In humans and other primates it has a major role as a principal source of sexual pleasure.

The **glans** is the very sensitive tip or head of the penis containing a high concentration of nerve endings. Behind the head is the bridge of skin, the frenum or frenulum, which is an even more sensitive part of the glans, linking it to the shaft.

The **prepuce** or **foreskin** is the fold of skin which covers the glans of the flaccid penis in an uncircumcised male.

The **testes** or **testicles** are the male gonads or sex glands which produce the characteristic male hormones and the reproductive gametes (sperm). They are equivalent to the ovaries in the female.

The **scrotum** is the sac of loose wrinkled skin beneath the penis which contains the testicles. They are loosely held in place by the dartos muscles attached to the scrotum, and the cremaster muscles attached to the testes themselves. The length of these muscles, and therefore the proximity of the testes to the body, is affected by temperature, emotions (fear, for instance, causes them to be drawn in), and by sexual arousal. The sac is divided into two sections to accommodate the two testes; the left testis often hangs slightly lower than the right, which may well be for comfort so they are not squeezed together between the thighs.

> Most men fear that their sex organs are too small.
> A woman's reassurance seldom helps to allay these
> fears, but business success sometimes helps.
> **THEODORE I. BUBIN**

Penis Size and Sexual Potency: Some Myths Dispelled

One of the greatest myths about sex relates to penis size.

The focus on the penis may well be due to the fact that this organ is to a great extent the source of male sexual pleasure. Perhaps it is also for this reason that it has been widely assumed in many male-dominated societies that the penis is equally the primary source of sexual pleasure for the female. This leaves many men preoccupied with the size of their penis.

Surveys suggest that almost all men – regardless of their sexual orientation – wish they had a larger penis. However, while some women may find a large penis attractive, many others are concerned about being unable to accommodate it or that they might find it painful. Generally, the girth of the penis is thought to be more important for sexual pleasure for females than the length.

The Examination of the Herald Illustration by Aubrey Beardsley (1872-98) From *Lysistrata*

A Few Basic Facts

• While there is some variety in flaccid penis size, the variation can be somewhat diminished when the penis is erect. Smaller penises can grow proportionally much more than larger ones, some even doubling in length.

• In a recent survey, carried out in an effort to reduce the number of men seeking penis extensions, the Parisian National Academy of Surgery, concluded that the average length of an unaroused penis is between 9 and 9.5 cm (3½ to 3¾ inches), a number that lengthens to between12.8 and 14.0 cm (5 to 5½ inches) when erect. Similarly, the average circumference, they discovered, is between 8.75 cm and 10.25 cm (3½ to 4 inches) – generally, much smaller than previously thought.

• The vagina has great capacity for expansion enabling most women to accommodate almost any size of penis, though a long penis may apply some pressure on the cervix. Some women find this painful but for others it is pleasurable; either way the depth of penetration may be controlled through the choice of certain positions for intercourse and the placing of the woman's legs. Above all it is important for men to recognise that, biologically speaking, the most sensitive parts of the female genitalia are the clitoris and, in some women, the G-spot.

- Amongst homosexual men, surveys suggest that almost equally as many consider penis size to be unimportant as consider it to be important. It is largely a question of personal preference, often influenced by culture.
- Ultimately, the variety in both size and shape of the penis is as great as in any other part of the body, and bears no relation to sexual potency or fertility.

Testes

While not as powerful a symbol as the phallus, the testes or testicles are often seen as the source of man's masculinity. A strong man is said to have "balls" or "big cohones". Physiologically, they are just as important as the penis, if not more so to male growth and the man's capacity to procreate.

Physiology of the testes

The testes or testicles are the male go-nads or sex glands. They are equivalent to a woman's ovaries and develop from the same tissue in the embryo. They are responsible for producing male hor-mones as well as the male reproductive cells, sperm.

They are situated inside the scrotum, the sac of skin beneath the penis where they are loosely held in place by the dartos muscles attached to the scrotum, and cremaster muscles attached to the testes themselves. To the touch, the testes are two firm, smooth, oval masses within the scrotal sac, which is divided into two to accommodate the two tes-tes. They are protected by four layers of covering which correspond to the lin-ings of the abdominal wall.

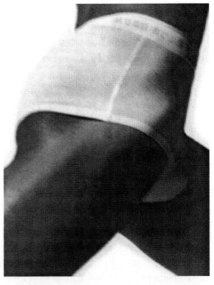

The testes are emphasised in some advertisements, even though the penis is the more common symbol of masculinity. The testes have also been associated with virility in other ways, as in the phrase "to have balls" meaning to have strength and bravado

The sperm are produced in what are known as somniferous tubules. There may be as many as a thousand tubules in each testicle, very narrow and tightly coiled together and each over 60 cm long. These tubules produce sperm constantly, maturing and nourishing each one for some 45 days in sertoli or nurse cells attached to the tubule's lining. They are then released into the epididymis, the duct where they are matured and stored until needed.

Sperm production and the position of the testes

Sperm are produced constantly, throughout the man's adult life. A typical ejaculation releases between 200 to 500 million sperm. The testes hang outside the

man's body because the sperm are produced
at up to 8°C below normal body temperature. For this reason, it has been suggested
that wearing tight trousers or close-fitting
underwear may reduce a man's sperm production, as tightly-fitting clothes hold the
testes closer to the body than normal, and
therefore at a slightly higher temperature.

Normally, the proximity of the testes to the
body is controlled by the dartos and cremaster muscles; they relax and contract to
keep the testes at the optimum temperature
for sperm production. Therefore, when the
man is cold, his testes are drawn closer to
the body.

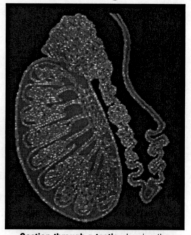

Section through a testis, showing the
tightly-coiled somniferous tubules in which
the sperm are produced, and the epididymis
into which they are released to mature and be
stored until needed. As many as 200 to 500
million sperm are present in each ejaculation

The height of the testes is also affected by
the man's emotions and by sexual arousal. In
the course of arousal the skin of the scrotum
may thicken and darken with the increased blood flow to the genital area, and
the testes are drawn tighter to the body, particularly just before orgasm. If pain
is inflicted on the testes, or even with the threat of pain, the testes are again
drawn closer to the body. The testes are extremely sensitive to pressure, which
can produce excruciating pain.

Self Examination

Self-examination is important for both men and women, for getting to know
one's genitals and in order to detect any signs of infection or lumps that may

indicate cancer. A testicular self-examination (TSE) is an inspection of the
appearance and feel of your testicles in
an effort to detect testicular cancer at an
early stage. Many testicular cancers are
first discovered by self-examination as a
painless lump or an enlarged testicle.

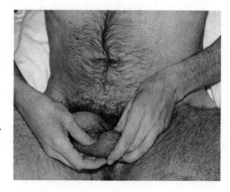

Lumps or other changes found during
a testicular exam aren't always a sign of
cancer but should be checked by a doctor.
Some testicular lumps are malignant and
will require immediate treatment.

- It is recommended that men aged 14 to 40 perform testicular self-examination once a month. While standing in front of a mirror, check for any swelling on the scrotal skin.

- Examine each testicle with both hands. Roll the testicle gently between the thumbs and fingers. Notice the feel of the testicles and note any suspicious lumps. This should be a painless experience. Signs of concern can include:
  - A painless lump or swelling in a testicle
  - Pain or discomfort in a testicle or in the scrotum
  - Any enlargement of a testicle or change in the way it feels
  - A feeling of heaviness in the scrotum
  - A dull ache in the lower abdomen, back, or groin
  - A sudden collection of fluid in the scrotum

- Locate the epididymis, the soft, tube-like structure behind the testicles. Once you are familiar with this structure you will not mistake it for a lump. Cancerous lumps usually are found on the testicles, not on the epididymis.

- If you find a lump or notice any changes to your testicles that may be a sign of testicular cancer see a doctor (preferably a urologist) right away.

Although the incidence of testicular cancer has risen in recent years, more than 95% of cases can be cured. Treatment is more likely to be successful when testicular cancer is discovered early. It is most often men themselves who are the ones to first detect most testicular cancers.

FACT

One testis usually hangs lower than the other, and may be slightly larger. Some studies have found that in right-handed men the right testis is generally higher, while in left-handed men the left is higher.

Slang terms for the testes: bags, balls, basket, bollocks, cobblers, cohones, family jewels, goolies, groceries, knackers, lunch box, marbles, nadgers, nuts, orchids, plums.

Sexual arousal begins in the brain as we react, consciously or uncon-
sciously, to certain stimuli. These are psycho-physiological responses,
manifesting themselves in a series of physical changes and sensations.
The nature and intensity of the sensations experienced vary greatly
from one person to another and may be affected by numerous inde-
pendent and circumstantial factors.

Sexual intercourse is the broad term for penile insertion between two
people; coitus is the specific term used for the penis-in-the-vagina act
between a man and a woman. This section deals with male and female
physical responses to sexual activity of all kinds.

The succession of changes may be broken down into the Masters and
Johnson's four stages: arousal, plateau, orgasm and resolution.

Penetrative Intercourse

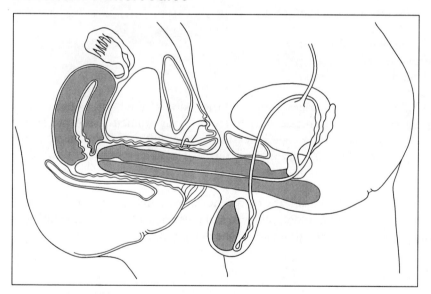

In heterosexual couples, when both partners are sufficiently aroused, the
man's erect penis is inserted into the woman's vagina. Movement of the
penis within the vagina leads to further arousal, which may culminate in
orgasm. Many of the sexual responses seem, in some way, to be geared
towards creating the ideal circumstances for fertilisation to occur until
finally, at ejaculation, the sperm is deposited as close as possible to the
cervix. Its passage to the uterus may be further aided by the uterine contractions which occur when the female reaches her orgasm.

Female Response

1. Arousal

Blood flow to the pelvic area increases. The vagina dilates and its walls darken and start to sweat a lubricating substance. The labia darken and swell: the outer lips, the labia majora, may separate, with the inner lips, the labia minora protruding between them. The clitoris emerges from beneath its hood, or prepuce, lengthening and thickening as it becomes erect. The uterus moves upwards and forwards so that the cervix protrudes less into the vault of the vagina. This movement lengthens the vagina, which also starts to distend to form a balloon shape at the upper end, near the cervix.

Physical responses to arousal occur in other parts of the body, as the nipples become erect and the areolae start to swell. Many women also experience a so-called sex flush, with a rash appearing on the skin of the abdomen, throat and upper chest. This may occur at any phase of sexual response but most often occurs in the build up to orgasm.

Excitement triggers the release of the hormone adrenaline into the bloodstream, causing a rise in blood pressure and pulse rate, muscle tensing, dilation of the pupils, heavier breathing and some perspiration.

2. Plateau

The labia may continue to swell, and their colour continues to darken. Vaginal lubrication may decrease, causing greater friction between the vaginal walls and the penis. The entire outer parts of the vagina – including the inner labia – swell to form what is termed the orgasmic platform. This is the area from where the sensations of orgasm will spread. The upper end of the vagina continues to expand, and the uterus continues to tilt and be drawn up into the body. Just before orgasm, the clitoris withdraws beneath its hood.

3. Orgasm

The orgasmic platform (see under *Plateau*) contracts rhythmically at intervals of 0.8 seconds (the same as in the man). There may be anywhere between three and 15 of these muscle spasms, gradually becoming less frequent and intense. The muscles of the uterus also produce involuntary contractions. These contractions dip the cervix, raised in the course of arousal, back into the vagina, which some have suggested may help draw sperm up and aid them on their journey to the ovaries. They also produce

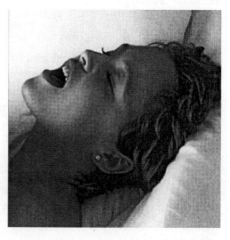

waves of intense pleasure throughout the body. At the same time, skin flushes may spread and deepen, and muscle spasms may occur in other parts of the body (such as the feet, hands, back and thighs). Blood pressure and pulse rate reach a peak.

4. Resolution

The sexual organs gradually return to their normal, unaroused state. Within five or ten seconds of the last vaginal contraction the clitoris returns to its normal position and the darker colour of the labia minora fades. It may take 10 or 15 minutes for the vagina to return to its usual size, shape and colour, and even longer for the swelling of the labia majora and the glans of the clitoris to subside.

If orgasm has not been reached, the congestion in the blood vessels in the pelvic area may not have been released. This can make the resolution process much slower and may cause some slight discomfort, but this usually passes within a few minutes.

Male Response

1. Arousal

The blood flow to the genital area increases, and the outflow of blood from the penis is reduced. The penis rapidly becomes engorged with blood, so that it stiffens, lengthens, and becomes erect. If the man is uncircumcised the foreskin is usually pulled right back, leaving the sensitive head or glans fully exposed. At the same time, the skin of the scrotum becomes thicker and firmer, and the testes are drawn visibly closer towards the body. The increased blood flow darkens the skin of the whole genital area.

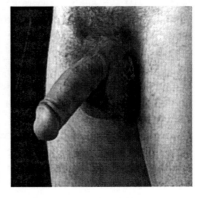

The skin may become flushed on other parts of the body (the sex flush), and the nipples may become erect. Adrenaline makes the pulse rate and blood pressure rise, the muscles tense, and the pupils dilate. Perspiration may increase and breathing becomes faster.

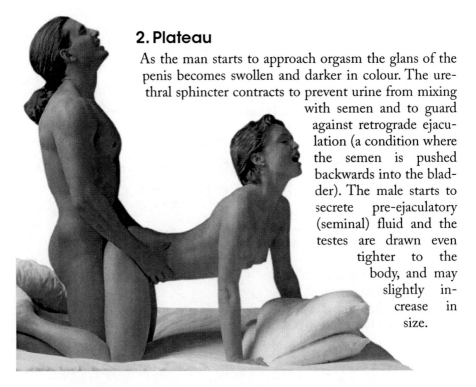

2. Plateau

As the man starts to approach orgasm the glans of the penis becomes swollen and darker in colour. The urethral sphincter contracts to prevent urine from mixing with semen and to guard against retrograde ejaculation (a condition where the semen is pushed backwards into the bladder). The male starts to secrete pre-ejaculatory (seminal) fluid and the testes are drawn even tighter to the body, and may slightly increase in size.

3. Orgasm

In men this has two stages. In the first stage the seminal fluid collects in the urethra, within the prostate. Involuntary muscle contractions are experienced in the pelvis, similar to the spasm that occur in female orgasm. This causes emission and is recognised as the period of "ejaculatory inevitability", the point of no return, just two to four seconds before ejaculation, when the man is aware that orgasm is imminent and that there is nothing he can now do to prevent it.

Finally, ejaculation occurs.

The muscles of the sex organs go into involuntary spasms, contracting rhythmically along the entire length of the urethra to expel the seminal fluid. The force of this may decrease with age, but in a young man the ejaculated semen can travel several feet and as fast as 30 mph. The muscles contract at the same rate as those of the vagina in the woman. They start at intervals of 0.8 seconds, and after three or four strong contractions rapidly reduce in force and frequency.

The greatest pleasure is felt with the first contractions, in which the largest volume of seminal fluid is ejaculated. Both gradually diminish with each contraction. The total volume of semen ejaculated is generally about 1 to 10 ml (for comparison, a teaspoon is 5 ml, a tablespoon is 10 ml) – with the average being around 2.5 ml or half a teaspoon. Adult semen volume is affected by the time that has passed since the previous ejaculation; larger semen volumes are seen with greater durations of abstinence.

Ejaculation is usually accompanied by the intensely pleasurable sensations and release of tension that occur with orgasm. Blood pressure, pulse and breathing rates reach a peak, skin flushes deepen, and muscle spasm may occur in many parts of the body as well as in the pelvic area. The man may perspire out of proportion with the physical effort exerted. However, it is possible both to ejaculate without orgasm, and to have an orgasm without ejaculation.

FACT
World distance record for ejaculating semen: 2.6 metres.

4. Resolution

After ejaculation the penis becomes flaccid again. This can occur more rapidly if the man removes his penis from the vagina immediately than if he remains in close proximity. The genitals return to their pre-arousal state, and any skin flushes fade. Breathing, pulse and blood pressure rapidly return to normal. Orgasm is followed by a refractory period, during which most men are unable to have another erection. The time varies from one man to another, and also depends on such factors as age and state of mind. As for the woman, though less usual in men, if orgasm has not been reached, the congestion in the blood vessels in the pelvic area may not have been released. This makes the resolution process much slower and may cause some slight discomfort, although this usually passes within a few minutes. Very few men are able to maintain their erection after orgasm.

Patterns of Arousal

In general the process of becoming aroused and approaching orgasm follows distinct patterns for men and women. While the man can reach full physical arousal quite quickly before the marked plateau phase, for many women the same process tends to be more gradual. However, while simultaneous orgasm is relatively rare, it can be achieved – particularly through getting to understand, and respond fully to, one's own and one's partner's sexual needs and arousal patterns.

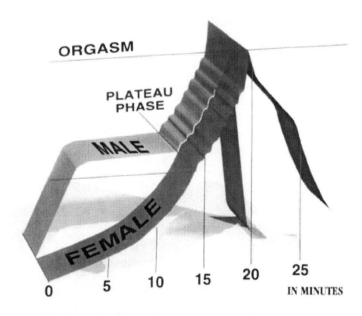

Timescales vary widely for different couples (many men may reach orgasm in a shorter time than is shown here). Also, simultaneous orgasm is relatively rare.

Differences Between Male and Female Response

The main difference between the male and female responses to intercourse is that some women are able to reach more than one orgasm during a single act of intercourse. Instead of passing from orgasm to resolution, the woman may repeatedly range between the plateau stage and orgasm several times. Also unlike men, women tend to experience increasing pleasure with each orgasmic peak. Some also experience no refractory period, and can become aroused again and again almost immediately after each orgasm. However, it may be possible for men to learn how to have multiple orgasms as well – but usually only with a good deal of training and practice.

Humans appear to be unique in their enjoyment of the reproductive act. Indeed, where contraception is available and acceptable, the original purpose of sexual intercourse – to produce offspring – may seem secondary to the pleasure we derive from the act itself. However, the two are intrinsically connected and it is most likely that our enjoyment has evolved principally as a means of reinforcing the instinct for procreation in the human species.

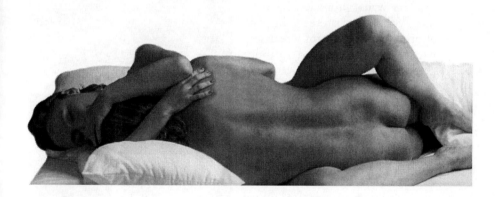

The force of the man's ejaculation helps ensure that the semen is deposited deep in the woman's vagina, close to the cervix. The muscle contractions of the female orgasm, while not necessary for sperm transport, can aid this process by dipping the cervix – raised in the course of arousal – back into the vault of the vagina and into the pool of semen. Further contractions in the uterus and along the Fallopian tubes carry the semen towards the ovum (egg). Substances present in the uterus act on the sperm to make it able to fertilise the ovum.

Fertilisation

Of the 200 to 500 million sperm ejaculated into the vagina, only 1,000 - 2,000 will reach the Fallopian tube, where conception usually occurs. Those that then meet the ovum drive their heads into its walls, propelled by their tails. When one succeeds in penetrating it, the ovum creates a barrier that the remainder cannot penetrate.

The moment of conception

Only the nucleus of the sperm cell passes into the inner parts of the ovum. Here the nuclei of the two cells fuse to create a single cell known as the zygote, containing half of the DNA taken from each of the parents to create a unique new being.

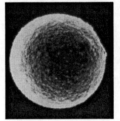

Human ovum   Human sperm

About a day after fertilisation this divides into two, and some 20 hours later the two cells become four. These divisions continue as the growing ball of cells travels down the Fallopian tube and into the uterus. There it becomes embedded in the lining of the uterus, connected by a protective placenta, where it is nourished as it continues to grow.

A month later the embryo will be 10,000 times the size of the ovum from which it developed.

Gender and Heredity

When the nuclei of the sperm and the ovum combine, so too does the genetic information (DNA) contained by each of them. In this way, when an ovum is fertilised a new identity – a unique new set of genetic information – is created, with characteristics from both partners.

This genetic information also determines the sex of the child. Each ovum contains what is termed an X chromosome, while each sperm contains an X or a Y chromosome. An X sperm produces a female

The extent to which genes determine our looks and personality remains a controversial issue

embryo, and a Y sperm produces a male - this is a fundamental working of gender. So it is the father who determines the gender.

In rare cases, there are several variations of X and Y combinations.

For various reasons, including chromosomal ones, the understanding of "sex" and "gender" remains a controversial issue.

Twins

There are two kinds of twin: fraternal (non-identical) and identical.

Fraternal twins are produced when two (or more) ova are released instead of one. Each of the ova can then be fertilised by separate sperm to form two separate embryos, both of which then develop together in the uterus, each with its own placenta. The tendency to produce fraternal twins is thought to run in particular families.

Identical twins are more rare. They are produced when a single fertilised ovum divides into two (or more in the case of

Identical twins from Asia

triplets etc) separate, equal parts. However many there are, these then continue individually to divide and grow to form embryos which share a single placenta and identical DNA.

Birth

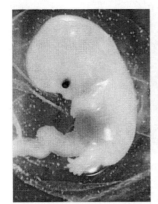

5 weeks

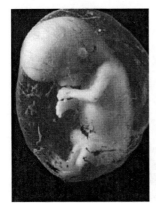

10 weeks

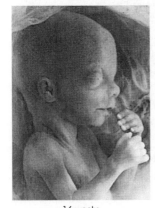

16 weeks

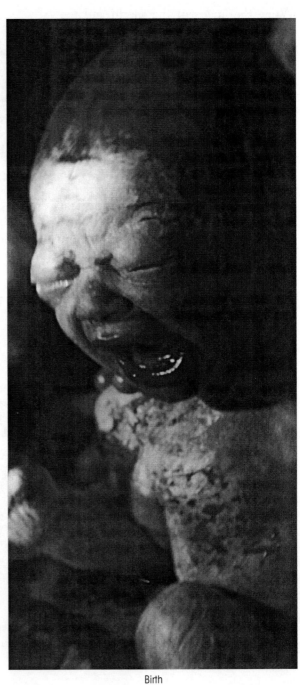

Birth

The course of our sexual development is marked by a series of watersheds. These are the key points which mark the movement from one stage of development to another. Each of these entails a range of physical and psychological changes.

The three watersheds are:

Sexual Differentiation (week 6 of pregnancy): reproductive organs start to develop

Puberty (age 10–16): the reproductive organs become active

Menopause (ages 40–61): the reproductive system decreases its activity

Sexual Differentiation

At six weeks of pregnancy male and female embryos are still alike. However, just six weeks later the sex of the foetus is already quite apparent. Even though the gonads do not take their final shape and position until the 34th week of pregnancy, by the 11th week the penis and the vulva are identifiable. At the same time, the female's Fallopian tubes and the male's prostate are also beginning to form.

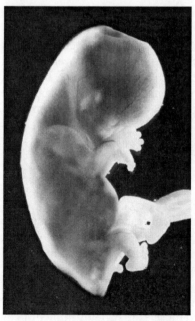

A foetus at 11 weeks

The changes initiated at this stage are caused by the production of the growth-stimulating hormone testosterone in the male and the growth-inhibiting hormone inhibin in the female. These and other sexual hormones are the key to our sexual identify.

Ultimately this identity is determined by the pair of sex chromosomes created at fertilisation, but its physical manifestations depend on the actions of the hormones. These are produced in the gonads at the stimulus of other hormonal messages originating in the brain, and bring about physical and emotional changes associated with sexual development throughout life.

Becoming Sexually Active

During childhood, both boys and girls grow in height (on average about eight to 10 cm per year). However, with the exception of their sexual organs there is little physical difference between the sexes at this stage. The major differences come with the onset of puberty.

Puberty can be a difficult time for both males and females. As well as physical change, there is substantial psychological and emotional development. They are becoming sexually aware and, in some cases, sexually active. Many feel acutely self-conscious.

Girl to Woman

For girls, puberty generally occurs earlier than in boys, usually between the ages of nine and 14.

Frame

One of the first signs of puberty is the growth spurt, starting around the age of ten. Over the following four years many girls will come within a few centimetres of their full adult height, often growing as much as 15 cm within a single year. At the same time, the shape of the skeleton will be developing. In particular, the pelvis will widen to create the space where a growing baby can be accommodated. The different bones involved rarely grow all at the same rate, leaving many girls feeling gangly or out of proportion for a few years.

Muscle and Fat

Women's bodies naturally have a higher fat content than men's; generally 20% - 25% as opposed to men's 10% - 20%.

At the start of puberty, usually when the growth spurt begins, fat accumulates particularly on the breasts, upper arms, hips, buttocks and thighs. The result of this is that women tend to have softer and more rounded bodies than men, with a more curved and defined waist. However, this is by no means a universal truth. The shape of the adult body is determined by a number of factors, in particular, by heredity. Puberty is also the time when many women start to build greater body muscle. The proportions of bodily fat and muscle are strongly influenced by hormones and gender, but also by health, diet, exercise and heredity.

The Maturing Body

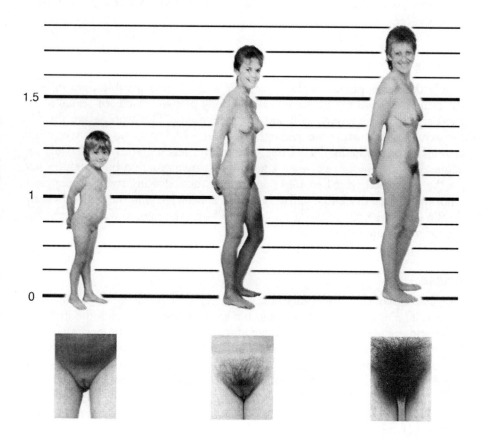

The differences in the bodies of three members of the same family demonstrate some of the changes that occur during puberty in women, as the pubic hair starts to grow and the vulva develops. The main changes in a woman's reproductive organs occur inside her body, in the ovaries and uterus.

Body Hair

Pubic hair, longer, darker, and coarser than other body hair, grows first on the vulva before spreading over the mons pubis and towards the stomach and thighs in an inverted triangle. Pubic hair is not necessarily the same colour as the hair on the head. Further, hair appears in the armpits, arm and leg hair will grow and the fine hair all over the body may also increase. The amount of body hair varies greatly from one woman to another. It is determined primarily by hereditary factors in terms of racial and family background, but is also influenced by any change in hormone levels.

Voice

As in men, women's voices tend to deepen during puberty, although to a much lesser degree.

Genitals

While the development of the genitals is much less noticeable than in boys, the same processes are in motion as the body prepares itself for sexual activity. Early in puberty girls will start to menstruate. The average age for first menstruation, known as the menarche, is around 12.5 years old but this average appears to be gradually decreasing. The ovaries reach maturity and ovulation begins, usually one or two years after the first menstruation but often sooner. As the menstrual cycle becomes regular over the following two to three years, a normal vaginal discharge will also start to appear, keeping the vagina healthy. At the same time, the uterus grows to its full size, the vaginal wall thickens and the external genitals develop.

Breasts

The first sign of the development of the breasts is the swelling or budding of the areolae. The nipple also enlarges, and the entire breast swells with the increased production of glands and fat. The size of the breasts depends on hormone levels and the amount of general body fat, as well as hereditary factors. They may vary throughout life with changing hormone levels, particularly in the course of the menstrual cycle. The breasts are often not of equal size or shape.

Boy to Man

In boys puberty occurs later than in girls, usually between the ages of 11 and 17.

Frame

The growth spurts associated with puberty begin around the age of 13 in boys. They may grow up to 10 cm each year at this time, coming close to their full adult height by the age of 18. At the same time, just as women's hips widen, men's shoulders tend to broaden. The proportions of the different parts of the body to each other may vary at this time, as growth rates are rarely even and consistent. Many boys will feel uncoordinated or gangly, but this tends to pass as they develop.

Muscle and Fat

In general, men's bodies tend to be made up of less fat and more muscle than women's. Muscle often accounts for as much as 40% of an adult man's body weight, with only 10-20% fat. This is largely due to the actions of the male and female sexual hormones, whose effects are first noted during puberty. Indeed, artificial male hormones have often been used to aid muscle building.

A boy's physical strength may increase dramatically during the course of puberty. At the same time, some body fat may accumulate, particularly on the upper arms, chest and abdomen. Some boys may develop breasts for a few months as the hormone levels readjust. While hormones play a significant part in determining the proportions of body fat and muscle, these are also dependent on general health, diet, exercise and heredity.

Skin

The hormonal changes in puberty also affect the skin and hair. The sebaceous glands become more active at this time, making both more greasy, and acne may appear on the face, chest and back. Body odour also increases as the sweat glands develop.

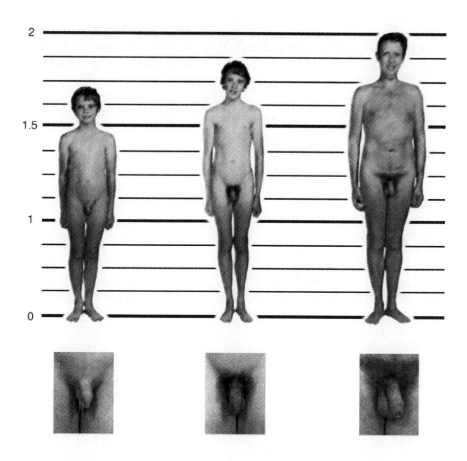

The Maturing Body

Three members of the same family show some of the visible differences to the genital area in the course of puberty as the pubic hair, the testes and penis develop. These changes – and other less obvious ones – usually occur between the ages of 11 and 17.

Body Hair

The coarse pubic hair appears early in puberty at the base of the penis. From here it spreads to the scrotum and sometimes to the anus and towards the stomach and thighs. It may be a different colour from the hair on the head, although it is likely to turn grey with age. Hair also appears in the armpits, arms and legs, and sometimes on the chest, shoulders and back. Facial hair will also darken and thicken, and again may not be the same colour as the hair on the head. Body and facial hair tend to be much more abundant in men then in women. It is determined primarily by hereditary factors in terms of racial and family background, but is also influenced by any change in hormone levels.

Voice

In men puberty often causes the voice to change dramatically or break. This can happen gradually or quite suddenly. It is caused by changes in the larynx: namely the elongation and thickening of the vocal chords, together with the growth of the Adam's apple from the thyroid cartilage.

Genitals

These are probably the most noticeable changes in males. Around the age of 10 or 11 the rate of growth of the external genitals increases dramatically. The testes grow in length and volume. The penis grows longer and wider, and its head or glans develops. The internal organs also develop and sperm and seminal fluid are produced (known as the spermarche). The penis can become erect (though it is believed that erections are possible in utero) and ejaculation can occur.

Frequent erections can occur at this stage, often without any sexual stimulus and at awkward moments. These tend to increase during puberty. Erections while asleep begin and spontaneous ejaculation may occur. This involuntary but perfectly natural experience is known as a nocturnal emission or wet dream.

FACT
Recent research has suggested that sperm counts in men are going down worldwide.

Hormones

Hormones affect every aspect of our lives. Originating in involuntary chemical signals in the brain, they control many of our bodily processes, including the cycles related to reproduction. At the same time it is widely believed that it is in the cycles and variations of our hormones – and particularly the sex hormones – that lies the source of many of our emotions.

Hormonal Action in the Mature Female

The Menstrual Cycle

The menstrual cycle is the method by which the female reproductive system is maintained. It is characterised by two hormones in particular, oestrogen in the first half of the cycle and progesterone in the second.

If there are no problems, this cycle ensures, along with hormones from the pituitary gland, that once each month at least one reproductive germ cell or ovum is released from an ovary, and that, if it is fertilised by its male equivalent (sperm), the uterus will be ready to receive it.

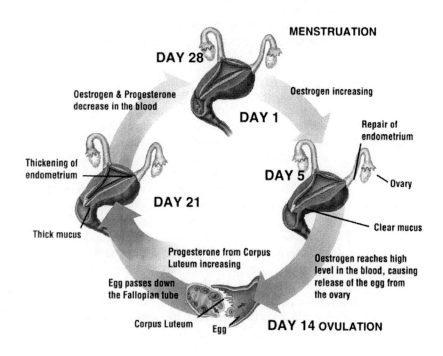

MENSTRUATION

DAY 28

Oestrogen & Progesterone decrease in the blood

Oestrogen increasing

DAY 1

Repair of endometrium

Thickening of endometrium

DAY 5

Ovary

DAY 21

Thick mucus

Clear mucus

Progesterone from Corpus Luteum increasing

Oestrogen reaches high level in the blood, causing release of the egg from the ovary

Egg passes down the Fallopian tube

Corpus Luteum   Egg

DAY 14 OVULATION

How the menstrual cycle works

Each ovary stores as many as half a million potential egg cells or ova. Each month the pituitary gland stimulates the growth of a follicle in one of the ovaries. In this follicle a single ovum is matured and oestrogen is produced. About half-way through the cycle the ovum is released, leaving an empty follicle, now called a corpus luteum, which starts to produce progesterone. This is the hormone that prepares the uterus lining for pregnancy. If the ovum is not fertilised, the levels of oestrogen and progesterone in the blood stream fall after about 14 days, at which time menstruation (menstrual period) will occur. The uterus lining is broken down and passed out of the body, ready for the cycle to begin again.

On average this cycle lasts 28 days, although cycles between 26 and 32 days are quite common. In a 28-day cycle, if Day One is the first day of menstruation, ovulation takes place around 14 days before. Menstruation itself generally lasts for three to six days. About 30 ml to 150 ml of blood are lost each month.

At times during menstruation some pain may be experienced. Known as dysmenorrhoea, this is a common occurrence which, if necessary, can be treated with pain killers or in extreme cases with hormonal preparations. There are various other disorders associated with menstruation, including amenorrhoea (stopped or missed periods), menorrhagia (heavy periods), and polymenorrhoea (over-frequent periods). These can often be treated. It is important to note that in some societies and religions, menstruation or menstruating women are considered to be unclean. This is a completely false notion of this natural cycle.

Other effects of the female hormonal cycle

The menstrual cycle is marked by certain physical effects of the changing hormone levels. The oestrogen produced in the first half of the cycle tends to create feelings of well-being. The hair and skin are in good condition. Vaginal discharge is minimal, becoming more profuse as ovulation approaches. The effects of progesterone in the second half of the cycle tend to be less positive. The breasts may become heavy and tender, spots may appear and hair may become greasier. Vaginal discharge becomes thicker and may have some odour. Many women suffer from water retention. Mood swings can also be acute with irritability, tearfulness and indecision.

These symptoms are collectively referred to as the pre-menstrual syndrome (PMS). In some extreme cases severe depression and even violence can occur. This is referred to as pre-menstrual dysphoric disorder (PMDD). Once surrounded by superstition, PMS and PMDD are now medically recognised. Symptoms typically may last up to nine days, but can be medically treated if necessary.

Hormonal Action in the Mature Male

In men hormones cycles also occur but in a 24-hour period as opposed to a month in women. In this pattern, testosterone is typically highest in the morning and decreases throughout the day. Through the day sperm are produced constantly and in vast quantities to maintain the 200 to 500 million sperm in each ejaculation. The male hormones sustain this production and maintain the whole male reproductive system.

How the male hormones work

The hormonal signals sent out by the pituitary gland act on the testes to aid and regulate the production of sperm and stimulate the production of testosterone. The sperm produced are matured and stored in the duct leading from each testis, called the epididymis.

Other effects of the male hormones

Testosterone is one of several androgens, the steroids that stimulate the development of the male sexual organs and secondary sexual characteristics. It raises the rate at which proteins are produced, and lowers the rate at which they are broken down. The effects of this are increased muscle bulk and accelerated growth. Testosterone promotes aggression. It also sustains the male sex drive, although this can be self-perpetuating, as sexual activity – whether through intercourse or masturbation – is itself the best natural way of maintaining levels of testosterone.

Menopause

This is the period in later life when the activity of the ovaries ceases. Menopause usually occurs between the ages of 40 and 56 in women and more gradually after the age of 40 in men. There is no real reason why it should mean the end of an active and satisfying sex life.

Women and The Menopause

The menopause is the term used to refer to the end of menstruation. It usually occurs between the ages of 40 and 56. There is some evidence of heredity in the timing of both puberty and the menopause. The period of change tends to last one or two years as the system re-regulates itself – this is similar to the time it takes for menstruation to become regular. It is at the menopause that the ovaries cease to be active. Ova are no longer released each month and the production of the sex hormones oestrogen and progesterone declines.

One of the first signs of the menopause is irregularity in the menstrual cycle, before menstruation ceases completely. All of the sex organs are affected: the uterus and ovaries shrink, the vaginal walls grow thinner, lubrication can be less, and the vulva may partially atrophy.

Physical responses to sex tend to be slower and sometimes less intense, but not necessarily any less pleasurable. The plateau stage of arousal may last longer. Orgasms tend to be less intense, but any decline in sex drive is usually gradual. Generally those who enjoy sex earlier in life will continue to do so for as long as their general health permits.

Women's experiences of menopause vary greatly. For some it is very straight-forward and even a relief, for others it can be quite traumatic. There are certain short-term symptoms caused by the change in hormone levels which can be disagreeable. These include:

- hot flushes
- night sweats
- palpitations
- headaches
- fatigue
- insomnia
- irritability
- mood swings
- depression

More importantly, lack of oestrogen can lead to some of the major health problems affecting women in later life, such as heart disease and the brittle-bone disease osteoporosis. Treatment, including hormone replacement therapy (HRT), may be recommended.

HRT replaces the hormones that the ovaries are no longer producing. It can eradicate the short-term symptoms of menopause, and reduce the risk of heart disease and osteoporosis by up to 50%.

However, HRT may not be suitable for some women, while others may prefer natural methods of easing menopausal symptoms. These include dietary supplements and various alternative therapies, such as reflexology, acupuncture, aromatherapy and homeopathy. More and more treatments are becoming recognised, as more is learnt about how to ensure that women can continue to enjoy good health through and after the menopause.

Men and the Climacteric or Male Menopause

The climacteric in men is less well recognised than that which occurs in women. This may be because it tends to be less dramatic.

On the whole, the production of testosterone decreases very gradually from the age of about 40. By 60 this may produce noticeable changes. The testes may shrink and become less firm, and the scrotal sac may grow looser and more wrinkled. Physical responses to sex may be slower and less strong. It

may be more difficult to obtain an erection as the blood vessels in the pubic area harden and slow down the blood flow. However, many men can maintain an erection for longer than in earlier life and the plateau stage of arousal tends to last much longer, even though orgasm is often more short-lived.

Along with testosterone, sperm production tends to decrease with age. However, both continue to be produced throughout life, with the result that they may remain both sexually active and fertile.

Ever since the connection between sexual intercourse and conception was first recognised, people have been looking for ways to prevent pregnancy.

Four thousand years ago Egyptian women were using pessaries of honey and animal dung, while Arabian women mixed pomegranate pulp with alum and rock salt. The Greeks used a concoction of cedar oil, frankincense and olive oil, and even experimented with intrauterine devices. In China and Japan disks of oiled paper were used as rudimentary cervical caps. It is said that the idea of the intrauterine device developed from the Arabic custom of placing a stone in the uterus of a female camel to keep it sterile, although how the method first came to be used in humans is not known.

At one time in Persia it was recommended that the woman should jump backwards nine times then sit on her toes stroking her navel! In Japan, men wore sheaths made from tortoiseshell, horn or leather.

However, it was in the 16th century that the Italian, Gabriel Fallopius, developed a sheath made from chemically-treated linen, although this was initially

From tortoiseshells to teasers – condoms have developed greatly from their origins. They are now available in an almost infinite variety of shapes, sizes, colours and flavours, and seem likely to remain one of the most popular forms of contraception.

developed to prevent venereal infections. This rudimentary version of the condom was later replaced with animal intestines, and eventually with latex rubber.

The condom and the diaphragm have been used widely since the end of the 19th century. Since then both the variety and the reliability of methods of contraception have increased dramatically. Intrauterine devices (IUDs) were used at the beginning of the century, but with frequent damage to the wall of the uterus.

Actually, it was not until the 1960s that a more modern and safer form of the IUD was produced – which was immediately popular. It was at this time that the first hormonal oral contraceptives were produced, as a result of research carried out in the mid and late 1950s. The pill, as it has simply become known, has become the major form of contraception since its discovery and now comes in a variety of types using different hormone levels. The first pill was the combined oral contraceptive pill (COCP), which contained both oestrogen and synthetic progestins. Since then the mini-pill has been developed, which is a supposedly progestogen-only pill (POP) – though it may actually contain several related chemical compounds – and can be taken every day, often by women who can't take the full pill. It also causes fewer health problems.

Many of the contraceptives available today are highly sophisticated, and continue to be developed further, providing us with a constantly-growing range of choices. The social acceptability of their use has also increased. The key to successful use of contraceptives lies in the combination of:

- having the motivation to prevent pregnancy
- knowing how to use the chosen method correctly
- being sufficiently happy with that choice to use it consistently

Contraceptives function in various ways: by preventing the production of sperm or egg, by preventing them from meeting, or by preventing them from surviving. Methods may be divided broadly into four main types: natural, mechanical, hormonal, and sterilisation.

Natural Methods

Natural methods of contraception do not involve any hormonal or mechanical intervention. Success or failure depends on using the technique correctly, and even then these methods may not be 100% reliable, especially for women with irregular periods. The guidance of a teacher fully trained in natural family planning methods is advisable.

Rhythm Methods

These are based on the woman's natural body cycles, determining when ovulation is likely to occur, so that the couple can avoid intercourse when conception is most probable. It is the only form of contraception acceptable to some religions. The lifetime of a sperm is estimated to be up to five or six days and of the egg just one or two, so the safe period is taken from six days before ovulation to two days afterwards. There are three different ways of calculating the time of ovulation that are described here only briefly.

The obvious advantage of these methods is that they are entirely natural. They also give a woman a greater awareness of her own body, and enable her to know when she is most fertile should she wish to become pregnant.

They are, however, far from reliable, especially for women who have irregular periods. Their effectiveness varies from 2% to 20% failure, meaning that in every hundred women using the rhythm method, between two and 20 will become pregnant during the course of a year. The calendar method remains the least reliable.

For greater safety, all three methods should be combined and, if possible, should be explained in more detail by a trained natural-methods teacher. None of them provide protection against sexually-transmitted diseases.

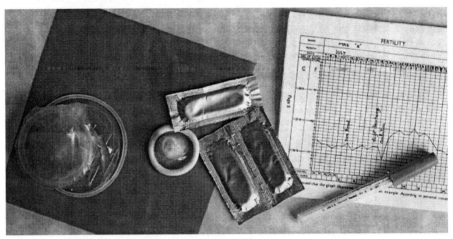

The range of methods of contraception continues to grow, under the influence of developments in scientific research and public demand. In many countries, a great variety is available, enabling most people to find a method appropriate to their own personal needs and preferences.

The Calendar Method

This is so unreliable that it is generally only recommended as a cross-check against other methods. A record must be kept of the length of the woman's menstrual cycle for at least six months, counted from the first day of her period to the day before the next period starts.

The first day of the fertile time is calculated by subtracting 19 from the number of days of the shortest cycle (i.e. 14 days after ovulation, plus five days to allow for sperm survival); the probable last fertile day is given by subtracting 10 from the longest cycle (i.e. 14 days after ovulation, minus four days to allow for ovum survival).

The cycle may change – and, if it does, then the calculations must be altered accordingly.

The Basal Body or Temperature Method

This involves taking the woman's temperature early in the morning (before getting out of bed and before having anything to eat or drink) and recording it daily. The temperature rises by about 0.2 - 0.4°C for three days immediately after

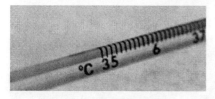

ovulation. However, body temperature may be affected by various other factors, making this a potentially unreliable guide on its own. With a record taken over some months, however, the safe period may be better estimated, but not infallibly.

The Cervical Mucus Method/Ovulation Tests

This involves observing the regular changes in uterine mucus. This increases in quantity and becomes more slippery and clear at the time of ovulation, so that the sperm can travel through it more easily. Intercourse is not safe until the discharge has become cloudy, sticky and thick once more. Ovulation tests, which are not unlike pregnancy tests, have now been developed to indicate when ovulation has occurred.

Withdrawal

In this method, also known as coitus interruptus, the man withdraws his penis from the vagina before ejaculation. While it has the advantages of other natural methods and is popular worldwide, it is probably the least reliable of all methods. It requires a degree of control which is not always possible and, even when practised, can result in extreme frustration for both partners. It is also very risky, as it is essential that not even a drop of sperm should be deposited in or near the vagina. Even the fluid that lubricates the penis in the earlier stages of arousal may contain sperm, so withdrawal prior to ejaculation may still be too late. It is estimated that each year as many as a quarter of the women regularly using this method become pregnant.

Non-penetrative Sex

This is a way of enjoying sexual activity while avoiding conception. It may involve kissing, stroking, mutual masturbation and other activities, but excluding any vaginal intercourse. Anal sex, though penetrative, is also used as a contraception method.

Mechanical Methods

These are designed to allow full vaginal intercourse to take place while preventing pregnancy. They function in a variety of ways and may be used in conjunction with one another or with other methods.

The Condom

The male condom or sheath is the most common of the barrier methods: that is, those that prevent the sperm from meeting the egg.

It is also the only widely-used male contraceptive. It is made of thin latex rubber, and functions by catching and retaining ejaculated semen. It must be rolled on to the erect penis before any contact with the vagina. This may be done either by the man or his partner, who may make it a part of foreplay. The air should be squeezed out of the end or the teat, if there is one, then the condom should be rolled gently over the tip of the penis leaving the teat (or the last half inch, if there is no teat) free to catch the ejaculate. The condom should not be pulled or tweaked, as this can damage it.

The base of the condom should be held on withdrawal to avoid spilling sperm

On withdrawal from the vagina, the condom should be held carefully in place at the base of the penis while it is still partially erect to prevent any sperm from escaping. A new condom should be used each time intercourse takes place.

For extra security and lubrication condoms may be used with spermicides; spermicidally treated condoms are also available. For lubrication, only a spermicide with a water or silicone-based jelly should be used, as other substances (such as petroleum jelly) may damage the condom or irritate the vagina.

The male condom is one of the most simple, straightforward, popular and widely available forms of contraception. Available in a variety of shapes, colours, textures and even flavours, its popularity has increased considerably in recent years as it also provides a high level of protection against sexually-transmitted diseases, including HIV infection.

The most common complaint is of reduced sensitivity, although this can be a benefit for those men who are prone to premature ejaculation. Another complaint is that the putting on of the condom can interrupt the growing excitement of sexual arousal, although many couples have found that they can counter this by making it a fun part of foreplay. Occasionally allergic reactions to the latex it is made of may occur; however, hypoallergenic condoms are now available.

Reliability is high: of 100 women whose partners use the condom as the sole method of contraception, only two to four will become pregnant in the course of a year - if it is used consistently and correctly. With less careful use, up to 15 women in 100 will become pregnant.

The Female Condom

The female condom is a thin sheath or pouch worn by a woman during sex. It entirely lines the vagina and helps to prevent pregnancy and sexually transmitted diseases (STDs) including HIV. The FC2 female condom is a nitrile sheath or pouch 17 cm (6.5 inches) in length. At each end there is a flexible ring. At the closed end of the sheath, the flexible ring is inserted into the vagina to hold the female condom in place. The other end of the sheath stays outside the vulva at the entrance to the vagina. This ring acts as a guide during penetration and it also stops the sheath from moving up inside the vagina. There is a silicone-based lubricant on the inside of the condom, but additional lubrication can be used. The condom does not contain spermicide.

The original version of the FC female condom (brand names included Reality, Femy and Femidom), was made of polyurethane. As this was a relatively expensive material, the makers of the FC female condom released the FC2 version, using the cheaper nitrile. Large-scale production of the FC2 began in 2007. Production of the original FC condom has now stopped.

Benefits of the female condom include:

- Women can share the responsibility
- Use if a partner refuses to use a male condom
- It protects against most STDs and pregnancy
- It can be inserted in advance of sexual intercourse
- Being made of nitrile, it can be used with oil-based as well as water-based lubricants

The Diaphragm and The Cap

These are also barrier methods, preventing the sperm from reaching the uterus. They both consist of a circular dome of thin latex or silicone placed in the vagina. The diaphragm fits behind the pubic bone and blocks the entrance to the cervix. It is kept in shape by a pliable metal, or firm rubber, rim. The cap is smaller and covers just the cervix; it is held in place by suction.

Both are available from doctors or clinics and need to be fitted correctly by a trained health professional. They should be checked by a qualified nurse or doctor every six months, as the vagina can change shape, especially with weight loss or gain. They may be inserted any time before intercourse. However, the spermicide used with them must be topped up if intercourse occurs more than three hours after insertion, or if intercourse is repeated.

Both caps and diaphragms must be left in place for at least six hours after intercourse, but should be removed before more than 30 hours have elapsed. With careful use, the diaphragm and cap have a failure rate of only four to 8%, which rises to 10% to 15% with less careful use.

Intrauterine Devices (IUDs)

The term intrauterine device refers to devices that are inserted (by a trained health professional) into the woman's uterus. They function largely by preventing the sperm from fertilising the ovum; additionally the presence of a foreign body inside the uterus appears to irritate the lining and wall and make it difficult for an embryo to implant. One type is made of plastic and thin copper wire; they have one or two fine threads attached to the plastic frame that extend through the opening at the cervix, where they can be felt by the woman's fingers. There are 10 types of copper IUDs in the UK alone. A second type (Marina) works by releasing the hormone progestogen. IUDs are also known as coils, Ts or loops, although these terms are no longer strictly accurate.

IUDs can also be used as a form of emergency contraception, since they partially function by making the uterus hostile to the implantation of an embryo.

IUDs have to be inserted by a trained health professional, but provide immediate protection and can be left in place for between five and eight years, depending on the type of device used. They must also be removed by a health professional.

Their advantages lie in the fact that they do not require thought or preparation before lovemaking and the copper type, at least, does not involve the use of any hormones.

However, there are possible problems:

*   they may slip out of the uterus. If this happens, pregnancy may occur, although this is most likely with young women or those who never had a baby

*   infection, typically when bacteria gets into the uterus during insertion of the IUD or one of the fine threads that lead through the cervix

*   in rare circumstances, when the IUD is inserted, it can push through the wall of the uterus.

If pregnancy does occur with the use of an IUD, ectopic pregnancy (where the embryo settles and starts to grow outside the womb, usually in a Fallopian tube) and miscarriage are more likely. In some women, they may cause longer, heavier or more painful periods or spotting in between periods. IUDs provide no protection against sexually transmitted diseases.

However, IUDs remain almost as reliable as the pill, with less than 1% of users becoming pregnant each year.

The IUD, marketed under the brand name Mirena, is an IUD with a hormonal implant, progestogen. It can be left in place for five years. This system is becoming increasingly popular, as it has been shown to reduce blood loss, and menstrual pain, so is often recommended in the treatment of cases of heavy menstruation or menorrhagia. It also appears to reduce the likelihood of some genital infections, as well as being highly effective as a contraceptive.

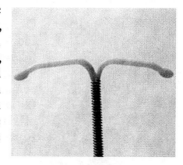

Contraceptive sponge

This is used in a similar way to the cap and the diaphragm in that it is placed in the vagina behind the pubic bone and over the cervix prior to intercourse. It functions by combining barrier and spermicidal methods by both blocking and killing the sperm ejaculated in to the vagina. However, it is less reliable than other methods and, whilst not very popular, three different brands are on the market, Protectaid in Canada and Europe, Pharmatex in France and French Canada and Today in the United States. Sponges provide no protection against STIs.

Spermicides

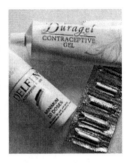

These are chemicals that kill the sperm inside the vagina. Available as creams, jellies, films, foams or pessaries, they are applied or inserted into the vagina before intercourse. On their own spermicides are not considered a reliable form of contraception, with a failure rate of 15% to 29%, and are generally used in conjunction with another method – in particular with diaphragms, caps and condoms – for extra security.

Hormonal Methods

These involve the use of synthetic hormones similar to those produced naturally by the body during pregnancy. Taken either by pill, injection or implant, they have been among the most popular contraceptives since the 1960s.

The Combined Oral Contraceptive Pill (COCP)

This contains both oestrogen and progestogen. Progestogen thickens the cervical mucus, making it less easy for the sperm to get through to meet the egg. It also makes the lining of the womb thinner, making it less likely to allow a fertilised egg to become implanted. Oestrogen alters the body's hormonal cycle to stop the ovaries from releasing an egg each month. The exact amount of oestrogen and progestogen used depends upon the type and brand of pill.

Use of the pill is based on a standard 28-day cycle. Hormonally-active pills are taken for the first 21 days, followed by a seven-day break to allow for the bleeding that takes place in normal menstruation. The most common type of combined pill is monophasic, each of the 21 pills in the packet containing the same amount of hormone. There are also bi- and tri-phasic pills, which vary the amount of each hormone taken over the 21 days to follow the body's natural cycle more closely.

Finally there is the everyday pill, each packet of which includes seven inactive pills. It is therefore particularly useful for women who have difficulty in remembering to take their pill, as there is no seven-day break.

Whatever the type or brand, the combined pill is usually taken at approximately the same time every day.

The advantages of the combined pill are considerable:

- it provides constant protection, with no mechanical devices and no interruption of intercourse
- many women find that it reduces bleeding, period pain and premenstrual tension
- more significantly, it offers substantial protection against cancer of the ovaries and the womb
- it can help prevent some pelvic infections and reduce the risk of fibroids, ovarian cysts and non-cancerous breast disease
- the pill can be used by most women, up to the age of the menopause if they remain healthy (with regular blood pressure and smear tests) and do not smoke.

However, the pill is not suitable for some women, such as those who are very overweight or have a personal or family history of significant heart or blood-pressure problems or blood clots. Research has suggested that use of the pill may slightly increase the risk of some cancers, but this is still very uncertain.

Many of the potential ill effects of the pill have been linked with smoking.

Generally speaking, the worst side effects experienced are:

- headaches
- weight gain or loss
- reduced interest in sex
- mood changes
- bleeding between periods.

If these occur they will usually disappear with the first few months, or may be eliminated by a change of pill. The pill does not offer any protection against sexually-transmitted diseases.

If taken regularly by suitable users, the pill is the most effective reversible method of contraception, with a failure rate of less than 1%. Apart from failing to take it, the only things that can reduce the pill's reliability are

- vomiting within three hours of taking it
- severe diarrhoea
- the effects of certain medicines.

The Progestogen-Only Pill (POP)

This is also known as the *mini pill*. It contains no oestrogen, functioning simply by thickening the cervical mucus and making the womb lining thinner, although it can affect ovulation in some women (see *The combined pill*). Otherwise it is similar to the combined pill, but with less likelihood of side effects and only marginally higher probability of irregularity in the menstrual cycle. It must, however, be taken at exactly the same time every day. Without oestrogen, it is not associated with increased risk of, deep vein thrombosis (DVT), or heart disease and is thus a good choice for older women who smoke and should not take the combined pill which carries these risks. The progestogen-only pill can also be used by breast-feeding mothers with no effect on milk production (oestrogen reduces the amount of breast milk).

When it is used carefully, the progestogen-only pill has a failure rate of only 1%, though this rises to 4% with less careful use.

Injections and Implants

Contraceptive injections give protection for either eight or 12 weeks. Implants, on the other hand, can provide protection for up to five years. They are small, soft tubes placed under the skin of the upper arm which gradually release a hormone into the bloodstream.

Like the mini pill, they use just progestogen, which thickens the cervical mucus and, in the injection method, stops ovulation. They are only available from doctors specially trained in their use.

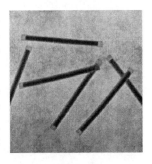

As well as the advantages of the progestogen-only pill, they have the great bonus of being effective for the full period, with no need to remember to take a pill at a specific time every day, or even to think about contraception.

The main disadvantage of the contraceptive injection lies in the fact that it cannot be removed, so any unwanted side effects will continue throughout the eight or 12-week period, whereas an implant can be removed at any time.

Both injections and implants are extremely reliable, with fewer than one woman in 100 becoming pregnant in a year. The statistics on implants suggest that about two women will become pregnant over the course of five years.

The Male Hormone Contraceptive (MHC)

Researchers around the world are very close to having success with male contraceptive pills, patches, implants and creams. It is now believed that an MHC in the form of a daily pill could be available on the market within five to seven years and implants could arrive even sooner.

It has been found that a combination of progestin and androgen implants are safe, effective, inexpensive and entirely reversible.

Researchers have tested several different products to find the best combination with the fewest and mildest side effects and then the least amount of medication required to get the maximum effect.

It is predicted that in some countries, a low-cost, reversible and long-acting form of an MHC could become commercially available within the next three years, however, it will probably be at least five to seven years before one is approved by the US Food and Drug Administration.

Controversy around the MHC is that there is concern that men may be less reliable in taking daily MHCs in that they are not the ones who risk pregnancy. Little is yet known about how these new birth control options will be received by men..

Sterilisation

Sterilisation of the male or female is a simple and relatively minor operation, which is highly effective. Failure rates stand at about one in 500 for women, and for men one in 1,000, or less, during the first year after the operation, dropping to one in 3,000 later.

Reversal of sterilisation is possible, but requires a more major operation; the success rates stand at about 70% for women, and between 10% and 90% for men. These figures vary according to the type of operation carried out and, for men, according to how long ago the original sterilisation was performed.

Sterilisation should still be seen as a permanent step.

Female sterilisation

This involves blocking or cutting and tying the Fallopian tubes, in which the sperm and ovum could otherwise meet. As in male sterilisation, the body's natural cycles are unaffected: an egg is still produced every month, even though it cannot be fertilised. Enjoyment of intercourse is also unaffected.

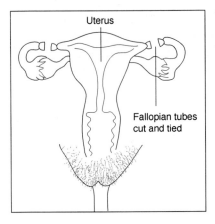

The operation is usually carried out under general anaesthetic as a day case. Afterwards there may be some slight bleeding or pain for one or two weeks, and a couple of weeks' rest may be required. After this time periods continue as normal.

Female sterilisation is effective at once, although some women are advised to use another method of contraception until their next period.

Male sterilisation (vasectomy)

This involves blocking or cutting and tying both of the tubes (the vasa deferentia) which carry the sperm from the testicles to where they are mixed to form the semen. Hormones and sex drive are unaffected, as are the man's orgasm and ejaculation. The sole difference is that there are no sperm in the semen, and this is only detectable under a microscope.

The operation is performed under local anaesthetic and takes about 10 minutes. The most common problem following the operation is bruising, swelling and pain, but usually this is slight and lasts no more than a week.

Vasectomy is completely reliable as a form of contraception after two clear semen tests, two to four months after the operation, to ensure that any sperm left in the tubes leading to the penis have gone.

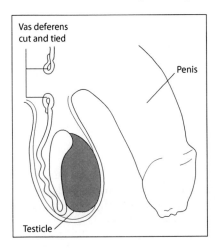

Failure of the operation stands at about one in every 1,000 within a few months of the operation, but can be easily detected by the post-surgery sperm tests. The chances of failure occurring some time later are estimated at between one in 3,000 and one in 7,000.

Some men report a drop in sex drive, though others – safe from the likelihood of fertilisation – report an increase. These responses are most certainly psychological as opposed to physiological responses to the surgery.

Emergency Contraception (EC)

In many countries emergency contraception is available for women who have had sex without contraception and do not want to become pregnant, or for women who suspect their method of contraception may have failed. It is essential to seek advice quickly.

Emergency Hormonal Contraceptive Pills (EHCs or ECs)

Even though this method is also known as the morning after pill, depending on the drug, it may be taken up to 107-120 hours after having unprotected sexual intercourse. It contains the same hormones as the combined pill but in larger quantities, functioning either by stopping an egg from being released or by preventing a fertilised egg from implanting in the womb. It is important to note that because it has its effect prior to the earliest time of implantation, it is not an abortifacient, or method of chemical abortion.

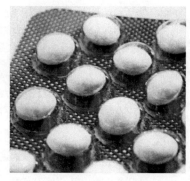

Early versions used to involve taking two doses 12 hours apart, but more recently is dispensed as a single dose. Side effects from taking it may include some nausea, and the emergency pill is not suitable for all women. It is 95% effective in preventing pregnancy.

IUDs as emergency contraception

IUDs (see under Mechanical methods) can also be used for emergency contraception, but must be fitted within five days of having unprotected intercourse.

Check-ups are usually made three to four weeks after using emergency contraception.

Part of enjoying a healthy sex life lies in taking proper care of the sexual and reproductive system. Sexual health is a responsibility: it affects both partners.

Natural, pleasant bodily odour can be attractive, though today's obsession with cleanliness has severely reduced the impact of personal odour as one of the most powerful sexual signals. However, it has also increased awareness of the importance of personal hygiene and helped eliminate offensive stale smells.

In fact, many parts of the body are looked after by the body's own processes. Nonetheless, minor problems can often be avoided by taking certain steps to maintain a basic level of hygiene, such as washing the genital area and anus every day and wearing clean underwear. Strong soaps should be avoided, as they may cause irritation in sensitive areas. Urinating soon after intercourse can also help prevent infections in the urethra.

Hygiene for Women

Some vaginal discharge is normal and necessary for maintaining a healthy environment in the vaginal and vulval area. However, its delicate balance may be upset by use of strong soaps, or too much soap, and by vaginal deodorants or perfumes.

Some slight yeasty odour is normal and healthy. However, any changes that do not coincide with the usual menstrual pattern may be a sign of infection.

After using the toilet, women should always wipe themselves from front to back (from vagina to anus), to prevent bacteria from the anus entering the vagina and possibly causing infection.

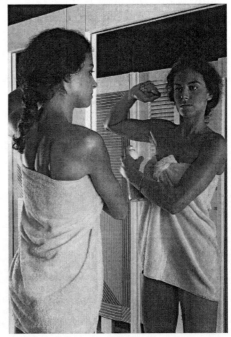

Body Odour - The Western obsession with cleanliness has severely reduced the impact of personal odour as one of the most powerful sexual signals. However, it has also increased awareness of the importance of personal hygiene and helped eliminate offensive stale smells

Hygiene for Men

Males of all ages should wash their penis at least once a day. Particular attention should be paid to the area just below the head of the penis, where a glandular secretion known as smegma can accumulate. If the man is uncircumcised, he should draw back the foreskin while washing. Penile discharge is not normal and any occurrence should be investigated.

This Japanese woodcut from the 19th century by Kunimori II shows a man's penis being cleaned by his female companion. Animals groom each other – and this can be a bonding part of human relationships as well

Circumcision

Male and female circumcision have been traditional in some cultures since ancient times, and are still performed today. Female circumcision, which has been outlawed by the World Health Organisation (WHO), is an emotive and much debated issue.

Male Circumcision

Male circumcision is both one of the oldest surgical operations (it was already well established in Egypt by 4,000 BC) and the most widespread. It is currently estimated that about half of the world's male population is circumcised but there is some evidence that that this number may be dropping.

There are several varieties of male circumcision, but the most common consists of the removal of the whole of the foreskin. This is mostly a religious practice amongst Jews and Muslims, and is also customary in many parts of Africa, the Middle East and

A Portuguese Jewish circumcision ceremony, depicted in an 18th century engraving. The child's father is standing at the back on the left, with a glass of wine in his hand, while his mother is not permitted to attend the ceremony

Circumcised Penis
(with trimmed pubic hair)

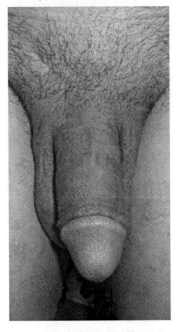

Uncircumcised Penis
(with fully shaven pubic hair)

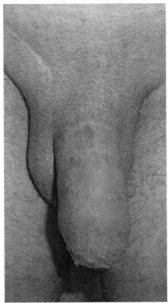

Australia. The operation may be carried out on babies or small children as a religious or other birth rite, or on adolescents to mark the passage into manhood.

By the 20th century it had become widespread in societies in which it had no traditional basis, in particular Britain and the United States because of recommendation by influential writers on childbirth and babyhood, such as Dr. Benjamin Spock with his bestselling *Baby and Child Care* guide book in 1946.

These days the main argument in favour of non-religious circumcision is hygiene, as removal of the foreskin eliminates any potential problems with the accumulation of the glandular secretion known as smegma.

Circumcision has also been linked with the prevention of various kind of cancer, as some surveys suggest that occurrences of both cervical cancer in women and penile cancer in men are significantly less frequent in societies where male circumcision is practiced. In Africa, there has been a major push on circumcision given that some studies have shown that it may lower rates of HIV infection.

In medical terms, aside from instances of such conditions as severe phimosis, where the foreskin or prepuce is closed up and cannot be retracted from the head or glans, the operation is almost always unnecessary. In adults it is intensely painful and there is a risk of complications, such as infections and withering of the penis. However, the use of anaesthetic and hygienic medical procedure reduces these dangers, so that this ancient custom can now be carried out more safely.

It should be noted that there continues to be controversy around such practices and even the British Medical Association has gone as far as issuing a statement that this procedure carries significant medical and psychological risks and no real medical benefits.

Female Circumcision

Female circumcision, female genital cutting (FGC), female genital mutilation (FGM) or female genital mutilation/cutting (FGM/C) is less frequent than male, but it is the subject of considerably more controversy. It is estimated that it has been carried out on 100 to 140 million women alive today typically between the ages of 10 and 14.

The most common forms of female circumcision are clitoridectomy and infibulation:

Clitoridectomy involves the removal of the clitoris and sometimes other parts of the vulva.

Infibulation is the sewing together of the labia majora, leaving only a very small hole for urination and menstruation; it usually involves the removal of parts or all of the clitoris and labia minora.

A circumcised girl from Somalia where female circumcision is still widely practised

Female circumcision is carried out in children or young women before puberty and marriage.

Clitoridectomy is quite common throughout Africa and in some Islamic groups. Infibulation is most common in eastern Africa. Both are also becoming increasingly common amongst some immigrant populations in Europe and the USA.

The origins almost certainly lie in a specific intention by men to reduce or eliminate women's sexual pleasure, as the operation holds no benefit for the women at all outside social convention. The number of deaths resulting from complications or infections remains high. The practice is surrounded by controversy as, on the one hand, it is seen as brutal and dangerous, inflicted on women by a male-orientated society but, on the other, it is also an ancient and deeply rooted tradition.

There have been several attempts by the World Health Organisation (WHO) to end the practice and the United Nations has declared February 6 as the *International Day of Zero Tolerance to Female Genital Mutilation.*

Safer Sex

Safer sex is the term used for the various ways of adapting sexual activity to reduce the risk of sexually-transmitted infections. These may range from minor infections such as thrush, to HIV, the virus which can lead to AIDS. The point of safer sex is to minimise these risks whilst attempting to make sexual activity as enjoyable and varied as ever – and possibly even more so.

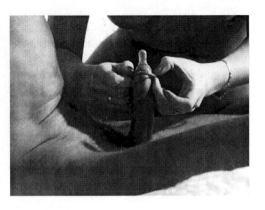

Basically, safer sex means sexual activity in which body fluids are not mixed. The forms that it can take are almost endless.

Condoms

The most common modes of transmission of STIs are vaginal and anal intercourse. If used carefully, the condom is one of the most reliable and widely available methods of making these activities safer. Condoms should be used with water-based or silicone-based lubricants only, particularly for anal intercourse. Oil-based substances such as Vaseline, body lotion or massage oil should be avoided, as they weaken the latex of the condom, often causing it to split. Many brands of condom are bought pre-lubricated with spermicides, which can themselves help kill some infections.

Extra-strong condoms should be used for anal intercourse. The female condom can also be used for both vaginal and anal intercourse. Made of polyurethane instead of latex, it is less vulnerable to damage from oil-based lubricants.

Spermicides and Microbicides

Spermicides are chemicals that kill sperm. However, as yet they are not sufficiently effective on their own, and are best used in conjunction with other methods such as condoms.

Research is also being carried out on chemicals that function not as contraceptives but just as microbicides: that is, chemicals which kill infection-carrying microbes or bacteria and so prevent STIs. Effective viracides are also being sought.

Non-penetrative Sex ('outercourse')

For a long time the term foreplay has been used to describe the activities that can take place before penetrative intercourse. However, the activities previously described as foreplay have acquired a new standing as potentially highly satisfying activities in their own right and not just before full-on intercourse.

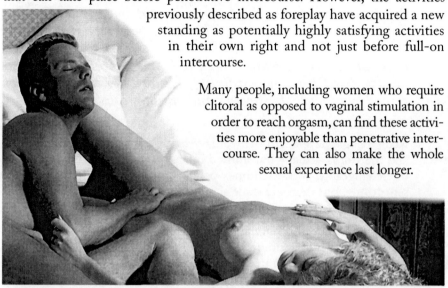

Many people, including women who require clitoral as opposed to vaginal stimulation in order to reach orgasm, can find these activities more enjoyable than penetrative intercourse. They can also make the whole sexual experience last longer.

Non-penetrative sex can include kissing, stroking, fingering, bathing, massaging, licking, biting, sucking, spanking, body rubbing (thighs, armpits, chests, breasts, buttocks, toes), sex toys, mirrors, magazines, videos, dressing up, bondage, fetishism, food, striptease, naked dancing, talking sexily, role playing, tickling, wrestling, watching, masturbating, fantasising…

Oral Sex

Oral sex does involve some risk of transmission of certain infections and diseases to the person performing the oral sex.

However, it is considerably less than the risk associated with unprotected penetrative sex and can be all but eliminated by using condoms or dental dams. A dental dam is a square of latex that is placed over the vulva or anus; a condom cut across the top and down one side can be used in the same way. Flavoured dams and condoms are available.

> Safe sex doesn't mean no sex – it just means use your imagination.
> **BILLY BRAGG**

References to sexually-transmitted infections (STIs) appear in the early writings of most cultures. They can be found both in the Bible and in early Hindu mythology. Two of the oldest are syphilis and gonorrhoea, which have been widespread for centuries. Their origins are unknown. They have been referred to as the French pox, Indian measles, the Italian disease, and the Portuguese illness - each country keen to blame another and thereby absolve itself from responsibility. Historically they have been spread by voyages of discovery and military campaigns.

Many people have heard the words sexually transmitted disease (STD) and the words sexually transmitted infection (STI); they are often used interchangeably, and oftentimes people just assume that they are the same thing. But there are some significant differences.

Fifteen years ago both these categories came under one name: Venereal Disease (VD). It was a common term to include all the various diseases and infections that are transmitted by sexual acts. To distinguish between them they were separated into infections (STIs) and diseases (STDs). Infection means that a germ, bacteria, parasite or virus is present in the body. Someone who is an infected person may not have any symptoms, meaning that they might be unaware that they are even sick. On the other hand, a disease is any abnormal condition of the body or mind that presents some type of symptom; in other words, your body tells you that you are unwell. For the purposes of this book, the more general term STI will be used as the generic.

Control and Elimination

Two major breakthroughs in the control and elimination of sexual diseases and infections were the discovery of the microscope, which facilitated diagnosis, and penicillin, which provided the first safe, reliable cure. Before these advances, diagnosis had been haphazard and treatment had been localised, unreliable or simply dangerous. The mass production of penicillin after the Second World War and the increasing availability and use of condoms brought new hope for the control of the gravest sexually-transmitted infections and diseases. With the scare induced by the spread of HIV/AIDS in the 1980s and 90s, the incidence of STIs dropped for a few years. However, recently their spread has gone onto the increase once more.

NOTICE: EFFECTIVE TREATMENT

Medical help should be sought if an infection of the sexual or reproductive organs is suspected. Treatment is effective in most cases, especially if initiated in the early stages of infection.

Infections Caused by Sexual Contact and Non-Sexual Means

Non-specific Genital Infections

These cover a large group of the most common genital infections. They include:

- cystitis (inflammation of the bladder)
- vaginitis (inflammation of the vagina)
- salpingitis (inflammation of the Fallopian tube)
- urethritis (inflammation of the urethra)
- balanitis (inflammation of the glans penis)
- posthitis (inflammation of the foreskin)
- proctitis (inflammation of the rectum)

Causes: various bacterial and non-bacterial germs, allergies or friction. They may also occur as symptoms of other infections or diseases.

Symptoms: any unusual discharge, irritation or discomfort in the genital area may indicate an infection.

Treatment: there are various options available for most non-specific infections, often including antibiotics.

Pubic Lice *(pediculosis pubis)*

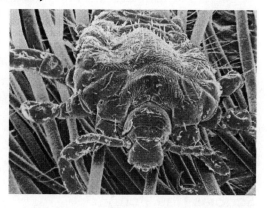

Cause: pubic lice are wingless parasites. They infest the hair in the pubic area and occasionally on other parts of the body. They feed on blood by biting into the skin. Eggs are laid and attached to the root of the hairs, hatching a week later. They are passed on from one person to another through close bodily contact and occasionally from infested clothes, towels or bedding.

Symptoms: the bites may cause acute irritation, but there are often no symptoms at all.

Treatment: DDT emulsion or powder. Shaving is not necessary, although it can provide a rapid cure.

Thrush

Cause: a fungus called candida albicans, a type of yeast that exists normally and harmlessly in the skin, mouth and gut. Under certain conditions it can multiply and cause burning discomfort in genital areas (in men this is known as balanitis) and sometimes in the mouth in both men and women. Factors that can lead to infection with thrush include:

- wearing tight trousers or nylon underwear
- using perfumed soaps or genital deodorants
- taking certain antibiotics
- diabetes
- pregnancy
- ill health
- sexual contact with someone who is infected with thrush

Symptoms in women may include:
- irritation and soreness around the vagina, vulva or anus
- thick, white, yeasty vaginal discharge
- swollen vulva
- pain on urinating or having sexual intercourse

Symptoms in men may include:
- irritation or soreness on the tip of the penis or under the foreskin
- thick, white discharge under the foreskin
- difficulty in pulling back the foreskin

Bacterial Vaginosis (also known as gardnerella)

Cause: multiplication of bacteria which occur naturally in the vagina, as in thrush. This bacteria seems to affect women only.

Symptoms: watery, grey vaginal discharge with 'fishy' odour, especially after intercourse.

Treatment: a short course of antibiotics.

Scabies (the 'Itch')

Cause: a parasitic mite. The disease is spread by close physical contact and poor hygiene, including infested clothes, towels and bedding. The mites survive by burrowing into the outer layers of the skin, most commonly on the hairy parts of the body, although they can also affect the hands, particularly the web of the fingers. They can also spread to other parts of the body. The female also lays eggs in these burrows.

Symptoms: the burrows appear as fine black or white lines surrounded by inflamed skin and with a blister at one end. The saliva and droppings produced by the mites cause acute irritation.

Treatment: application of a lotion such as benzyl benzoate or malathion all over the body from the neck down. The treatment may have to be repeated several times.

Genital Herpes

Cause: the *herpes simplex* virus, which affects the genital and anal areas and occasionally the mouth. It is passed through genital or oral-genital contact. People are particularly infectious when they have the characteristic genital blisters or oral cold sores, and intercourse should be avoided at this time; however it is also possible, although more rare, for the virus to be passed on when there are no symptoms. It can be passed from the genital area to the mouth and from the mouth to the genital area.

Symptoms may include:

- in the genital or anal area small, painful blisters form then burst to leave red ulcers. These usually heal within one to two weeks
- stinging, tingling or itching in the genital or anal area
- (particularly in women) pain or burning sensation when passing urine
- cold sores on the mouth
- general, flu-type symptoms such as headache, backache, fever or swollen glands.

These symptoms tend to occur within a week of infection. Relapses are common, but the first outbreaks are usually the worst.

Treatment: no cure for herpes has yet been found so, once infected, it remains for life. However, with a new generation of antiviral drugs such as aclivovir, there are various remedies which can ease the symptoms and help ward off attacks.

Hepatitis B

Cause: a virus present in the blood and other bodily fluids of an infected person, causing inflammation of the liver. It is passed on by sexual contact and contact with other fluids, including blood, saliva and urine.

Symptoms occur in three stages, although in some people no symptoms are apparent.

Stage One:
• one to six months after initial infection
• flu-type symptoms
• fatigue and loss of appetite
• aching joints

Stage Two:
• jaundice, stage, lasting two to eight weeks
• yellowish colouring of skin and whites of eyes
• dark brown urine and light-coloured faeces
• pain in the abdomen
• weight loss

Recovery Stage:
• skin and eye colour return to normal
• urine and faeces return to normal

Treatment: rest and a healthy diet, excluding alcohol. Complete recovery may take several months. In some people there may be long-term liver damage.

Infections Caused by Sexual Contact Only

Genital Warts

Cause: certain types of virus called the human papilloma virus. It is passed through skin-to-skin contact with the wart, primarily through vaginal or anal intercourse. Once a person has been infected by the virus, it can take from two weeks to a year for the warts to appear.

Symptoms: the warts appear as fleshy growths of various sizes, on their own or in clusters. In women they are found in the vulva, vagina, cervix and anus, and have been implicated in cervical cancers. In men they are found in the penis, urethra and anus. They may itch but are seldom painful.

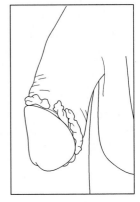

Prevention: There are two HPV vaccines which should be administered before infection by the virus.

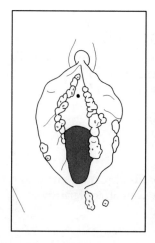

Treatment: Depending on the sizes and locations of the warts, as well as other factors, there are several ways to treat them. The first line of treatment, due to its low cost, is usually by painting with a liquid called Podofilox, several applications of which are necessary. Imiquimod is a topical immune response cream, applied to the affected area. It causes less local irritation than podofilox. Sinectechins is an ointment extracted from green tea. It appears to have higher clearance rates than podophyllotoxin and Imiquimod and causes less local irritation, but clearance takes longer than with Imiquimod. Genital warts can also be removed surgically, or by lasers, or electrocauterisation and by cryosurgery with liquid nitrogen.

Trichomoniasis

Cause: a small parasite which infects the vagina. It is almost always passed through sexual contact. Men are only rarely infected, in the urethra. They can be carriers.

Symptoms: in women are sometimes unnoticeable, but may include:

- a change in vaginal discharge, which becomes more watery or frothy, slightly yellow or green in colour, with a strong odour
- soreness or irritation in the vaginal area

If untreated, it can cause other infections such as non-specific urethritis (NSU) in men and vaginitis (inflammation of the vagina) in women. These are also curable.

Treatment: a course of tablets of the drug metronidazole for both partners.

Chlamydia

Cause: a bacteria which infects the genitals and sometimes the eyes and throat. It is passed primarily through sexual contact, but can also be passed from mother to newborn baby, causing lung disease and eye infection. Chlamydia may lie dormant for some time before symptoms become evident.

Symptoms: there are usually no symptoms, and chlamydia often passes unnoticed. In women there may be vaginal discharge or pain on urinating. In most cases chlamydia is only noticed when it spreads elsewhere, in particular to the urethra where in men it is the most common cause of urethritis. In women it may lead to pelvic inflammatory disease (PID), which can cause infertility.

Treatment: a seven to 14-day course of antibiotics.

Non-Gonococcal Urethritis (NGU)
(also known as non-specific urethritis or NSU)

Cause: NGU is an inflammation of a man's urethra, NSU an inflammation of a woman's sexual organs, caused by a number of different germs. The germs can be in the body for some time before any symptoms become evident.

Symptoms (there may be no symptoms at all) may include:

- discomfort or burning pain on urinating
- white, cloudy discharge from the tip of the penis

Without treatment the inflammation can spread to the prostate gland and sometimes to the testes. This can be painful, and can even affect fertility.

Treatment: a 17 – 14-day course of antibiotics.

Chancroid

Cause: a bacterial infection which rarely occurs outside tropical and sub-tropical areas.

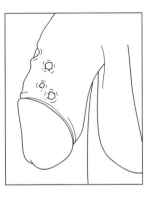

Symptoms: In men these appear about a week after infection, when a soft, inflamed ulcer appears on the genitals. It bleeds easily, and often spreads extensively, causing acutely painful destruction of the flesh. In extreme cases the foreskin and the head of the penis can be ulcerated away. Abscesses may also develop. Symptoms are seldom evident in women, as the lesions can be vulval or even within the vagina.

Treatment: antibiotics, sulphonamide drugs.

Gonorrhoea

Cause: a bacterium called the gonococcus. It can affect the cervix, urethra, rectum, and occasionally the throat if it is passed by oral-genital contact. Its incubation period is usually two to 10 days. It attacks the mucous membranes, causing inflammation and the production of pus.

Symptoms in Men:

These are usually obvious and may include:

- discharge of white or yellow fluid from the tip of the penis
- burning pain when urinating
- discharge or irritation in the anus
- a sore throat

Symptoms in Women:

These are usually slight and may even pass unnoticed. They can include:

- a change in the vaginal discharge, which may increase in quantity, become more watery, or turn slightly yellow or green in colour
- pain or discomfort when urinating
- pain in the abdomen
- discharge or irritation in the anus
- a sore throat

If untreated, in men gonorrhoea can lead to acute or chronic inflammation of the urethra, testes and prostate gland. These can cause difficulty in urinating and even sterility.

In women it can cause pelvic inflammatory disease (PID), which can lead to sterility. During childbirth it can be passed on to the baby as an eye infection.

Treatment: penicillin and other antibiotics are very effective in treating most cases of gonorrhoea, but early diagnosis is essential if the disease is to be cured completely.

Syphilis

Cause: a bacteria called the treponema. This enters the body through tiny cracks in the skin or by penetrating mucus membranes, then lives and multiplies in the blood and other body fluids of the infected person. It is passed on by the fluid secreted from the characteristic sores or chancres.

Symptoms: the development of syphilis occurs in three stages. The symptoms are the same in men and women.

Stage One: between one and 12 weeks after infection a hard, painless sore develops on or near the penis or vagina, or sometimes in the anus or mouth. It usually lasts two to three weeks.

Stage Two: two to six months after infection a skin rash appears all over the body. It may develop to form pimples or pustules. Flu-like symptoms may also occur. This lasts for two to six weeks. Sometimes these first two stages are not even noticeable. Natural antibodies are also produced in the body, which in some cases are sufficient to cure the disease.

Late Stage: this may occur long after the other symptoms have disappeared, many years after infection. If untreated the treponema, the bacterial genus responsible for the disease, can affect other parts of the body, and damage the heart and brain in particular. Disfigurement and death can occur, though nowadays this is rare.

Treatment: syphilis can be treated very effectively with penicillin if the disease is diagnosed early.

HIV and AIDS

AIDS, the Acquired Immune Deficiency Syndrome, is caused by the Human Immuno-deficiency Virus, HIV. In an infected person (someone who is HIV positive, or HIV+) HIV prevents the immune system – the body's defence mechanism – from working effectively. It does this by attacking the cells (known as CD4 cells) that co-ordinate the fight against infections. This makes the body vulnerable to potentially fatal infections that the immune system would normally destroy.

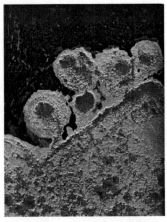

The Human Immunodeficiency Virus, HIV, the virus that causes AIDS

Without intervention, progression from HIV infection to AIDS takes, on average, nine to 10 years. Before successful drugs were discovered, average survival time once AIDS had developed was 9.2 months. The disease remains officially a pandemic. As at 2009, there were 33.3 million people around the world living with HIV/AIDS, with 2.6 million new infections occurring per year, 1.8 million deaths annually from the disease and a total of 25 million deaths up to that year.

Warren Hills Cemetery, Harare, Zimbabwe. It is estimated that at the end of 1997, AIDS peaked in Zimbabwe with 26.5% of the adult population HIV positive. By 2001 this had dropped to 23.7% and by 2010, down to 14.3% (World Health Organisation)

Defining AIDS

The precise definition of AIDS varies from one authority to another, and continues to evolve as understanding of the disease develops. Generally, a person is considered to have AIDS if they are suffering from one or more of a specific group of diseases associated with HIV infection, or if the CD4 cells fall from a normal count of 800 to below 200.

Symptoms

It is impossible to give an exhaustive list of the symptoms of AIDS, as the forms taken by the disease are so varied. However, pneumonia, with shortness of breath, is the most common opportunistic infection and often the first to appear. Other common minor symptoms, known as the AIDS-Related Complex (ARC), include weight loss, diarrhoea, fever, rashes, fatigue, coughing, insomnia, nausea and memory problems. Some of the other major symptoms of AIDS are recurrent herpes simplex, persistent generalised lymphadenopathy, a form of skin cancer called Kaposi's sarcoma, and cryptococcal meningitis.

The History of AIDS

AIDS was first recognised as a distinct syndrome in the USA by the Center for Disease Control and Prevention in 1981. The disease was discovered as a result of an increasing number of unusual infections, primarily amongst the homosexual population, caused by a form of immune deficiency. It was only later that it was directly associated with other groups. Since that time the disease has spread to all sectors of society.

It was not recognised that the condition was cause by a virus until HIV was discovered in 1983. The main ways in which HIV is spread are now well understood.

The origins of the virus now seems clear from genetic research which suggests that it developed in Sub-Saharan Africa in the late 19th or early 20th century. It appears to have been spread by contact with the non-human primates where it first began.

Dance with Death, the ballet about HIV and AIDS choreographed by Mathew Hart and performed by The Royal Ballet, London, 1996

Transmission

HIV is carried in various body fluids; in particular blood and semen, vaginal and cervical secretions, and breast milk. It can be passed to another person through open wounds, broken skin or mucous membranes such as those in the urethra, vagina, cervix and rectum. There are four proven, substantial routes of transmission of HIV.

These are:

- unprotected sexual intercourse (vaginal, anal or oral – see under Safer Sex)
- shared, unsterilised injection equipment in intravenous drug use
- blood transfusion or organ donation (thorough screening is now carried out in most countries to eliminate this risk)
- more rarely, from mother to baby in womb, during childbirth or breast-feeding

Other activities, which are potential routes of transmission, include oral sex and sharing sex toys, as well as any activities that might involve shared blood, such as piercing and shaving.

NOTE

It is particular behaviours that carry risk, not particular groups of people.

Treatments

As of yet there is no full cure or vaccine for HIV. However, various medical treatments are available, functioning in a number of different ways, attacking the virus itself by reducing the speed at which it reproduces or by preventing it from fulfilling other functions. Antiretroviral drugs both alleviate the symptoms and reduce the mortality of HIV infection and many patients see remarkable improvement in their health and quality of life. However, these drugs are expensive and not available throughout the world.

These treatments and preventions include:

- highly active antiretroviral therapy (HAART), a cocktail of three drugs belonging to at least two types of antiretroviral agents
- preventing opportunistic infections with safe sex and needle-exchange programmes
- complementary and alternative medicines (CAM) or therapies (i.e. non-scientific treatments such as homeopathy, acupuncture, massage and visualisation) are also available, which may fulfil the above functions and help reduce stress, improve psychological health, and relieve pain, but the effectiveness of these has not been established, despite widespread use.

In the meantime, research on the virus, its causes and possible cures, continues.

- HIV has not been detected in urine, faeces or vomit (except where these contain blood) or sweat. Only negligible quantities, insufficient for infection, have been detected in saliva, tears and blister fluid

- HIV cannot be passed through casual acquaintance

- Touching and kissing involve no risk provided that body fluids are not exchanged

- HIV cannot be passed through shared cups, glasses, plates, cutlery, beds, baths or bed clothes

- HIV cannot be passed on toilet seats, in swimming pools, or by sharing an office or classroom with an infected person

- HIV cannot be passed by mosquitoes or other insects

- HIV cannot be acquired by donating blood

- HIV can only be passed during First Aid if substantial quantities of blood from an infected person come into contact with an open wound, cut or graze

- HIV has never been known to be passed through mouth-to-mouth resuscitation.

Testing

The HIV test is based on the detection of HIV antibodies in a sample of blood. Antibodies are substances produced by the body in response to a particular infection: the presence of the antibodies indicates the presence of the virus. It may be several months after exposure before the antibodies can be reliably detected, so it is often necessary to carry out two tests a few months apart. Testing on a regular basis may be advisable if a person is considered to be at risk.

It can be impossible to tell whether a person is HIV+ by their appearance

FACT

Various pre-1980s cases have been retrospectively (and controversially) diagnosed through descriptions of specific patterns of symptoms and stored blood samples. It is not known for how long the virus has existed in humans. It is thought that HIV might have escaped diagnosis in the pre-1940s period in the midst of many infectious diseases in existence at that time.

Sexual harassment is the use of sex to threaten or intimidate and/ or as a means of gaining power over an individual.

Sexual harassment can occur anywhere: at work, at home or in public places. It may come from family members, strangers, acquaintances, colleagues, friends or sexual partners. It can include anything from wolf whistles to rubbing up against a stranger's body in a crowd (frotaging), from obscene comments or phone calls to overt demands for sex: the key is that the behaviour in question is sexual in intent and that it is unwanted and unprovoked. Victims are usually women, but men may also be affected; in either case the harasser is more commonly male but can be female.

The harm which it does is not usually physical, so much as psychological and emotional. In many societies and social groups sexual harassment is barely even acknowledged, because of the way women are treated generally in a culture, or because there is no physical evidence or because the victim is seen as somehow responsible.

This often has to do with the victim's class, race or social status: being seen as inferior in any way damages credibility. In some countries sexual harassment in the workplace is a criminal offence, but cases are notoriously difficult to prove as they tend to amount to one person's word against another's.

Child Abuse

Sexual abuse of children is one of the most disturbing forms of abuse. While most children have some degree of sexual awareness, child sexuality is quite distinct from adult. A child may be aware of certain sexual issues but is rarely able to control them or make informed, mature decisions about them. Child abuse implies coercion and dominance, however subtle this may be. "Child grooming" is a type of abuse when a child is befriended as a means of establishing an emotional trusting relationship in order to lower the child's inhibition for preparation for sexual activity (or exploitation such as prostitution or pornography). Social networking services on the internet can be used for this.

Child abuse can be incestuous or non-incestuous.

Statistically, incestuous abuse is most commonly between father and daughter, although it has been suggested that this is less likely to occur where the father takes an active role in the day-to-day care of the child or children. Incestuous abuse may also be instigated by an elder sibling or, more rarely, the mother.

Non-incestuous abuse is that perpetrated by a non-relative, be they a stranger, an acquaintance or a carer.

The immaturity of the victim makes it more difficult to prove that abuse has occurred. A child cannot always be relied upon to be able to tell fact from fiction: they are also more suggestible than adults. This becomes more complex still when members of the family are involved.

Victims of abuse often suffer long-term consequences, such as a difficulty in forming stable, trusting, loving relationships. If the abuse is incestuous it can affect the entire family. However, counselling can be helpful, both for the victim and sometimes for the family as well.

Rape

Rape is the act of forcing a person to have sexual intercourse against their will. Sexual assault encompasses all forms of forced sexual activity, including those which do not involve penetration or the vagina or anus with the penis.

Sexual assault involves extreme physical and personal violation. In many cases physical violence is used, but the victim may be forced into sexual activity by many other means, such as threats, fear, shock or exhortation. It has been linked to tolerance of other forms of violence, both in daily life and in the media, where physical violence can acquire a false sense of acceptability.

Sex Crimes - detail from *The Rape of the Sabines* by Peter Paul Rubens (1577-1640)

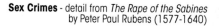

For the victim the effects can be devastating. Initial reactions can include anger towards the assailant, shock, fear, self-blame, shame and humiliation. There may also be fear about sexually-transmitted diseases and pregnancy.

There is also the question of how and whether to tell anyone. The American Medical Association considers rape to be the most under-reported violent crime. One of the greatest deterrents against reporting a rape or assault is that it may be suggested that the victim provoked the crime in some way. The way a woman is dressed, her sexual history, whether or not she had been drinking, if she entered a bar alone, or was walking alone at night – all these points have been mentioned in legal defence of alleged rapists; however, there are now laws against using this as admissible evidence in some countries.

Ultimately the only relevant question is whether or not consent was given for sex to occur (so it can occur within a marriage). The term statutory rape may be used to refer to sex with someone who is below the age of consent (and thus not accepted to be mature enough to give legal consent – whether they actually have or not), or who has been made unconscious or incapacitated by means of drugs, such as the date rape drug, Rohypnol.

Victims of rape can be male or female, of any age and social background. Statistics show the majority to be female, but in recent years more cases of male rape have been reported.

The US Bureau of Justice estimated that 91% of rape victims are women and 9% male. Rapists are almost always male (99%), although cases of sexual assault by women have also been reported.

No conclusive psychological profile of a rapist has been produced. The majority of convicted rapists are not mentally ill and have nothing to distinguish them from others. Their relationship to their victim can be as stranger, acquaintance, friend, family member, date, lover or long-term partner or spouse. It is estimated that at least 50% of rapists know their victims. It is very prevalent in prison, as it also is during warfare.

Motives for rape are varied, circumstantial and individual. It may be an isolated act or part of a consistent pattern of abuse. No universal rules exist. However, it has been suggested that there is a link between the incidence of rape and sexual assault and the power relationships between the sexes. In some societies where women are subordinated – professionally, domestically, and/or economically – rape seems more common. Certainly rape often involves a desire to overpower or dominate the victim, and is considered a crime of violence more than a crime of lust.

SEXUAL FEELINGS

2

The notion of gender goes far beyond the straightforward male/female distinction. Although based in biological differences, gender distinctions in humans incorporate innumerable social and psychological influences. Each person's understanding of gender identity affects every aspect of his or her life.

What is gender?

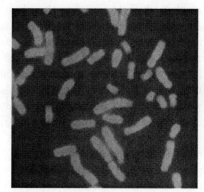

- **Sex** refers to the basic biological distinction between male and female, determined by sexual organs and hormones, the secondary sexual characteristics (that is, the distinctive, visible, physical features) and the chromosomes that determine them.

- **Gender** is the associated sexual identity; it is the state of being male or female.

Chromosomes XX for females XY for males

- **Gender identity** is the conscious sense of which gender one belongs to. This usually develops between the ages of two and six years, and involves recognising one's own gender as distinct from or aligned with that of other people.

- **Gender role** is the outward expression of this gender identity.

Sex is biologically determined at conception but gender identity develops between the ages of two and six years

How does gender identity develop?

A person's sense of their gender identity is a central part of his or her psychological makeup. There are two major influences in its formation.

Firstly, and principally during childhood, there is the influence of parents and/or other gender role models. A child observes their behaviour and usually comes to associate particular activities or characteristics with each gender. He or she generally follows the example of his or her same-sex parent or carer, unless a conscious decision is made to reject it. Carers themselves also have an active role to play by encouraging or discouraging different types of behaviour in boys and girls.

Secondly, society and socially-ascribed gender roles have their impact, as the child becomes aware of the norms of behaviour outside the home environment. This includes the ways in which gender identity is expressed and, more particularly, notions of masculinity and femininity or what is considered appropriate to each gender. This can affect everything from attitudes to the opposite sex to forms of dress.

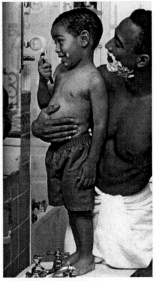

Observing the behaviour of parents or carers can be one of the main ways that children learn about gender identity.

Masculine and feminine

Certain personality traits have come to be associated with each gender. In many cultures men are expected to be active, assertive and tough, and women to be more passive and gentle. Such criteria often form the basis of people's notions of 'masculinity' and 'femininity'.

These classifications may have a certain basis in biology, but they are also highly restrictive and in many cases completely unrealistic. For example, they can preclude the possibility of female assertion and male sensitivity.

Masculinity and femininity cannot be defined in this way as there are few, if any, characteristics that can be seen as exclusive to men or women. In spite of this, many people feel obliged to fulfill such roles to the point where they may experience a sense of failure or abnormality if they do not.

This also applies to sexual orientation. In many parts of the world, there is a sense that masculinity means being attracted to females and that females ought to be attracted to males. As in other assumptions about gender identity, in many cases this rule simply does not apply.

Variations of sex and gender

In some cases genetic variations can cause a person's gender to be less clearly defined. This is often recognised at birth by the individual having genitalia that are not clearly male or female. The term currently used to describe this condition is intersex. Intersex is the presence of intermediate or atypical combinations of physical features that usually distinguish female from male. An intersex individual may have biological characteristics of both the male and the female sexes. This is usually understood to be congenital, involving chromosomal, morphologic, genital and/or gonadal anomalies. This presents as a diversion from typical XX-female or XY-male presentations such as sex reversal (XY-female, XX-male), genital ambiguity, or sex developmental differences.

Intersex individuals sometimes choose their own gender identity but often their gender identity has been prescribed for them at birth, so they sometimes need multiple surgeries to conform to an anatomical image of the gender chosen. As they develop, some people do not identify themselves as either exclusively female or exclusively male.

Though each society has distinct names for intersex individuals, some cultures revere intersex individuals as special, such as the two-spirit healers of the Native Americans in North America.

Though gender variations may be attributed at times to a variation in sex, it may also be due to other congenital conditions, such as in someone who is transgender (see section on transexualism).

In addition, there is a spectrum of gender roles which may lead to gender ambiguity - the various ways in which our gendered behaviours, activities, dress and identities do not match prescribed assumptions of the binary categories - male and female.

Character dolls such as these are based on stereotypical views of masculinity and femininity in the West. These and other toys can be powerful influences in the ways that children develop a clichéd understanding of what 'masculine' and 'feminine' mean

Female Sexual Feelings

Endless generalisations have been made about male and female sexual psychology, many of them contradictory. The reality is that such contradictions are inevitable. Each individual's sexual psyche is determined and influenced by a unique combination of biological and psychological factors. Development begins before birth and continues throughout life, although gender role models in early stages are important influences.

> The great question … which I have not been able to answer, despite my thirty years of research into the female soul, is 'What does a woman want?'
> **SIGMUND FREUD**

A common mistake is to assume that men and women are the same psychologically. Whilst there are clearly some basic similarities, there are also some fundamental differences.

Biology and evolution

Beginning with menarche (puberty), each month a woman produces one ovum in contrast to a man's almost infinite supply of sperm; and women tend to lose their fertility (although not their sex drive) earlier in life.

One man's vision of femininity – Egon Schiele's *Seated Woman with Bent Knee* (1917) (detail)

There are competing theories on how and why each gender has evolved. What seems to be consistent is that women have a limited reproductive capability, while men are usually capable of reproducing throughout their adult life. Despite this difference, both men and women have the ability to maintain healthy and enjoyable sexual involvement throughout life.

However, due to a change in hormone production in menopause, women may struggle with some variations such as vaginal dryness, bone brittleness, loss of skin softness and, for some, decreased libido.

The sexual act

Sex can mean anything from kissing to anal sex to bondage and beyond. However, typically it is meant to describe vaginal intercourse. The sexual act is replete with various emotions, skills and abilities. Much like good dancing partners, individuals need to know their own bodies and teach their partners what feels good for them. With some practise and effort, they can learn many dances.

Sexual roles can be difficult to understand as culture has dictated that men need to be the aggressors and women more passive. Many couples do not fit into these prescribed gender roles and, therefore, women are just as

likely to desire and ask for sex and want fulfilling orgasms as are men. However, some women feel under pressure to climax in sex and that can lead both to disppointment and the phenomenon of the faked orgasm (which is not wholly a female phenomenon). Ultimately, good sex usually takes good communication, trust and lots of caring practice.

Arousal

Sexual arousal for a woman may be more complex than for a man. The whole body can be an erogenous zone, with areas of particular sensitivity varying greatly from one woman to another. Visual stimuli are important but in a different way than for men, as women tend to respond more to atmosphere and situations. Research also seems to suggest that women can reach a more elaborate state of arousal from fantasy than men. Perhaps this is because women are more in tune with sexual process rather than simply aesthetics.

Notions of femininity

For a long time, ideas of femininity have been centred on a woman's appearance as the source of her attractiveness, above all in the West. Consequently, a woman's self-image is often influenced by how she feels about her looks and, in particular, her figure. Changing perceptions of the place of women in society have had a positive impact in this regard.

Firstly, they have given greater value to a woman's own sense of personal achievement. Secondly, while in the past women were seen as either *sexy* and desirable or *nice* and suitable for marriage, now other factors can play their part just as much as they do for men and such divisions are no longer clearly distinguishable.

Toilette of a Courtesan (detail), after Aubrey Beardsley

Male Sexual Feelings

Biology and evolution

From an evolutionary perspective, the fact that a woman mostly has only one ovum available for fertilisation each month, while a man has an almost infinite supply of sperm, may affect his attitude to his sexual partner(s), creating a tendency for him to be less bound by emotional commitment until he finally decides to settle down with a single mate.

Until this point there is no biological, nor may he feel any, need for commitment.

This may explain why, statistically, men have traditionally been more likely to have casual sex and to be able to enjoy sex without an ongoing commitment – although these days, in liberal societies, both genders generally have sex with a number of partners (some research has suggested typically nine for males and three for females, though, without a massive difference in the proportion of males to females, this cannot statistically be so – and the number for both must be around six). Studies have also shown that men tend to fall in and out of love more quickly and easily than women.

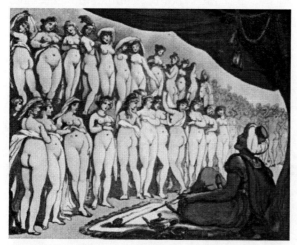

The Harem (detail) by Thomas Rowlandson. It has been suggested that men are biologically predisposed to have higher sex drives than women – they have a constant supply of sperm and their natural instinct is to make use of it

The sexual act

Popular culture puts great emphasis on intercourse and it is broadly assumed that *all* men are *always* ready for sex. The widespread stress on this single aspect of sex can put great pressure on heterosexual and homosexual men alike. The man may feel that he has to produce and maintain an erection at will and perform in a dominant and essentially aggressive manner.

Depending on his attitude to his partner, he may also feel under pressure to successfully penetrate his partner sufficiently enough for him or her to orgasm at each sexual encounter. This pressure may lead to personal, relational and sexual problems.

In addition, many men are also concerned about the size of their penis. This can contribute to sexual vulnerabilities based on poor notions of personal attractiveness and performance capability.

The ideal image of sex, with its stress on intercourse and male performance, is both unrealistic and, in many cases, undesirable, as it eliminates many of the more engaging, exciting and sensuous, as well as the more satisfying, aspects of sex play.

Arousal

Male sexual arousal is, relatively speaking, direct and immediate in most healthy men. The erogenous zones are specific and men tend to respond to specific triggers. Both stimulation and arousal are focused more on the genitals. Visual stimuli also tend to be more important for men than they are for women, which may be why pornographic magazines and films tend to be more popular with, and mostly orientated toward, men. Many men tend to have strong voyeuristic tendencies for perhaps the same reason.

Notions of masculinity

Each man has his own idea of what it means to be masculine. This is deter-

mined both by cultural influences and by gender role models. The macho man has long been a powerful image in the West. However, women's liberation has called out for men who are more in touch with the feminine side of their nature, who are more sensitive and openly caring and not afraid to express their emotions. The balance between these two sides has been liberating for many many men but has left others confused as to how they should behave, and in particular how they should behave toward a sexual partner of either gender.

The Lacedemonian Ambassadors (detail), by Aubrey Beardsley, 1896 illustration for Aristophanes' Lysistrata. The penis – and penis size in particular – has always played an important role in the male sexual psyche

Sexual Orientation

The terms homosexual, heterosexual and bisexual are commonly used to classify people in terms of their sexual orientation. However, the terms really refer not to people but to types of behaviour; their use to classify people has led to countless cases of misunderstanding and misrepresentation.

Sexual orientation is not a simple matter: human sexuality cannot be divided into distinct groups. Understanding these terms and what they really mean can help people to express their own sexuality more completely as well as to understand that of others.

> I can't understand why more people aren't bisexual. It would double your chances for a date on a Saturday night.
> **WOODY ALLEN**

Describing sexuality

Homosexuality refers to sexual attraction to, or relations with, a member or members of the same sex; heterosexuality is with the opposite sex; bisexuality is with members of both sexes. These behaviours can encompass anything from the occasional fantasy to full sexual relations.

Dr. Alfred Kinsey, a major US sex researcher, devised a seven-point scale from 0 to 6 to describe human sexual orientation more precisely:

- 0 represents people who were exclusively heterosexual
- 3 applies to those equally attracted to men and women
- 6 represents those who were exclusively homosexual

1, 2, 4 and 5 deal with all other degrees of preference, and take into account such factors as fantasies and isolated or one-off experiences outside a person's usual sexual preference. The system also deals with changes in attraction throughout life. Many people are curious about other kinds of sexual experience and experiment at some time with different kinds of sexual activity. Ultimately, those who rate themselves at 0 or 6 are relatively few.

The demographics

Kinsey's studies, mainly carried out in the 1940s and 1950s, produced statistics suggesting that about 37% of males and 19% of females surveyed had had some kind of overt homosexual experience in the course of adult life (though many on the religious right have called his work into question, the methods he used for gathering information, in terms of statistically social and geograph breadth, were robust).

It is estimated that exclusively homosexual males comprise about 5% of the adult population. The proportion of homosexual women is suggested to be marginally less than this. A recent study in the UK indicated that 91.6% of men and 90.3% of women self-describe their sexual experience as "only heterosexual". However, studies have also shown that same sex fantasies are common among people of all sexual orientations.

What determines sexual orientation?

There has historically been a great deal of prejudice about sexual orientation, though a spectrum of sexual attraction has always been part of human sexuality. There are a number of factors that suggest that non-heterosexual sexualities are natural consequences of biology and/or psychology:

- Records of homosexual activity have been found in all periods and a wide diversity of cultural groups. Even where it was not socially acceptable, it seems that it still occurred.

- Proportions of different types of sexuality seem to be approximately the same across all cultural and racial groups.

Which Way? It is increasingly believed that few, if any, people are exclusively homosexual or heterosexual. Human sexuality does not work within tight definitions or limitations – it can take many different forms and is fluid and flexible

- Homosexual activity has been observed and documented among other higher primates (see *Biological Exuberance* by Bruce Bagemihl and *Evolution's Rainbow* by Joan Roughgarden), including at times when opportunities for heterosexual activity were clearly available.

- Various pieces of research point to some genetic basis for sexuality. Studies of identical and non-identical twins (identical twins have identical genetic makeup) show that if one twin is homosexual, an identical brother is much more likely to be homosexual than a non-identical brother. More recent research claims to have identified the relevant gene.

- Male homosexuality has also been linked to the number of male siblings: a study has shown that the greater the number of elder brothers that a man has, the more likely he is to be homosexual. The reasons could be biological or simply an effect within the family.

Homosexuality and Society

A great deal of acceptance is beginning to sweep through Western cultures where the same kind of rights – such as visitation, inheritance, benefits and marriage – are being given to homosexual couples and often being seen as a human rights issue. In addition, there is growing appreciation for the talents and contributions of people who identify themselves as gay or lesbian. However, too much prejudice, often due to myths and misunderstandings, still prevails.

Some myths dispelled

The term homosexual strictly applies to any kind of sexual behaviour – from fantasy to intercourse – with a member of the same sex, but it may be used to refer to a person who is exclusively or primarily attracted to or involved with same-sex partners. Whilst in some cultures there are strong taboos relating to all forms of homosexuality, these are largely due to misunderstandings and misconceptions.

The term gay is frequently used to describe homosexuals, particularly men. The term lesbian is used for homosexual women.

It is not reliable to identify a person as gay or lesbian by appearance. Some gay men and women play up to camp or butch roles, but many do not. There are no specific gay or lesbian types; people who enjoy same sex activity are as varied in terms of occupation, social class, dress, religion and education as anyone else.

Openly gay expressions of love are finally becoming accepted in many – though mainly Western – societies

Same sex relationships are as varied as heterosexual relationships in terms of affection, physicality and commitment. Similarly, gay sex is just as varied, if not more so as heterosexual sex. Practices include kissing, touching, body-rubbing, oral sex, masturbation and anal intercourse.

Contrary to some prejudices, gay people are not more likely to carry out sexual crimes than non-gays. Indeed, homosexual men are statistically less likely to abuse children than heterosexuals. Partly because of this mistaken belief, some heterosexual people fear, and a few even abuse, gays and lesbians. In some Western cultures the law has elevated such violations against homosexuals as hate crimes, and added more severe sentencing than a crime of violence would carry alone.

Gay and lesbian culture

Gay rights have become an increasingly prominent social and political issue – and are frequently the subject of mass campaigns. Major gay pride marches are now held annually in many Western cities and attract crowds of all orientations

In many societies, gay and lesbian culture is being openly welcomed and incorporated. Overtly gay themes in literature, film, drama, ballet and the visual arts are now accepted as part of mainstream culture. However, particularly where homosexuality is illegal, social intolerance has forced homosexuality into a form of sub-culture. Even in apparently liberal societies, acceptance tends to be greater where there are fewer religious restraints and where larger, more cosmopolitan groups of people congregate, such as in major cities.

LGBT or Gay Pride, is a major movement where gay, lesbian, and transgender people assert pride in their sexual orientation and gender identity. The belief that diversity is a gift to be welcomed, and the view that sexual orientation and gender identity cannot intentionally be altered, are the principles on which it is founded. Today many countries celebrate the LGBT Pride movement with major annual parades; the one in New York commemorates the date of the infamous Stonewall Riots in 1969 when gay activists fought back against oppression by the New York Police Department. The movement has become influential in furthering gay rights within the political system on such matters as same-sex marriage and being openly gay in the military.

In many larger towns and cities, gay and lesbian-specific meeting places have been created. As for heterosexuals, some are for general socialising while others are intended specifically for finding partners, sometimes for casual sex. These venues include bars, restaurants, and occasionally steam baths and specific public lavatories.

While more and more people are coming to accept homosexuality, others can react judgementally to overt homosexual or bisexual orientations, making the decision to *come out*, that is to reveal one's sexual orientation, difficult. Some homosexuals believe they can strengthen their case and influence others by *outing* (publicly revealing) the sexual orientation of well-known and highly-regarded gays or lesbians. This remains a controversial issue.

Gay and lesbian double marriage

Same-sex marriages

Same-sex marriage is not currently legal in the UK. However, since 2005, same sex-couples have been allowed to enter into civil partnerships, a union which provides virtually all the legal consequences of marriage. In the US, the federal government is currently considering recognising same-sex marriage, though individual states, such as New York, do have laws which now recognise these marriages. The legitimisation of same-sex marriages continues to be driven by court rulings and legislative action on the basis of equal civil rights.

SLANG TERMS FOR HOMOSEXUALITY

Homosexual Female: dyke, lesbian, bull dyke, butch dyke, diesel, radish, sophist, gay, femme, Amy-John, bull dagger/bitch

Homosexual Male: faggot, fag, queen (closet, drag, wrinkle, chicken), dairy, fruit, pouf, Nancy, poor, poorter, radish, daily, queer, quntie, Nellie, fem, belle, swish, latent, bender, woofter, brown-hatter, pansy, fairy, flaming, butt pirate

Adjectives: gay, bent, camp

Transgender

Transvestism and Transsexualism

Transvestism and transsexualism are two areas in which the gender boundary is blurred. Both transvestites and transsexuals are born anatomically complete as one sex or the other. However, in a minor way in the case of transvestites, and in a more fundamental way in the case of transsexuals, members of both groups are drawn towards living as the opposite gender.

Females dressing in 'male' attire have rarely been seen as controversial. From an illustration in *La Vie Parisienne* (1926)

Transvestism (Cross-dressing)

Transvestites are men and women who like to dress in the clothes associated with the opposite gender, either occasionally or, in a few cases, all the time. Most transvestites are male and heterosexual; many are married with children.

In a high percentage of cases the motivation behind cross-dressing is a form of fetishism, with a sexual attachment to the clothing and accoutrements of the opposite sex. This may produce strong sexual arousal and even involve reaching orgasm.

Other cases have to do with a man wishing to express the feminine side of his personality, with women's clothing providing him with a sense of freedom and security, together with a release from the demands of the male gender role. This seems to be particularly common among homosexual transvestites.

The same behaviour may also be interpreted as a way of challenging the traditional gender roles ascribed by society, where many forms of dress and other aspects of behaviour are determined by gender.

Audition at Madame Jo-Jo's – many of the more flamboyant transvestite men go to enormous efforts to perfect their looks

Cross-dressing may be practised in public or in private, with or without the knowledge of a sexual partner. Though the term transvestism was not coined until 1910, the phenomenon is not new; indeed, it is referred to in the Bible and no doubt goes back to human beginnings. And, whilst it is believed that it is usually carried out in secret, it is not thought to be particularly uncommon.

The term drag is sometimes associated with transvestism. Homosexual transvestites are sometimes referred to as drag queens, particularly if their style of dress is very flamboyant. The term is also used in its original sense to mean men dressing up as female characters in theatrical productions.

FACT
Miss Vera's Finishing School for Boys who want to be Girls, the first transvestite academy, opened in 1994 in New York. The academy's courses include: *What Every Girl Should Know About Her Five O'clock Shadow* and *How To Prevent Your Evening Gown Being Ruined by a Bulging Penis.*

Transsexualism

Transsexualism is quite distinct from transvestism – it is more deeply rooted and more complex, and widely misunderstood. However, society at large is increasingly coming to understand, and ultimately to accept, this relatively rare condition.

Transsexualism and Gender Identity Disorder (GID)

Transsexualism is a rare condition and the term Gender Identity Disorder or GID is a formal diagnosis used to describe a person who experiences significant gender dysphoria.

Male-to-female transsexual

Being transsexual means having an overwhelming sense of having been born with the body of the wrong sex; that is, the biological sex and the gender identity of the person concerned are opposed. Transsexuals may cross dress, but their attitude to their body and in particular their genitals, is completely different from that of a transvestite. Transsexuals tend to disassociate themselves from their bodies, even to the point of wishing to change them into that of the opposite sex with hormone therapy and having their physical genitalia reassigned to those of the opposite sex by means of surgery. Not all people with gender dysphoria wish to transition surgically, though; many see their condition as inborn, and live their lives as transgender individuals in various stages of transition.

Transsexuals are often conservative in their perception of gender – seeing males and females as quite distinct. They mostly see themselves as heterosexual, attracted to members of the opposite sex in terms of their believed inner sexual identity - even though this is actually the same biological sex. There are also bisexual and homosexual transsexuals.

Once a person is convinced that he or she is transsexual, there are various courses of action open to him or her. For many, the ultimate goal

Female-to-male transsexual

is to have surgery to bring their body into line with their sexual identity: this is known as a sex change or gender reassignment procedure.

There are a number of less severe measures which can be taken, and which are usually obligatory as preliminary steps before the final operation on the genitals. These can include removal of body hair or hair transplants, silicone implants to change the body shape, and treatment with male or female sexual hormones (affecting the secondary sexual characteristics). Before the reassignment operation is carried out, transsexuals are usually expected to have lengthy counselling and assessment and to live as the other gender for at least a year.

The reassignment operation for male-to-female transsexuals consists of removing the testes and using the skin of the scrotum to line a surgically-created vagina. For female-to-male transsexuals the breast tissue is removed and a hysterectomy is performed, removing the internal female reproductive organs. In some cases, a penis is created with skin and muscle tissue taken from another part of the body. The urethra can be extended with the use of a catheter and, in some cases, implants can be included to make vaginal penetration possible. In any of these procedures, sexual sensitivity may or may not be preserved.

While the law in many countries permits and acknowledges the process of gender reassignment, few countries legally recognise a person's new alignment and he or she will seldom be permitted a legal marriage or a passport appropriate to the reassigned sex. However, in other parts of the world such people are coming to be accepted and their new identity respected.

The female-to-male gender reassignment operation

An artificial catheter is used to extend the urethra ❶ , covered with skin taken from the abdomen ❷ . This is attached at the perineum and forms the body of the new penis (❸ - ❺). The other external genitals are removed.

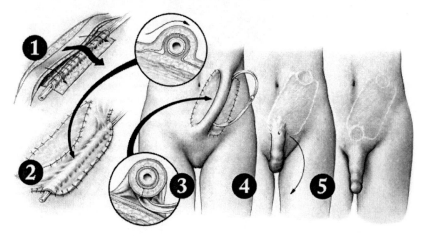

The male-to-female gender reassignment operation

A cut is made to the base of the penis ❶ ; the skin is peeled back and the main body of the penis is removed ❷ . The penile skin is used to line a vagina, made in the region of the perineum ❸ . A cut is made in the scrotum ❹ and the testes are removed, the scrotal sac being used to form the labia ❺ . Lastly, the urethra is moved to just above the vagina ❻ .

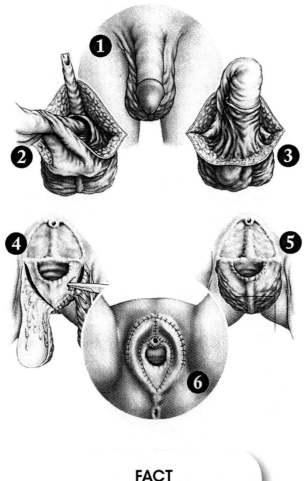

FACT
The first male-to-female gender reassignment surgery was performed in Denmark in 1952.

It is often thought that humans become sexually aware only when they reach puberty. However, sexual consciousness – both physiological and psychological – appears to begin at or even before birth, and infancy and childhood are crucial stages in its development. In spite of this, infant and childhood sexuality continues to be surrounded by ignorance and embarrassment.

Pre-birth and infancy

It is now known that male foetuses have erections, in many cases fairly frequently, for some time before birth. This continues after birth in boys and, for girls, this is when vaginal lubrication has also been observed.

The extent of unborn or newborn children's consciousness of this activity is not known, but it is certain that their awareness of their body develops rapidly from birth. The earliest stages of learning are based on two things: exploration of the body and senses, and interaction with other humans. It is these things that form the basis of sexual awareness.

An infant rapidly starts to take interest and pleasure in his or her body and bodily processes, and this is entirely natural. Freudian psychoanalysts point to three early stages of development of physical awareness, described in terms of oral, genital and anal fixation stages. Feeding and excreting are of obvious and immediate interest, but so too, it appears, is genital sensation; between the ages of six and 12 months most infants show an interest in their genitals by fondling or exposing them.

Basic elements of infant care, such as rubbing, stroking, patting and breastfeeding, are important in creating physical awareness and a sense of security and intimacy with carers.

Demonstration of loving relationships between parents, family members, other carers and children are an important basis for establishing a sense of security in relationships and aids the child's ability to form loving attachments.

Childhood sexuality is more openly accepted in some cultures than others. This detail of a poster advertisement for Sadoga-shima shows kids enjoying themselves. That the boy is holding his genitals is not seen as shameful or something to be hidden, but is a symbol of innocent fun and joyousness

Childhood

Much early sexual exploration takes place with peers, not uncommonly with same sex play. Additional learning comes from advertising and the media. While masturbation used to be something that was discovered by accident or through peers, much discovery is now coming from social media and via the internet. By early adolescence, nine out of 10 boys are masturbating, though it is less common at that stage among girls.

Children become aware of relationships – and the social practices affecting them – while still very young

Many boys and girls are also naturally curious about the genitals of the opposite sex. Mutual kissing and fondling are common, as are pelvic thrusting, simulated intercourse and mutual masturbation. Intercourse is more rare, but has been known to occur. Activity may be heterosexual or homosexual, but the choice of partner or orientation is unlikely to be significant at this stage. It may be spontaneous or it may be imitative, influenced by sexual activity seen on television and the internet or from witnessing intimacy between parents or other adults. Surveys suggest that as many as 85% of adults recall some sort of sex play with peers between the ages of six and 12. Personal, romantic attachments before the age of six are also not uncommon.

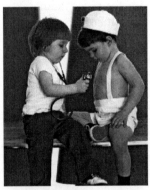

Sexual learning begins during childhood as children learn to interact with each other – and even seem to flirt here, playing doctors and nurses. In spite of this, they are still a long way from puberty and full sexual awareness

Attitudes to childhood sexuality

In many cultures childhood sexuality is either ignored or repressed. Those in which it is openly accepted as natural and healthy are relatively few, although tolerance does seem to be increasing. Certainly, Western societies have progressed from the days when children were often forcibly restrained or punished for innocent masturbation. In a few cultural groups, sexual activity is actively encouraged from an early age.

The attitudes of parents and other carers to children's sexuality can be very powerful. Children learn from them how they ought to behave and if they are taught that sexual feelings are dirty or shameful this impression often remains with them for life. A parent or carer who is comfortable with his or her own body and sexuality will pass on this message to the child, who will learn that sex is natural and to be enjoyed without guilt or shame, though in an appropriate place and at an appropriate time.

Sexuality in Adolescence

Adolescence is a time of change - physical, emotional and psychological. The physical changes are the most immediately noticeable, but they bring with them the need for psychological and social adjustment. It is often a time of intense confusion but it can also be exciting, heralding the change from childhood to the challenges and opportunities of adulthood.

Adolescence has been described as the second stage of the process of individuation. The first stage occurs in infancy and childhood and is based on an individual's relationship with his or her family, or carers and companions, and immediate environment. At this stage individuation is likely to be entirely unconscious. However at adolescence individuals are likely to be acutely – even painfully – conscious of some of the changes that are occurring to him or her, even if other changes are dealt with instinctively.

Adolescence can be a crucial time for exploring and developing sexual identity

What is adolescence?

Adolescence begins with puberty, when the adult hormonal cycles are set in motion, bringing with them the range of physical and psychological changes that herald the development from child to young adult.

Physical changes

Puberty usually lasts between three and five years, from the ages of nine to 13 in girls and 10 to 15 in boys. Some studies have suggested that the age at which puberty occurs is gradually getting lower worldwide. Puberty sees the development of the secondary sexual characteristics differentiating male and female, and is marked by the menarche or first menstruation in girls and the first ejaculation (spermarche) in boys.

It is usually at puberty that young people start to become sexually aware and/or active. Watersheds such as a girl's first menstruation or a boy's first ejaculation can be exciting or traumatic, depending on the kind of attitudes and information which the girl or boy has experienced.

The development of other physical characteristics also has its impact. Physical awareness increases, as does a sense of personal and sexual attractiveness that may acquire a disproportionate amount of importance at this time. Adolescents who do not consider themselves attractive may find it harder to relate to their peers.

Social and psychological changes

Adolescence includes the development of identity, both personal and sexual. It is a time for developing personal, social and sexual confidence and learning to relate to prospective partners.

Adolescence also signifies a shift away from the family for emotional support and personal influence, in favour of peer groups and other, non-familial, role models. An enormous variety of influences are experienced, and young adults have to choose between them as they forge their own identity and attitudes. This is part of becoming more individual and independent.

At the same time, sexual identity, attitudes and values are forming. Adolescence is often a time of experimentation as people try out different gender and sexual roles until they find those with which they are comfortable. This search for identity may continue until much later in life; social pressures may prevent a person from exploring his or her identity and sexuality, particularly at this delicate stage of development and, above all, if the kinds of identity in question are perceived as outside the norm in the cultural group.

Adolescents may try out various sexual roles

Attitudes to adolescent sexuality

In some cultures, children can be expected to assume adult roles even before puberty. This may be a question of tradition or sheer necessity, as when children are required to rear younger siblings or work to augment the family income.

The situation in the West is usually much less repressive, as the transition to adulthood mostly involves formal education and has become prolonged to the point where a strong, independent youth culture has developed. This can influence anything from changing trends in fashion and music to attitudes to sex and sexuality.

Learning About Sex

Learning about sex is a fundamental part of human development. What people learn about sex as children may influence them for life. People learn about sex at all ages and from a variety of influences. However, in some cultures it is almost a taboo subject. Attitudes to sex education can be one of the clearest indications of a culture's attitudes to sex in general.

Sex education is now taught in schools in many countries, although the issue remains controversial. The young people themselves are, on the whole, enthusiastic, but feel that most sex education is 'too little, too late'

What is sex education?

The term sex education can refer to anything from the first discussion of human reproduction with a young child to the provision of clear, broad information on sexual practices and techniques for adults. It can come in the form of conversations with parents, siblings or peers, specific sex education classes, books, DVDs, and magazines. Much of the time it is learned less formally through media and the internet.

The importance of sex education

In its early stages, sex education for children can explain the differences between the sexes and the processes of human reproduction. As puberty approaches, it helps young people to recognise and adapt to the changes in their bodies and emotions, and to prepare them for different kinds of interpersonal relationships. At later stages, it is important for developing knowledge, skills and attitudes in all areas of sexuality.

At all stages, sex education can provide a broad understanding of the whole range of human sexuality. It entails personal and social education as well as information about health issues.

It can include:

- the mechanics of reproduction: sexual intercourse, conception, pregnancy, childbirth
- all aspects of sexual health: sexual hygiene, infections and diseases, unintended pregnancy, contraception and safer sex, abortion, sexual abuse
- aspects of sexuality: gender roles, sexual orientation, giving and receiving sexual pleasure, masturbation, sexual practices, notions of normality and individuality
- aspects of relationships: sex, love and commitment, casual sex, sex and relationships, sexual technique, sexual responsibility
- attitudes to sex: religious and cultural beliefs, one's own and other people's personal beliefs

Sex education for young people sometimes focuses simply on the mechanics of sex and the potential dangers, with comparatively little attention being paid to personal relationships, love, sexual attitudes and sexual pleasure. It may be riddled with euphemisms and, consequently, fail to deal with issues clearly and frankly.

Adult sex education has existed for a long time in many cultures, in some cases being elevated into an art form. In the East, in particular, the art of loving has long been taken very seriously, and is the origin of such works as the *Kama Sutra, The Perfumed Garden,* the Japanese *Pillow Books* and many Taoist and Tantric works.

Attitudes to sex education vary enormously from one cultural group to another. While this particular form, as depicted by the 11th century Chinese artist Su Shih, may be taking liberal attitudes to an extreme, the importance of sex education for people of all ages cannot be underestimated

The importance of sex education is often seen more clearly where it has been inadequate. Poor sex education has been shown to be directly related to higher incidence of STDs, unintended pregnancies and abortions. It can also produce a fear of sex and other relationship problems.

Despite some opponents' claims, there is no evidence that sex education increases early sexual activity or promiscuity – indeed quite the opposite. And ignorance is very often the source of prejudice.

Sex education not only helps people enjoy sex and form positive relationships, but it can also help build consideration and respect for others.

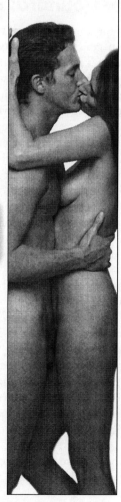

The essence of attraction between individuals remains the most elusive of all aspects of human relationships. Authors, poets, artists and philosophers have devoted their attention to it for centuries. More recently they have been joined by anthropologists, psychiatrists, psychologists and sociologists, gossip columnists and advice columnists, not to mention most socially or sexually active people. Still, it continues to evade identification, in spite of lying at the heart of sexual relationships. That unidentifiable spark of attraction is the key to our interaction as sexual beings.

Physical Attraction

This is the most immediate and powerful level of attraction. It dominates our first impressions and, if a sexual relationship develops, may continue to be a powerful force.

The power of physical attraction is most significant in first impressions. Consciously or unconsciously, we make fundamental decisions about a person's suitability as a sexual partner within the first four minutes of meeting him or her. These early decisions are based entirely on physical criteria, although, as relationships develop, many other factors naturally come in to play.

> Being a sex symbol has to do with an attitude. Not looks. Most men think it's looks, most women know otherwise.
> **KATHLEEN TURNER**

These early stimuli can range from being attracted to the way someone smells, to their tone of voice - but of course a major element is also appearance. Almost all people mention good looks as something they look for in a potential partner. Men in particular – regardless of sexual orientation – consider physical attractiveness to be essential: statistically the vast majority of men point to good looks (though what counts as good looks is relative to the eye of the beholder) as the most important attribute of a sexual partner.

The essence of attraction remains the most elusive facet of human relationships

Research carried out in Europe and the USA has pointed to a number of possible explanations for this. They include:

- biology and evolution, incorporating the idea that the instinct to reproduce is a response to a series of physical signals
- the impression created in particular by the advertising, magazine, television and film industries that the best relationships are formed with a physically attractive person
- the association of good looks with a good personality; the impression may originate in children's literature, in which evil characters such as witches tend to be described as ugly and beautiful characters are generally virtuous
- the idea of an attractive partner being seen as a status symbol

Cross-cultural comparisons

Focusing on Western developed countries with few cultural differences, allow certain generalisations possible, but with regard to other cultures, less data is available. There may be some truth in Darwin's theory that people are attracted to the physical characteristics that they are most used to. He gave the example of beards being greatly admired in populations in which there is a genetic tendency towards hairiness. However, many ideas of attractiveness seem to be more socially rooted, in what certain particular attributes signify to a certain social or cultural group. The power of this kind of social conditioning is seen in the range of attitudes toward physical build. For example, in some cultures, body fat is seen as an indication of health and high social status or wealth, while in others it can suggest quite the opposite.

Male teenager from Wodabe tribe, Nigeria.
Notions of attractiveness, including those relating to notions of masculinity and femininity, vary greatly from one culture to another. In this tribe, painting the body and face – as well as other forms of body decoration – is an important aspect of male attractiveness.

In some cases, without understanding a particular culture, many of its peculiarities could be written off as oddities, such as the preferences for cross-eyes (Mayans), flattened heads (Kwakiutl), black gums and tongue (Maasai), black teeth (Yapese), joined eyebrows (Syrians), absence of eyebrows and eyelashes (Mongol), enormously protruding navels (Ila), pendulous breasts (Ganda), gigantic buttocks (Hottentot), fat calves (Tiv) and small feet (Chinese). To understand the origins of these preferences it is important to understand the cultural background.

Same-sex Sexual Attraction

There is little definitive research on same-sex sexual attraction in terms of what specifically gay men and women look for in a partner. It may be fair to assume that attraction, though a highly subjective experience, shares commonality based on cultural and regional customs.

Male attractions

What seems to be suggested by the research is that men tend to be attracted in a similar way to other men as straight men are to women - they look for sexually dimorphic faces. That is, gay men look for well-defined physical features such as strong masculinised facial features. Interestingly, according to research studies, the types of faces that gay men find attractive generally typically do not mirror the types of faces that straight women find attractive. However, pheromone research finds that gay men respond similarly to women in the (masculine) scents that they are most attracted to.

Female attractions

Research on female to female attraction suggests that women are attracted to other women in a very similar way to men's attraction to women as well as the way in which women are attracted to men.

Therefore, it seems that women who are attracted to women have a broader attraction template, at least to physical attraction. However, in pheromone research, lesbian women showed similar brain activity (in terms of attraction to women) to sexual scents as did heterosexual men.

Bisexuality

Since at least the middle of the 19th century, behavioural scientists have noted bisexual attraction in men and women and debated its place in the development of sexual identity. Some experts, like Freud,

> My feeling is that we are all bisexual. I don't believe there is anyone who could honestly say at some point in their lives they have not been attracted to a member of the same sex.
> **KEN LIVINGSTONE, FORMER MAYOR OF LONDON**

concluded that humans are naturally bisexual. In his landmark sex surveys of the 1940s, Dr. Alfred Kinsey found many married, publicly heterosexual men who reported having had sex with other men. In fact, research suggests that the majority of people may be truly bisexual.

Despite one's sexual orientation or gender, the ways in which we choose to express our sensuality and sexuality are incredibly diverse. Ultimately, it is important to recognise that attraction is a natural expression of our sexual and sensual self. For many people, attraction is more about the person's character than it is about any other one physical attribute.

Western stereotypes: what women look for in men

In surveys, women frequently point to height, well-muscled upper bodies and small, firm buttocks as attractive features in men. These attributes echo the patterns of choice of mate followed by our most distant ancestors; the females then had to look for a mate who would provide healthy offspring, protect them, especially during pregnancy, and hunt for food.

Consciously or not, and regardless of women's changing role in society, the attributes which women tend to seek in prospective partners suggest that they look for a mate who can be relied upon in all these aspects, though it may now be more subtle. Intelligence appears to have taken over from brute force to provide good offspring, a decent home and a good lifestyle.

Women may now be attracted to men's bodies more for what they represent in terms of this reliability – power, protection, and security – than for the bodies

This body builder seems to have got it wrong – generally speaking, women are more interested in non-physical attributes in partners.

themselves. This theory may account for the fact that many women can be more strongly attracted to non-physical attributes such as occupational success and power, or personality traits such as confidence, assertiveness and independence.

Survey of attraction: attributes valued in men, by women

1. Intelligent
2. Sense of humour
3. Successful
4. Good in bed
5. Reliable
6. Physically attractive
7. Sensitive
8. Kind
9. Handsome
10. Similar interests

Notions of attractiveness in the West

It may, ultimately, be impossible to generalise about what people find attractive. In particular, when a relationship is formed a great many other, non-physical factors influence people's attitudes. However, a great many surveys have been carried out in Europe and the USA with regard to what physical features people find attractive in prospective partners. From these, certain trends emerge, many of which can be explained by the influence of evolutionary patterns.

Men tend to be much more orientated towards the physical – even though the specific type of looks or body that a particular man finds most attractive is entirely a matter of personal preference.

Western stereotypes: what men look for in women

Evolutionary patterns also seem to have a significant role in dictating men's choice of partner, in that purely physical attributes – including youth – are considered much more important, as they search for a child-bearer.

Again, an impression of health – suggesting fertility – is often considered attractive. However, the film, television, fashion and advertising industries have led to the perception of a narrow stereotype as the current Western ideal of female physical beauty. But in the same way as many, if not most, women are not over-preoccupied by penis size, a woman with blonde hair, long legs and large breasts is mercifully not the ideal for all men.

For men, physique is a priority, but the nature of that physique is much more a question of personal preference. In many cases men will describe themselves as 'breast', 'bottom' or 'leg' men.

Some research has suggested that sporty extrovert men prefer large breasts whereas intellectual introverts prefer smaller breasts.

Survey of attraction: attributes valued in women, by men

1. Physically attractive
2. Beautiful
3. Kind
4. Sensitive
5. Sense of humour
6. Intelligent
7. Similar interests
8. Reliable
9. Sporty
10. Successful

Opposites Attract

It is often said that 'opposites attract'. However, in psychological terms, it is increasingly thought that we are attracted to people similar to ourselves, though when it comes to physical attraction, it is the *differences* that play a key role. The biological differences between the sexes – women's softer skin and more rounded bodies, for example, and men's firmer bodies and greater body hair – can be deeply attractive to a member of the opposite sex.

Sexual Attraction and Smell

Smell is possibly the most evocative of human senses, possessing an emotional potency that other senses may not. Smell can affect mood, stir memories and evoke fantasies.

Moreover, some experts now believe that smell can be as important as appearance and personality in determining choice of partner. Within seconds of meeting someone we may draw intuitive sensory conclusions about him or her; if they possess the right smell, a process of olfactory bonding may occur at a conscious or unconscious level.

The mechanism of smell

Human beings can distinguish more than 10,000 different odorous chemicals. However, each person's sense of smell is completely unique. Smell is learned by association, and based on personal experiences.

The sense of smell functions in a part of the brain that controls learning, memory, appetites and basic emotional states such as fear, hate, love and sexual arousal. All smells have a chemical shape that fits like a key and locks into smell receptors inside the nose. The smell message is then passed directly to the brain, triggering an immediate signal in the centre of moods, emotions and long-term memory patterns.

Human bodies are among the most sophisticated smell-producing systems in the animal kingdom and each person's personal smell is as individual as his or her fingerprints or DNA makeup. Humans possess some three million scent glands. Most are found in the armpits and genitals, with others in the navel, nipples, scalp, mouth and eyelids. Musky smells are contained in armpit and pubic odours along with scents which are linked to sexual attraction. These may produce unconscious erotic responses or memories of certain events in the past.

Provocative perfumes

The secret of any strong sensual appeal in a perfume has always been ascribed to the animal base notes in it and consequently humans have plundered the animal kingdom for its precious scents for centuries. The most potent perfumes contain ingredients which produce erotic responses. One group of smells which are arousing to humans are odorant secretions released from the skin around

> One should wear perfume wherever one expects to be kissed.
> **COCO CHANEL**

the sexual organs. From the animal world these include musk, civet and castor. Ambergris, the 'pearl of the whale', has a smell similar to human hair. All of these substances are used in the manufacture of provocative perfumes. In higher concentrations the odours of musk (from deer) and civet (from the cat) resemble human sex-attractant smells.

Some plant scents have much the same impact on the human sexual response as animal ones. Frankincense resembles the body oils of dark-haired people and myrrh that of fair-haired people. Gum resins have a musky smell, henna blossom has the odour of semen and vanilla that of warm, human skin. Costus and mace, though, are the only two plants which have scents that are actively erotic to humans.

Pheromones

Pheromones are 'odour-hormone' chemicals emitted from the skin's surface, conveying messages that produce responses, often sexual, in others. In the animal kingdom pheromones are widely used in communication and some can be turned on an off at will. A female silk moth can sexually excite every male for miles around by emitting one type of pheromone.

That pheromones exist in the human world is undisputed. They fall into two categories, attractants and primers. Primers cause biological changes in women and account for such phenomena as menstrual synchrony among women living together. Attractants can cause sometimes overtly sexual personal attraction between individuals.

The female sex hormone, oestrogen, sharpens a woman's sense of smell, making it keener than a man's. Apparently, the scent women are best able to detect is musk, associated with the deeper-note smells of the male body.

> Scents are surer than sights and sounds to make your heartstrings crack.
> **RUDYARD KIPLING**

However powerful a human pheromone or a particular scent is, it is unlikely that it will produce an instantaneous response of passion and sexual receptiveness, as it can in the animal kingdom. Instead, pheromones and provocative scents are likely to work as part of a much broader and more sophisticated picture.

Psychological Factors

The nature of attraction is hard to identify even in terms of relatively straightforward physical criteria, but it becomes more complex still when the innumerable psychological factors are taken into consideration. These include the obvious elements such as common interests, but also other factors which can influence our choice of partner. Although we may be completely unaware of them, these may be the more powerful influences.

Personality

It is impossible to define universally-attractive characteristics of personality. An impression of vitality, a positive outlook, humour or enthusiasm are often considered appealing, if for no other reason than that they suggest health and energy. These characteristics can be linked to the influence of evolutionary patterns as we are, if heterosexual, probably subconsciously searching for a mate who appears best equipped to provide healthy offspring.

Sensitivity is also often mentioned as being important for both men and women. However, it is more likely to be the more individual characteristics, the idiosyncrasies and mannerisms, which attract us to a particular person.

> Love looks not with the eyes, but with the mind.
> **SHAKESPEARE,**
> *A MIDSUMMER NIGHT'S DREAM*

Social and Cultural Pressures

There are various psychological factors of which we may be only partially aware. These include a range of social and cultural pressures, varying from one population group to another, such as the socio-economic status or the religion of a prospective partner.

The Role of the Imagination

There is also a less practical side, in which the imagination can play a key role. This is seen in the idea of attraction based on previous sexual experience, real or imagined. According to this theory, we have in our subconscious a particular image of attractiveness to which we unconsciously relate our current experiences. The role of film, television, literature and other media may be fundamental here. As love and sex feature so frequently in the media, we are regularly presented with examples of all kinds of views about what constitutes attractiveness and what constitutes the ideal relationship. These powerful images often create a fantasy model of what our partners should look and act like. Unfortunately, fantasy is often better than the reality of the people available to us and with whom we may form relationships.

Attraction and Childhood

This takes us into the realms of unconscious influences, and brings us to one of the oldest, though also most researched, theories of attraction: that of the influence of childhood and the family.

Cases of people feeling sexually attracted to members of their immediate family appear in the Bible and in much classical literature. The common terms for sexual attraction to a parent of the opposite sex, the Oedipus complex and the Electra complex for boys and girls respectively, are taken from Greek mythology. These complexes, and many other links between family relationships and sexual identify, were first investigated by Sigmund Freud at the turn of the 20th century. Freud was the first to recognise sexuality as a powerful source of human will and to recognise that the source of sexuality occurs in infancy.

The idea that what attracts us to a potential sexual partner may be linked to certain characteristics of our parents is still widely accepted. Many theorists now believe that it is not only our parents who influence our choice of partner, but also the whole family structure. Tests have consistently shown that even before speaking to one another, people are often attracted to those whose families have a similar structure. This can be in terms of levels of affection, strictness of discipline, parental expectations, or significant changes or losses at particular ages. Whether we wish to copy or to escape the characteristics of our families in our own relationships, the influence of the family background may be as inevitable as it is pervasive.

La Belle Dame Sans Merci (detail), by the late 19th century painter, Sir Frank Dicksee

Situations

The media plays a similar part in the theory of attraction determined by particular situations. The *knight in shining armour/damsel in distress* scenario is somewhat clichéd, but may mirror everyday personal interactions, with the associated erotic feelings. At its core lies the idea of one person rescuing another from a difficult situation, a pattern that is reflected in the common sexual fantasy involving doctors or nurses or people in positions of power.

Linked to this is Dutton and Aron's *heightened emotion = arousal* theory that suggests that people are more likely to be attracted to a potential partner or to become aroused when in a situation which makes them anxious. This has been demonstrated by studies in which subjects have been forced into prolonged eye contact, threatened with electric shocks, and questioned in other potentially tense situations. The subjects consistently show greatly enhanced attraction to potential sexual partners.

Body Language

The spoken word accounts for only a small percentage of our communication with other people. Most of our communication (figures between 60 and 90% have been claimed) is through what is known as body language, the facial and bodily movements which – consciously or unconsciously – express our thoughts and feelings.

> They heard the wave's splash, and the wind so low,
> And saw each other's dark eyes darting light
> Into each other – and, beholding this,
> Their lips drew near, and clung into a kiss.
>
> **BYRON,** *DON JUAN*

Just as the meaning of a single, isolated word is limited, an independent gesture or movement may reveal relatively little. However, combinations of words form sentences and combinations of movements may be even more expressive. An understanding of the way the different aspects of body language function can make us more aware both of the way people react to us and of the way we appear to them.

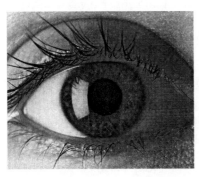

Eye Contact

In surveys on notions of attractiveness, time and time again people mention the eyes as the most important facial feature, and often (particularly among women) as the most important attribute of the whole person. This is more than merely part of a physical assessment. Our eyes are frequently more eloquent than our voices, and can reveal more than we intend or realise.

The eyes can be a clear indication of emotion in the very earliest stages of any relationship. They are often the best way of establishing initial interest or rapport: hence the well-worn clichés of 'love at first sight' and 'eyes meeting across a crowded room'.

Generally speaking, when they talk, people look at each other for no more than two-thirds of the time, their eyes meeting for barely a second at a time. People who like each other maintain more eye contact, and if they are attracted to each other, eye contact becomes greater still. Games may be played, as two people each try to catch the other's unguarded gaze.

> The eyes are the windows to the soul.
> **JOHN BUNYAN**

Men tend to look for longer and more openly, for, if women do the same, it may sometimes be interpreted as a blatant sexual signal. Women tend to look away then back at a person in whom they are interested. In both cases, eye contact can establish a sense of openness and sexual attraction.

When a person looks away to break his or her gaze the direction to which they turn can also be significant. It has been said that looking downward indicates strong inner emotion; looking up suggests an active imagination; looking sideways can imply rehearsing or recalling words or thoughts.

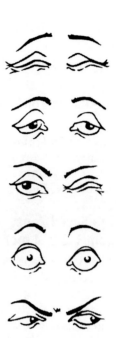

> Drink to me only with thine eyes
> And I will pledge with mine.
> **BEN JONSON,** *TO CELIA*

Attraction may also be betrayed by the appearance of the eyes themselves. With sexual attraction they tend to widen and the pupils dilate. With sexual arousal the pupils remain enlarged but the eyes may narrow and become less focused. This may be considered a strong sexual signal – a fact recognised by Italian courtesans in the 16th century, who used small quantities of the drug belladonna to dilate the pupils; the word belladonna means 'beautiful lady' in Italian. Eye decoration has been common in many cultures.

> Speech happens not
> to be his language.
> (attributed to Mme De Stael on being
> asked what she found to talk about with
> her new husband, a hussar)

Eye contact can be a powerful way of conveying feelings – these people are clearly enjoying each other's company

Personal Territory

Research into people's reactions to the proximity of other individuals in specific situations has led to the classification of four zones of personal space.

The Public Zone: over 4 metres

This zone relates to public performances. This may be in the context of the theatre, the Church or education. Audience and performers are separate and defined, and any interaction between the two can be disconcerting, as when actors move into the audience, or a single member of the audience is singled out by a performer.

The Social Zone: from 1.2 to 4 metres

This is the zone occupied by strangers and distant, professional acquaintances. It may include shopkeepers and domestic workers with whom interaction tends to be on a formal, or arms-length level.

The Casual or Personal Zone: from 0.5 to 1.2 metres

This is the zone in which we operate at social gatherings and in offices. It allows casual interaction, enabling people to get to know each other though with no sense of threat or invasion of each other's space.

The Intimate Zone: up to 50 cm

This is the zone to which only lovers and close friends, associates and relatives are admitted. If anyone else tries to enter this zone it can seem hostile and invasive. The body reacts to this degree of proximity with a rush of adrenaline. This increases the pulse rate and blood flow through the body, preparing it to fend off or flee an invasion, or to respond warmly to the closeness of a loved one.

These zones vary from one person to another - for instance, the distances tend to be reduced between two women and increased between men. They also vary greatly from one culture to another. Movement from one zone to another can occur as situations change and relationships develop, but crossing a boundary too soon can be threatening. The movement from social to intimate zones can be eased initially with socially acceptable excuses - dancing is a good example of this.

Posture, Gesture and Attraction

Posture and gesture can also form a strong indication of one person's feelings for another. This is another area where animal instincts come into play, as we preen ourselves for courtship and react to basic, subtle sexual signals. Open body movements combined with sensitivity to other people's body language can be very attractive. Likewise, negative or *closed gestures* can be surprisingly powerful and barriers can easily be created with a crossed leg or arm, a lack of eye contact or the turn of the body.

We use posture and gesture to make ourselves more attractive, to emphasise our best points and to indicate our interest in a specific person in a group by pointing our body, or even just a knee, towards the person in whom we are most interested, whether sexually or socially. We may also touch ourselves or each other. However, there are also specific uses of body language employed by men and women – consciously and unconsciously – to attract or to demonstrate attraction to a prospective partner.

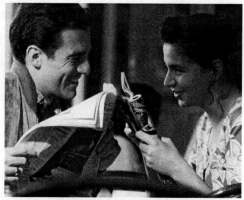

Actions speak louder than words – the posture of this man and this woman, and the echoing in the way they are holding their newspaper and magazine, clearly show warmth and attraction.

Echoing

One of the more remarkable forms of unconscious communication is posture and gesture echoing. Research has shown that we tend to copy the body language of people we like. The closer the relationship the more evident this behaviour becomes, as emotional and psychological rapport and trust develop. A conscious form of this echoing, by subtly following a person's posture or gestures, can also be used to establish a connection with an otherwise distant or unfriendly person, without them realising why.

Though most kinds of echoing behaviour are generally quite unconscious, in an intimate relationship it can extend to bodily processes over which we have no control at all. It is quite common for lovers to develop synchronicity in their heartbeat, breathing rate, body temperature and even blood pressure.

> There's language in her eye, her cheek, her lip,
>
> Nay, her foot speaks; her wanton spirits look out
>
> At every joint and motive of her body
>
> **SHAKESPEARE, *TROILUS AND CRESSIDA***

The smile is friendly; but her body is upright and slightly angled away, whilst her arms and legs are closed, suggesting that she is slightly apprehensive

Female Courtship Gestures

The woman will want to make a good impression, but her gestures may be subtler than the man's and she may be hesitant to make the first moves. General appearance, body language and the use of voice and touch are all significant.

If she is attracted she may:

- cross her legs and point them towards the person to whom she is attracted, or cross and uncross them

- straighten her body, drawing attention to her breasts

- touch or stroke her hair during conversation and tilt her head

- look briefly at the person then look away again

- lean forwards with interest during conversation

- lower and soften her voice

- smile warmly and open her eyes wider

- touch the person, sometimes by brushing something off his or her clothing

'Preening' – classic female courtship signals: the legs are crossed towards you, the head is tilted, and one hand is on the knee whilst the other preens the hair, revealing the subconscious desire to look youthful and attractive

1. He is making the first advances – his posture is relatively open, though the left hand shows he is slightly guarded. Her gestures are closed, but her smile is inviting

Closed, uninterested body language is indicated by the firmly crossed arms, the legs crossed and directed away, her eyes looking up and away

2. She is opening up her facial expression and hand gestures, turning her hand and wrists upwards and angling her body further towards him, whilst he is angled closer towards her – the ice is breaking

Male Courtship Gestures

The man will want to make a good impression. That impression will involve general appearance, body language and tone of voice as well as actual spoken words and touch. It may also include specific preening gestures.

If he is attracted he may:

- smooth his hair or clothing

- flatten his abdomen and stand/sit tall

- thrust his hips and chest forward, sometimes with hands on hips

- maintain eye contact

- lower and soften his voice

- touch the person he is attracted to, perhaps with a hand around the shoulders or on the elbow

- sit with his pelvis tilted upwards and legs apart

- smile warmly and open the eyes wider

For a female, a hand on the leg could be come-on, but for a male, it is more likely an indication of stubbornness His outer arm and leg form a defensive barrier against close interaction

 3. His gestures are open but he is leaning away. She is angled towards him and her raised eyebrows intensify eye contact

His legs are open suggesting that he is not nervous. However, he is rubbing the back of his neck and has a closed facial expression, both of which indicate that he is fairly uninterested

4. Their bodies are open and turned towards each other. Eye contact is strong, and they have bridged the gap between them with their hands

His exposed palms, forward-angled body, open legs and smile all give a strong message of interest

SEXUAL BEHAVIOUR

There are many elements to making love, which mostly refers to an enhanced form of having sex with another. It covers the wide spectrum of sexual activity and expression from kissing and touching to oral sex and all the various ways to engage in sexual intercourse.

True making love involves something beyond the basic urges of having sex. It is more selfless, placing the desire to give the other pleasure above simply satisfying one's own desires. It happens when two people feel so strongly for one another that they want to express that love in a deeply intimate, physical demonstration of their mutual involvement.

Touching

Touching is one of the most basic forms of communication. As newborn babies, we first come to know our environment and form bonds with other people through touch. Touch – or the lack of it – continues to be a significant aspect of all our relationships.

In terms of where and how we touch another person, different kinds of touching are appropriate in different situations. Above all, this is determined by the nature of the relationship between the people concerned. Completely distinct kinds of touching may take place between, for example, close relatives, business associates and lovers. In some cases the distinction may be less clear, for example between lovers and close friends.

However, there is a boundary between the two, the nature and location of which vary from one person to another. This boundary must be respected. Even allowing someone to come close to it is a gesture of trust. If the boundary is crossed in the wrong way, or at the wrong time, it can seriously damage a relationship. But, if both people feel comfortable with the boundary being crossed, it can take the relationship to a whole new level of intimacy.

Lovers (detail), by Egon Schiele (1911)

> **Touching includes...**
> stroking, scratching, pressing, pinching, rubbing, tickling, smacking, feeling, squeezing, patting, caressing, massaging.

Types of touch

The various kinds of touch may be classified into five levels of progressive intimacy. These help to define what kinds of touch are acceptable in specific situations.

- **Level 1** – the touch of professionals, including teachers, beauty therapists and medical practitioners, dentists, oculists and physiotherapists. It may be soothing and reassuring, even sensual, as in the case of massage, or stressful, as in some kinds of medical examination.

- **Level 2** – touch in social situations, as in the many forms of greeting and farewell, some 60% of which involve some physical contact.

- **Level 3** – any form of contact between friends, from a reassuring touch on the hand to an open and enthusiastic embrace. The extent of this kind of contact with which people feel comfortable depends largely on what they are used to: some families and some cultural groups are more tactile than others.

- **Level 4** – the more intimate touch which may be permissible between parent and child, close friends, and lovers. It is a clear demonstration of trust in the relationship, although it is also affected by cultural factors.

- **Level 5** – the sensuous touching between lovers as part of sexual arousal.

Touch in a loving relationship

As a relationship develops and trust is built up, the kinds of touch that are appropriate may move through the five levels of progressive intimacy. Most relationships begin with the distant and formal social touch before moving on to friendly touch; only occasionally does this develop into the more intimate loving or sexual contact.

The movement from one level of intimacy to another often comes through trial and error. We try to interpret each other's body language before attempting any kind of physical contact; then, when we touch, we observe the person's reaction. Any kind of backing off shows that the person is not comfortable with our touch; if, however, they return the touch, this is clearly a more positive signal. Any individual may have certain no-go areas where they do not like to be touched for personal or cultural reasons. Excuses for touch, to test the water, can also be found, such as passing something from hand to hand.

FACT
The skin of an average adult covers more than two square metres and weighs up to four kilos. It contains millions of nerve endings which relay all kinds of sensory information to the brain. It is considered to be the largest sexual organ (the brain is considered the most powerful).

Once intimacy has been established, touch can take many forms and can be a fundamental part of any sexual relationship. It is largely through touch that we come to know our sexual selves. In the same way, touch can be the key to getting to know someone sexually.

Sexual touch

Sexual touch is distinguished from friendly or loving touch by where and how people touch each other. The significance of touching particular parts of the body may vary from one cultural group to another. For example, while in the West rubbing noses is something people in a close personal relationship might do for fun, in Polynesia it used to be a formal greeting and in the Eskimo tradition is an intimate way of breathing in the other person's spirit.

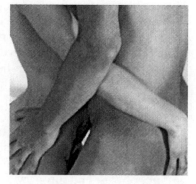

Generally speaking, the more intimate the touch, the more intimate the relationship. People tend to start by touching the parts nearest to them, such as hands and perhaps shoulders or knees. Touching the face, or allowing another person to touch one's own face, can be quite a powerful signal of affection and trust. Touching the thighs, the trunk of the body and anywhere near the breasts or genitals makes the gesture overtly sexual.

Erotic touch comes into its own when clothes are removed and skin-to-skin touch begins. This can take many different forms, and can develop as intimacy grows. Ultimately it can become a powerful and sensuous facet of lovemaking.

The skin responds to all kinds of stimulation and each individual has specific parts of the body which are particularly sensitive. Some seem to be gender-specific while others vary from one individual to the next. They may include anything from the fingertips to the genitals themselves. These are known as *erogenous zones*.

Pressure, temperature, speed and rhythm can all be varied to produce an enormous range of sensations. Touch can be with the fingertips, the hands, the feet, the lips and tongue or any other part of the body.

While the sensation of skin on skin can be highly arousing, further sensual sensations can be produced by touching with other objects or materials, such as hair, feathers, fur, velvet, silk or satin, rubber or leather, water or ice or sexual aids such as a vibrator.

Kissing

A kiss is one of the most common gestures of affection. It can also be one of the most intimate and erotic.

Human beings are the only animals able to kiss in this way: the J-shaped muscles in the lips contribute to this purpose. This may be because evolutionary processes required the development of sexual signals on the front of the body when humans started to stand upright and mate face-to-face.

A passionate kiss can burn up as many as 12 calories.

However, the origins of the practice of kissing mouth-to-mouth lie not in mating but in caring for the offspring, in mouth-to-mouth feeding. Many animals feed their newborn offspring in this way, making it one of the most natural gestures of trust and intimacy. Even now the sensual side of the experience of eating is often linked to, or combined with, more overtly sexual activity.

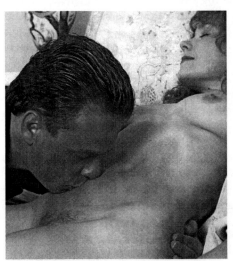

Kissing can be addictive - the glands at the edge of the lips and the mouth produce chemicals that enhance and stimulate desire during kissing. The very action of kissing boosts the production of these chemicals

Kissing and relationships

Kissing on the cheek can mean many different things, depending principally on cultural factors. Social kissing by way of greeting is common in many countries; it is more common between women but is also becoming increasingly common amongst men.

The first mouth-to-mouth kiss is generally taken as a specific sign of the beginning of an intimate relationship. Even after this stage kissing can continue to stand as an indication of the affection between the two people concerned. According to Relate, Britain's relationship guidance and counselling organisation, unhappy couples tend to stop kissing even before they stop having sexual intercourse. Many sex workers (prostitutes) refuse to kiss their clients on the lips. For many people full-on, mouth-to-mouth kissing is even more intimate than sexual intercourse and may therefore be reserved only for the most meaningful relationships.

Ways of kissing

The mouth is a highly mobile and responsive organ, allowing for great variety in types of kiss. Kisses can be anything from soft and tender to deep, passionate and even rough. Kisses can mimic intercourse, the tongue penetrating the mouth, ears or vagina. The entire body can be explored with kisses.

Eyes open or closed?

It is believed that kissing with your eyes open can create a greater sense of closeness, perhaps because we are using more senses. Some people however, prefer kissing with their eyes closed; perhaps to create greater focus on the connection and inner sensations.

Lips open or closed?

Different kinds of kiss are appropriate in different situations. However, it has been suggested that certain types of mouth-to-mouth kiss may reveal certain character traits or attitudes to the relationships in question. For example, an unwillingness to kiss with open lips may suggest some kind of fear of intimacy, while kissing with closed lips then opening the mouth for more lingering kisses, indicates increased sensuousness and passion. Kissing with open lips and using the tongue may imply generosity or the desire to create a strong and intimate bond (though, too early, may indicate over-eagerness).

Other variations

Differences that make each person's way of kissing unique include the varying degrees of rhythm, speed, pressure and moisture, the softness or firmness of the lips and tongue and the amount of movement of the lips and tongue. Sometimes the teeth can be used and kissing can include nibbling or biting. Any part of the body can be kissed, in any way.

"A kiss can be a comma, a question or an exclamation point. That's basic spelling every woman ought to know"
Mistinguett

"The sound of a kiss is not so loud as that of a cannon, but its echo lasts a great deal longer"
Dr. Oliver Wendell Holmes

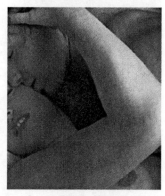

"... we did one of those quick, awkward kisses where each of you gets a nose in the eye"
Clive James, Unreliable Memoirs (1980)

Erogenous Zones

Any part of the body can be sexual. Any touch can be sexually arousing, particularly when the people touching each other are emotionally
involved. However, some parts of the body are especially sensitive. The
genitals are the most obvious example, but other, apparently non-sexual
parts of the body can be extremely erotic. These areas of high sensitivity
are usually known as the erogenous zones.

The sensitivity of different parts of the body can also be governed by psychological factors. These may be influenced by past experiences and associations,
or by culture-specific taboos. These may make a certain part of the body a
no-go area, or they may make it that much more sensitive or erotic.

Female erogenous zones

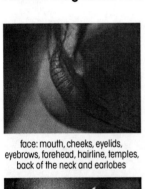
face: mouth, cheeks, eyelids,
eyebrows, forehead, hairline, temples,
back of the neck and earlobes

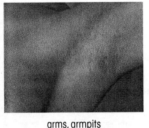
arms, armpits

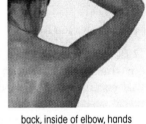
back, inside of elbow, hands

breasts, nipples

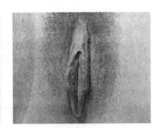
abdomen, navel

genitals: inner lips, clitoris

base of spine, perineum, buttocks,
anus, legs, inside of thighs

backs of knees

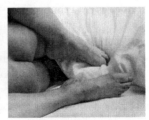
feet and toes

Male and female

The erogenous zones in the male tend to be more clearly defined and more uniform from one man to another than they are in the female. The genitals are by far the most sensitive parts and male arousal tends to depend more upon genital stimulation than anything else.

For women, however, stimulation of almost any part of the body can be highly arousing. There is also considerably more variation from one woman to another. Some women have been known to come close to, or actually reach, orgasm through stimulation of the breasts, mouth or even the earlobes alone. In spite of this, the effects of arousal are still most strongly felt in the genital area, primarily in the clitoris.

Male erogenous zones

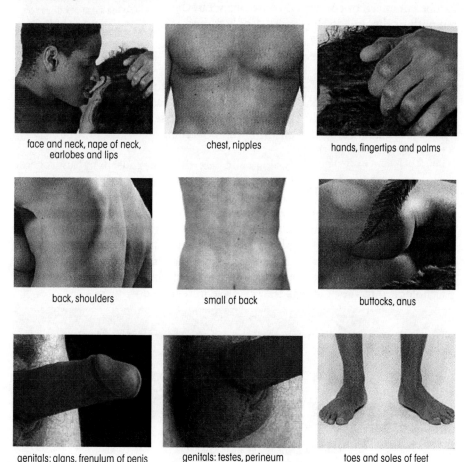

face and neck, nape of neck, earlobes and lips

chest, nipples

hands, fingertips and palms

back, shoulders

small of back

buttocks, anus

genitals: glans, frenulum of penis

genitals: testes, perineum (area between penis and anus)

toes and soles of feet

Sex Drive

The term sex drive refers to the strength of a person's desire to have sex. It influences the amount and the kind of sex a person needs in order to feel sexually satisfied. It is an innate, instinctive urge common to all animals, but which varies greatly in degree from one person to another. It can also be affected by external influences, causing it to change throughout a person's life and even from one day to the next.

What determines a person's sex drive?

Sex drive is instinctive: it is not a conscious force. It can be enhanced or controlled consciously, but the strength of the urge itself is more deeply rooted.

Having the same sex drive can make a couple's sex life highly satisfying. However, if people find that differing sex drives are a problem, mutual understanding and flexibility can often resolve it

> ### FACT
> Freud was the first person to use the term *'libido'*, the Latin word for desire, in a sexual sense. He was the first to point to sex drive as a fundamental source of human motivation.

At one level, sex drive is about reproduction: it is the instinct that ensures the continuation of the species. It has been suggested that the human enjoyment of sex evolved as a means of ensuring reproduction.

Biologically, sex drive is caused by androgenic hormones, in particular testosterone. This is produced in the adrenal glands and the testes in men, and the adrenal glands and the ovaries in women. In men testosterone is produced in greater quantities and is responsible for the male secondary sexual characteristics such as greater body and facial hair, and the occurrence of more muscle and less body fat than females. Anything that affects the production of testosterone – such as castration and use of synthetic hormones, as well as psychological factors – affects the sex drive in men and women.

Incompatible sex drives can be a problem for some couples, but through good understanding and teamwork this can often be resolved. It can help to see a qualified sex therapist to work with this issue

The links between state of mind and hormone production are still not fully understood. However, the two are connected and can affect sex drive. Stress and anxiety are known to reduce sexual desire, just as happiness and a sense of security can boost it. Negative influences may be specifically to do with sex or apparently quite unconnected, but they can be very powerful. Many are rooted in sexually repressive attitudes during childhood, in cultural background or upbringing.

Two Athenian Women in Distress (detail), by Aubrey Beardsley, 1895 illustration for Aristophanes' Lysistrata. The picture depicts women of fifth-century Athens, who went on a sex strike when annoyed about their men always being at war. They ended up as sexually frustrated as the men – if not more so

Throughout history, people have been searching for effective aphrodisiacs, that is, substances or products that increase sexual desire. Although a fail-safe aphrodisiac has yet to be found, many people believe that certain substances, a balanced diet, regular exercise and good general health will boost sexual appetite, capacity and enjoyment. It is unclear whether drugs which are used to treat erectile dysfunction, such as sildenafil citrate (Viagra), tadalafil (Cialis) and vardenafil (Levitra) also increase desire, though they are likely to have some influence on sexual outlook when an erection becomes readily achievable.

Differences in sex drive

Attitudes to female sexuality have always been somewhat ambivalent. Men have almost always been expected to have strong sexual desires; though some cultures have recognised, and even worshiped, female sexuality, others have completely denied it. In the West in the 19th century, women were seen as divided into two types: those who had sexual desires and were loose or immoral, and those who were chaste and suitable for marriage. Sex drive was not considered an acceptable part of the ideal of femininity.

The Sultan (detail), by Thomas Rowlandson, from a 19th century series of caricatures of the English aristocracy

It is now acknowledged that both sexes have a sex drive, although some stigma can still wrongly linger for women. A man with many partners may be admired for being sexually successful while a woman is more likely to be criticized for being tarty. However, statistically, women are more likely than men to have low sexual desire, although amongst men, too, it is by no means uncommon. A study carried out in the USA estimated that 26% of the population is suffering from Hypoactive Sexual Desire Disorder (HSDD).

Masturbation

According to 2010 data from the Kinsey Institute in the US, up to 64% of women and 85% of men masturbate regularly at some time in their lives. As with all studies on masturbation, these are self-reported behaviours and it is likely that the actual percentage is significantly higher. Indeed, some have said that all but asexual men have masturbated at some point in their lives and that figures for women actually approach 90%. Sue Johanson, for instance, a US sex educator and counsellor has gone on record to say: "99% of men of all ages masturbate regularly and the other 1% are liars."

Masturbation can provide uncomplicated and quick sexual relief and pleasure. It can also contribute to sexual health by keeping the sexual organs healthy and working properly when there is no sexual partner and, in men, it maintains levels of testosterone. It can also aid treatment of some sexual problems, such as premature ejaculation and vaginismus

Masturbation is a wholly natural, normally instinctive sexual practice, yet for centuries the practice of masturbation was condemned as wrong or dirty in cultures throughout the world. Even now that most people understand that masturbation is not only common but also at worst harmless and at best helpful, people are still trying to free themselves from the legacy of guilt which these attitudes have created.

Masturbation means using the hands, other (non-genital) parts of the body or an object, to stimulate the genitals. Most commonly it refers to stimulating oneself, usually to orgasm, but it can also mean arousing a partner in the same way. Mutual masturbation means partners masturbating one another at the same time.

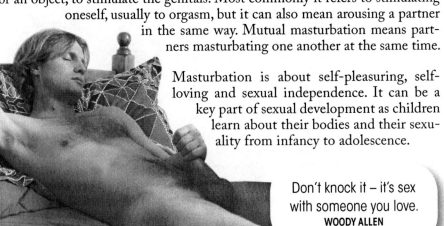

Masturbation is about self-pleasuring, self-loving and sexual independence. It can be a key part of sexual development as children learn about their bodies and their sexuality from infancy to adolescence.

Don't knock it – it's sex with someone you love.
WOODY ALLEN

In adult life masturbation can perform a similar role as people explore their sexuality. It enables people to learn what they find most arousing and what kind of stimulation they need in order to reach orgasm, which may be particularly useful for women.

Masturbation is often triggered by, or accompanied by, fantasising or the use of pornography.

It has a part to play both in single life and within a relationship. Many people may, at least occasionally, wish to have sexual release without commitment or dealing with another person's needs and emotions.

Masturbation within a relationship

Within a relationship, whether permanent or not, masturbation can be part of arousal before moving on to another kind of lovemaking, or it can be enjoyed in its own right, and perhaps continue to orgasm. It can be used to give both partners a chance to orgasm, and can be used to redress the balance in a relationship where partners have different sex drives.

Mutual masturbation can be an alternative to intercourse when this is not possible or not wanted. It does not involve concerns about pregnancy or STIs.

Some people also enjoy masturbating in front of their partner or watching them masturbate as a part of learning about each other. In a long-standing relationship, masturbation can provide pleasure if either partner is absent or ill or just because one feels the wish to do it.

> You know what I like about masturbation? You don't have to talk afterwards.
> **MILOS FORMAN**

Masturbation can be an intimate way of getting to know your partner and learning what kinds of stimulation arouse them most. It can include stimulating the clitoris – the key to sexual arousal for many women

Masturbation can be one of the most exciting forms of stimulation – especially as, for a man, most of the erogenous zones are focused on the genital area

Masturbation need not be just with the hands – any part of the body can be used

Taboos about masturbation from 'self-abuse' to self-loving

Masturbation was historically condemned for two reasons: on religious grounds, because sex was supposed to be only for procreation and not for pleasure, and on medical grounds, on the basis of a perceived health risk. Eminent and respected physicians and psychologists of the time issued serious health warnings, as every kind of mental or bodily disorder – '*from pimples to insanity*' (Kinsey's reporting) – was ascribed to masturbation.

'Cures' included such extreme measures as castration, various forms of male and female circumcision and vicious restraints. Children were sometimes tied or chained at night to prevent them from touching their genitals in their sleep; bizarre and painful penis harnesses were also used. Indeed, the *New Orleans Medical and Surgical Journal* railed

19th century coloured woodcut (detail) by Kunimori II of Japan. Masturbation has always been part of human sexuality, for both individuals and couples.

in 1850 that: "Neither plague, nor war, nor smallpox, nor a crowd of similar evils have resulted more disastrously for humanity than the habit of masturbation: it is destroying the element of civilized society."

Towards the end of the 19th century, masturbation among adolescents came to be more accepted, although among adults it was taken as a sign of immaturity, senility, insanity or an inability to form, or maintain, a normal heterosexual relationship. The major breakthrough came with Kinsey's study of male sexuality in the late 1940s. This revealed that 92% of men had masturbated at some point in their lives, generally with no adverse effects. (Intriguingly, female masturbation was not investigated until later.)

The only substantive negative effect of masturbation was, ironically, the way people had been affected psychologically because of its fervent condemnation. For many people, this legacy of guilt still survives. Though it is now known that masturbation is not only harmless but can also have significant

positive sexual and health benefits; it is also probably the most common of all genital sexual practices.

There are a plethora of masturbatory devices on the market today and a continued rise of sex boutiques and websites for both the amateur and the experienced to explore.

Slang terms: to wank, to jerk off, to beat off, to toss off, to beat the meat, to choke the chipmunk, to spank the monkey, to diddle/flog the poodle, to jerk the gherkin, to knock oneself off, to wack off, to bash/beat the bishop, to milk, to jill off, to play solitaire, to pound the pud, to pull the pudding, to do it yourself, to punish Percy in the palm, to have one off the wrist, to touch oneself up, finger job, pocket pool, hand jive, hand shandy, wrist job, Jodrell Bank, J Arthur Rank

Oral Sex

Oral sex means using the mouth to stimulate a
partner's sexual organs. Oral sex can be one of
the most sensuous and erotic forms of lovemaking. Like masturbation, it has been common
in many cultures for centuries and yet, in some
cultures and circles, it remains controversial.

> You know the worst thing
> about oral sex? The view*.
> **MAUREEN LIPMAN**
> [*we disagree - Eds.]

Oral sex can be part or all of a lovemaking experience. It can likewise be used
to satisfy either partner before or after the other has reached orgasm. What
distinguishes it from other sexual practices is the intense and intimate awareness of the sight, feel and smell of one's partner's genitals which it allows.

Cunnilingus

Cunnilingus is stimulating the female genitals with the
mouth, in particular the tongue. Kissing and caressing
the clitoris and vaginal lips with the tongue can be
highly sensuous and arousing – the tongue is soft and
moist and can be more mobile and exploratory than
fingers. The sensitive inner and outer vaginal lips
can be licked and sucked. The vagina itself
can be penetrated with the tongue and the
G-spot can be stimulated with a finger
at the same time, but to bring about
greater arousal most attention should
be focused on the clitoris.

Cunnilingus may begin with the women's partner caressing her inner thighs
and the area around the genitals, moving on to stimulating the clitoris with the
tip of the tongue, or to penetrating the vagina with the tongue. Oral pleasuring
of the female can be intensely pleasurable for both partners. However, it is
important to discuss and identify what each partner finds most exciting.

Fellatio

Fellatio is stimulating the male genitals with the mouth and tongue. It may
involve kissing, sucking and licking the
penis or testicles or taking the shaft
into the mouth; if this occurs then the
penis can be sucked and the tongue
used to stimulate the sensitive ridge
(the frenulum) on the underside of the
head (the glans) of the penis.

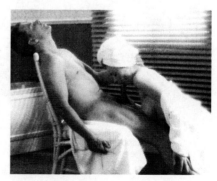

The mouth can be moved to stimulate the movements of vaginal or anal intercourse, and the fingers and hand can be used to stimulate the penis and testicles further. The partner may wish to thrust simultaneously.

Some people fear gagging or choking, but this can be avoided by not allowing the penis to be pushed too far into the mouth using a hand. Others, in deep throat fellatio, have learned to repress this reflex.

Taboos about Oral Sex

There are, however, often taboos surrounding oral sex. Personal taboos may include a sense of inhibition about this kind of intimacy. Some fear it may be unhygienic - although if proper personal hygiene is maintained, there are generally actually fewer bacteria on the genitals than there are in the mouth after eating. Many people feel ashamed of their genitals, or conscious of their natural, healthy genital odour, and are for this reason reluctant to let anyone come into such close contact with them. Others have more practical concerns such as fear of choking or being unable to breathe.

The sexual mouth. The mouth is the only part of the body capable of rivalling and even exceeding the genitals in terms of sensuousness and sensitivity. It is associated with not one but two of life's potentially most sensuous experiences: sex and eating. As well as this, it is mobile and expressive, and can convey anything from doubt or displeasure to excitement, delight and seductiveness. In oral sex, the penis, scrotum and perineum of the male and the vulva of the female – like any other part of the body – can be licked, sucked, kissed, stroked with the lips or lightly nibbled. These factors give the mouth a unique capacity for both giving and receiving oral stimulation

Cultural taboos are not unlike those relating to masturbation in that many are associated with religious beliefs. Certain religions only sanction intercourse when it is for reproduction: thus any other kind of activity – including homosexuality, anal intercourse, masturbation and oral sex – may be condemned.

Japanese woodcut showing a gymnastic display of the 69 position

By contrast, a number of cultural groups have celebrated oral sex quite openly. Images of people engaged in oral sex have been featured on Chinese perfume bottles and ceramics, Japanese sexual manuals, Hindu temples and Amerindian pottery, as well as, albeit less openly, in Western art and literature.

Oral Sex facts

The amount, consistency and taste of seminal and vaginal fluid produced varies from one person to another. There are, however, some things that can affect the nature of the taste. Cigarettes and alcohol make bodily fluids more bitter; red meats, spinach and foods high in iron give them a sharper flavour; the fluids of vegetarians tend to have a more moderate taste.

69 or Soixante-neuf Position

This is called the 69 position (or *soixante-neuf* in French) because of the shape of the bodies when they are both positioned mouth to genital area at the same time.

Simultaneously performing cunnilingus and fellatio can be highly satisfying and exciting for both partners. A number of positions can be used, with the man on top, the woman on top, side-by-side or even standing; in most of them, the hands can be used to caress the partner's body.

The 69 position may be difficult for partners who are very different from each other in height or physique. Also, some couples prefer to stimulate each other in turn, concentrating on the distinct sensations of giving and receiving oral sex. This may be either as a prelude to penetrative sex or in order to induce orgasm.

> As for that topsy-turvy tangle known as soixante-neuf, personally I have always felt it to be madly confusing, like trying to pat your head and rub your stomach at the same time*.
> **HELEN LAWRENSON**
> [*we disagree, again - Eds.]

Slang terms - Cunnilingus: cunt sucking, Frenching, eating out, going down, eating at the Y, muff diving, clam diving, tonguing, cat lapper, plating, licking, blowing, pussy nibbling, box lunch, head job, breakfast in bed, cake eater
Slang terms - Fellatio: cock sucking, blow job, BJ, giving head, deep throat, sucking off, going down on, nob job, Frenching, plating, basket lunch, copping a joint, Derby picnic, Hoover

Anal Sex

Within the range of common sexual practices, anal sex is probably the most controversial of all. However, those who explore this highly sensitive part of the body often find interest in its unique delights.

Anal intercourse seems to have been a common sexual activity in all ages and cultures and yet can remain a taboo subject, often even between close friends or lovers. For many people it is a highly rewarding sexual experience and fantasy, for many others the mere idea is considered repulsive. Amongst some groups it is used as a method of contraception.

Attitudes

The notion of anal sex as a taboo may begin in infancy. A child's interest in his or her bodily functions – described by psychologists as the oral, anal and genital fixation phases – is natural and healthy. The interest in the genitals has been re-pressed in some cultures but tolerance is now growing once more. However, the interest in excretion – and hence anything to do with the anus – is often frowned upon and repressed.

Pleasure and Practicality

It is estimated that as many as 25% of het-erosexual couples and 66% to 75% of male homosexual couples include anal sex as part of their sex play. During anal sex, the anus is stimulated with fingers or hands, mouth and tongue, the penis, or any other part of the body, with or without penetra-tion. Sex aids and sex toys can also be used, including those that are made specifically for use in or around the anus.

19th century coloured woodcut (detail) by Kunimori of Japan. The anus is an area of natural curiosity – as well as an erogenous zone of many people

Like the vagina, the tissue of the anus and rectum contains many nerve endings, par-ticular in the outer parts. Stimulating this area can be highly pleasurable. The tightness of the anus can provide great pleasure, especially for the giver.

Anal stimulation by hand or penis is the only way to stimulate the prostate directly. It also provides homosexual men with a means of having penetrative sex.

Anal sex can also answer certain practical needs. Firstly, as a method as contraception, as long as the semen does not come into contact with the vagina, it cannot lead to pregnancy. Secondly, having anal sex avoids breaking the hymen, which is taken as all-important proof of virginity in certain cultures (although the hymen can in fact be broken in other ways). People may engage in anal sex for any of these reasons, as well as out of simple sexual curiosity.

The risks of anal sex

Practised carefully, in many cases anal sex need cause no problems. However, there are a few risks involved. The walls of the rectum are much thinner and more fragile than those of the vagina and can be damaged comparatively easily.

Anal sex can also be painful, though this can be eased by using plenty of lubrication, the one penetrated relaxing fully, and aided with gentle dilation of the anal sphincter with a finger or a small object beforehand.

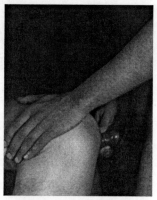

Anal intercourse between homosexuals is illegal in many countries and often subject to taboos. It is, however, a common form of sexual fulfilment between homosexual men

Anal sex carries greater risk of spreading infections and sexually transmissible diseases including HIV, principally because of the fragility of the walls of the rectum which makes contact between semen and blood that much more probable.

The use of a condom with plenty of water-based lubricant substantially reduces this risk. Also, bacteria, which exist naturally and healthily in the anus, can cause infection when passed to the vagina or mouth.

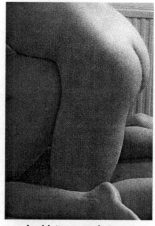

> **FACT**
> A survey suggested that at least 16% of British women have tried anal sex, compared to 49% of Russian and 52% of Italian women.

Anal intercourse between heterosexuals is illegal in many countries. It was legalized in the UK at the beginning of 1996

Woman on top

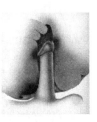

The woman-on-top positions can provide intense pleasure for both partners. In addition, the woman can control much of the lovemaking. The depth of penetration can be regulated by the woman, as can the rhythm and pace. If the woman is pregnant, these positions may be more comfortable for her. And if the male partner is very heavy this may also be true. These positions allow for many parts of the genitalia to be stimulated as shown in the diagram.

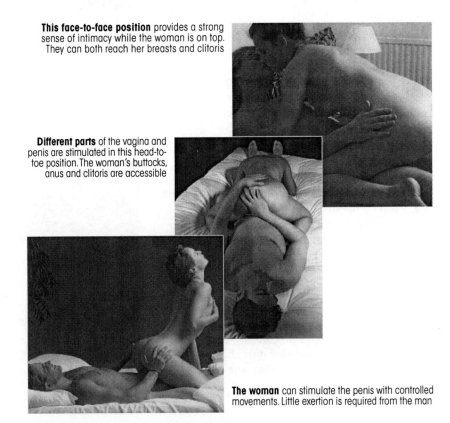

This face-to-face position provides a strong sense of intimacy while the woman is on top. They can both reach her breasts and clitoris

Different parts of the vagina and penis are stimulated in this head-to-toe position. The woman's buttocks, anus and clitoris are accessible

The woman can stimulate the penis with controlled movements. Little exertion is required from the man

Man on top

The man-on-top positions, and in particular the missionary position, where the woman's legs are apart with the man between them, are traditionally the most common positions. The woman has less control and less ability to move sensuously, but variation is possible to increase the pleasure received by each partner. Deep penetration and stimulation of the penis and clitoris is possible in all these positions. Couples will need to experiment to discover which positions and actions give them most pleasure. Generally the positions in which the woman's knees are bent allow for deeper penetration and those where the woman's legs are together give stimulation to the penis and clitoris.

The penis and clitoris receive stimulation in this position. The woman can squeeze the penis with the vaginal lips and muscles. She can exert some control of movement with her hands on her partner's buttocks

The knees up position allows for deep penetration. The woman's buttocks can be raised slightly to increase depth of penetration

In this position, the clitoris and G-spot receive intense stimulation. The woman's legs can help control movement

Deep penetration is possible in this position and it is easy for partners to fondle each other's bodies with their hands

This position allows for deep penetration. The woman's feet around her partner's neck give good balance and control whilst the kneeling position of the man enables him to thrust forcefully if desired

Rear entry

Rear entry positions can be enjoyed while crouching, kneeling or standing. Either partner can be on top. There is freedom to move and to caress a partner's body with the hands. These positions are also comfortable for the pregnant woman. Penetration and the areas most stimulated are shown in the diagram.

The penis can be squeezed by the woman's buttocks. The man can reach to stimulate the clitoris with his fingers

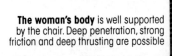

The woman's body is well supported by the chair. Deep penetration, strong friction and deep thrusting are possible

The vagina is tilted upwards slightly which allows for deep penetration. The man's hands are free to caress his partner's body

The woman can move as she pleases; her leaning back allows for deep penetration. The man can hold his partner's waist or caress her legs

Side-by-side

Face-to-face

The face-to-face positions can be intimate and sensuous. Looking at, kissing and caressing one's partner on the mouth, face and upper body is possible. The hands of both partners can be used to stroke and caress the body of the other. It is a comfortable position if the woman is pregnant or if her partner is heavy. The clitoris can be stimulated by the partner's fingers. The areas stimulated are shown in the diagram.

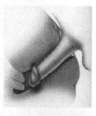

The woman can open her legs to allow penetration and then grasp her partner with her legs to control the rhythm of movement and increase stimulation

Face-to-back

The face-to-back position where the man enters the woman from behind can be relaxed and sensuous. Both partners can move easily. The man can stimulate the woman's clitoris and breasts with his hands and the woman can caress his testicles. If the man leans back, greater penetration is possible. This is sometimes called the Spoons position. The areas stimulated are shown in the diagram.

The penis stimulates the sides of her vagina and G-spot. Penetration can be deep

Sitting and kneeling

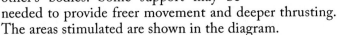

The sitting and kneeling positions for sex are close and intimate. Many people find them relaxing. In the face-to-face positions both partners can caress each other's bodies. Some support may be needed to provide freer movement and deeper thrusting. The areas stimulated are shown in the diagram.

Both partners are kneeling, they can see, kiss and caress each other's bodies easily

The chair gives support to the man, who can then support his partner. She can control the penetration and thrusting movements

The bed and pillows give good support and alignment for penetration

In this position, the woman leaning back aligns the vagina with the angle of penetration. The woman's clitoris and breasts can be caressed

Standing and advanced positions

These positions are worth exploring for the sense of challenge and novelty that they provide. They may require a certain amount of agility, and in some cases concern about balance and other factors may affect sexual performance. Some couples find them more athletic than intimate, but others find that they add variety and excitement.

This 'wheelbarrow' position, requires fairly gymnastic capability for the woman, a strong man and a good sense of balance for both

The **woman's buttocks** and anal area can be stimulated while the man can control movement with his hands on her hips

The **man's buttocks** and anal area are accessible, enabling the woman to stimulate his G-spot. The angle of the penis gives both interesting sensations for him and strong back wall stimulation for her

The **woman squatting** on a chair allows penetration from below. The penis stimulates the G-spot and the man can fondle his partner's breasts and body

The **woman's body** is supported by the man's, allowing her to set the pace. She can use her pelvic muscles to stimulate his penis

Man to man

In male to male sexual practices participants can be gay or bisexual men, though some prefer to refer to themselves as "men who have sex with men" or MSM and dispense with any specific sexual identification. As in any relationship, physical expression of intimacy between men depends on the context of the relationship along with many other influences.

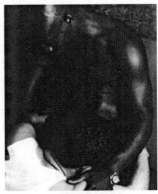

Gay lovers performing oral sex

Rubbing penises can bring both partners to orgasm without penetration

Sex between men shares many of the same characteristics as other gendered sex with a few additional considerations. Factors that may play a role in MSM sex include internalised homophobia, homo-negativity, heterosexism, male socialisation, safer sex, addiction, influences of gay subculture, and ambiguity in gay relationships. Because of these factors, good communication is even more important for a healthy sexual relationship between men.

Historically, anal sex has been popularly associated with male homosexuality and MSM. However, many MSMs do not engage in anal sex, and may preferably engage in oral sex, frotting (rubbing bodies) or other forms of mutual masturbation. Among those who do have anal sex, the insertive partner is referred to as the "top" or active partner. The man being penetrated is referred to as the "bottom" or passive partner. Preference for either is referred to as "versatile".

The Spoons position allows for good penetration. The penetrated partner's (or bottom's) penis can also be stimulated manually by him or the penetrator (or top)

Many men feel, however, that penetrative anal sex and orgasm is a sensual way of expressing intimacy and love, and of satisfying sexual desires. Because of the openness needed between gay men, sex is often more diverse and may be more experimental and adventurous than heterosexual sex.

Woman to woman

In lesbian sexual practices, participants can be lesbian or bisexual women, though some prefer to refer to themselves as "women who have sex with women" or WSW and dispense with any specific sexual identification. As in any relationship, physical expression of intimacy between women depends on the context of the relationship along with many other influences. WSW can be as varied as the partners who wish to have it, with scope for great imagination and inventiveness.

Undressing a partner can be an erotic part of arousal

Research indicates that WSW sexual behaviours have qualities that produce a greater sense of sexual satisfaction than their heterosexual counterparts. These include a focus on sensual pleasure including full-body sexual contact, rather than genital-focused contact, less preoccupation or anxiety about having an orgasm, increased communication about sexual needs, and longer-lasting sexual encounters.

Licking or sucking the breasts can be exciting for both partners

WSW sexual activities may include both penetrative and non-penetrative activities. Sexual expression may include fingering (digital stimulation - which may or may not be penetrative), cunnilingus (oral sex - that may or may not be penetrative), penetration of the vagina or anus with fingers, tongue, vibrator, dildo or strap-on dildo, and other stimulation of sensitive and erogenous body parts including the lips, nipples, breasts, anus, vulva and clitoris. Sex toys may also be used to enhance pleasure and creativity. Common forms of sexual positioning involve tribadism (aka scissoring) and other various sexual positions.

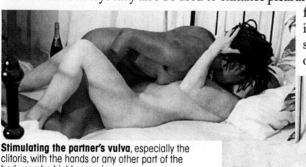

Stimulating the partner's vulva, especially the clitoris, with the hands or any other part of the body, can be highly arousing

Self-pleasuring may be part of arousal together

Orgasm

Orgasm, for most people, is the highest point of sexual excitement and represents the release of sexual tension built up in the course of arousal. It is also arguably the most complex part of sexual responsiveness, both in its nature and in the way it is perceived.

Orgasm can be anything from purely physical sensations experienced in the genital area to a psychic experience in which immediate, physical consciousness of the body is lost. Many attempts have been made to classify orgasm, but the reality is that it varies enormously from one person to another and from one sexual act to the next.

The importance of orgasm

The main difference between male and female orgasms is that men's are more reliable and happen faster. This does not mean that women are condemned to sexual dissatisfaction, but it does mean that a woman's partner may need to learn what she needs in order to achieve orgasm so that the partner can help by giving her that kind of stimulation. This may involve a partner learning to delay his or her own orgasm or using other – non-penile – kinds of stimulation first.

However, it is also important to note that placing undue emphasis on orgasm as the sole indicator of successful sex can detract from sexual pleasure. The media in general – and films in particular – frequently portray orgasm as the primary objective in sex: the message often conveyed is that orgasms should be frequent, simultaneous and preferably multiple.

For many, orgasm may well be the ultimate sexual experience, but often it is not possible and pursuing it single-mindedly can prevent people from enjoying many of the other satisfying aspects of sex. Some Eastern sexual practices are even based on delaying orgasm or preventing it completely.

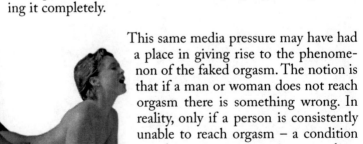

This same media pressure may have had a place in giving rise to the phenomenon of the faked orgasm. The notion is that if a man or woman does not reach orgasm there is something wrong. In reality, only if a person is consistently unable to reach orgasm – a condition known as anorgasmia – may there be cause for concern, and the condition is often treatable.

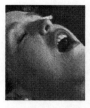

Female orgasm

Orgasm in females is much more complex, mainly because women rarely reach orgasm through vaginal penetration alone. For most women, sexual arousal is focused on the clitoris rather than the vagina and it is direct or indirect clitoral stimulation that allows the woman to achieve her orgasm.

The debate about the differences between clitoral and vaginal orgasms has yet to be resolved. Biologically there is no difference between the two as they involve the same muscles.

Some women also report intense G-spot orgasms. They suggest that many have an area of highly sensitive tissue, or G-spot, located on the front wall of the vagina and that stimulation of this can create an orgasm which is more intense and powerful than that which is created from one focused solely on the clitoris.

Most women do not reach orgasm with every sexual act; indeed surveys suggest that only about 50% of women have regular orgasms. The reason for this may be evolutionary in that female orgasm, unlike male, is not necessary for reproduction. On the other hand, women are also more likely to be able to achieve multiple or prolonged orgasms, possibly because they do not have to maintain an erection and have no refractory period such as that experienced by men. A woman's ability to have an orgasm can also vary, as can the nature of the orgasm itself: both can be affected by the menstrual cycle, by emotional stress and by innumerable other factors, both physical and psychological.

Male orgasm

For men, sexual activity involving extended friction with an erect penis, will – if uninterrupted – usually lead to an orgasm, which is generally accompanied by ejaculation. The pleasure experienced tends to be focused on the genitals and is closely linked to the ejaculatory process. A refractory period during which re-arousal is not possible usually follows ejaculation. The duration of this period is variable, but generally increases with age.

It was long thought that there was only one kind of male orgasm. However, research has revealed considerable variation, including the incidence of male orgasms without ejaculation. Some men are able to delay orgasm, whether by halting stimulation for a few moments when orgasm is felt to be approaching, by mental exercises or by using conscious muscle control to prevent ejaculation. Either technique can make it possible for men to experience more than one orgasmic peak, similar to the multiple orgasms experienced by some women, or the so-called orgasmus or prolonged orgasm in which the sensations of orgasm can last for as long as a minute. Delaying ejaculation can anyway also help a man to maintain his erection long enough to ensure that his partner reaches her orgasm, or to help enable the couple to achieve simultaneous orgasm if desired.

Après Sex

In the rounding off of a session of satisfying sex, it can be useful for both partners to understand exactly what happens to men and women after orgasm, emotionally and physically. There are differences, and they can lead to misunderstandings that can leave either partner hurt or resentful.

For a woman, resolution from orgasm can be slow as she drifts her focus back into the world. She likes – and, some would even say, needs – to feel her partner embracing her, and enjoys loving kisses and words to make truly intimate lovemaking end warmly.

For a man, however, with his erection fading soon after ejaculation and his penis feeling very sensitive, his sexual arousal may quickly desert him. This, with the tiredness that comes with orgasm, makes many men want simply to withdraw, roll over and go to sleep.

Keep talking

In bedrooms all over the world this is what happens night after night, leaving most men ignorant of the damaging emotional effect this can be having on their partner. She can feel neglected, unloved and lonely, especially if she is left unsatisfied. The whole relationship, emotionally and sexually, can very soon begin to suffer.

A sensitive man should try to be tender, and talk to and cuddle his partner even if he feels this overriding need to sleep. It is also up to the woman to keep her lover interested and awake by touch and conversation.

Try making love at other times of the day occasionally, so that neither of you is tired; you will have more energy to cuddle and talk. Avoid talking about mundane things such as shopping or problems with the car; concentrate on each other, the experience you have just had, and how much you enjoyed it.

Forms of sexual expression are so many and varied as to be almost beyond counting. Sex is amongst the most personal of all human activities and the most intimate form of expression; it is therefore potentially an arena for forms of expression inappropriate in any other situation.

This section covers a whole spectrum of practices – from places where to make love, through the devices, food (aphrodisiacs), drugs and fantasies used to heighten or enhance sexual response. It covers personal body alteration, including tattooing, scarification and piercing and the wilder shores of bondage and fetishism.

Locations

The bedroom is regarded as the most suitable place for sex by the majority of people. There are many reasons for this, including comfort, privacy and convenience. However, where people have sex is another case in which personal preference, sexual expression and cultural norms can vary enormously.

In certain cultures sex outdoors is forbidden and strictly punished. At the other extreme are some tribes of Papua New Guinea among whom sex indoors is taboo. Between the two come certain parts of Africa and Oceania where both are considered normal and acceptable.

Even though the norm in the West is to have sex at night, indoors and mostly in the bedroom, people have always experimented with other options. This may be out of necessity (such as, to avoid problems with those with whom accommodation is shared) or simply to add excitement.

For many, a sense of the forbidden or the taboo can be highly arousing. In the right circumstances and with due forethought, great variety in terms of location can be brought into lovemaking.

Outdoor and Public Places

Making love in the open air is the wish of many and hence a common sexual fantasy. While those who have an enclosed garden can be assured of privacy, sexual activity in any other place outside the home or

Spontaneous lovemaking in the kitchen, study or elsewhere is possible. The living room is one of the most popular choices. Over 90% of women and men have made love in the living room at least once

A desk in a home office can provide a firm support for sex

The bathroom often has the added advantage of having a lockable door. Making love in a shower or bath may be highly sensuous, and candlelit baths are very romantic

hotel room carries its risks – of discovery and of prosecution. Most countries have some laws against sexual activity in public. For many people these risks, and a sense of doing something forbidden, are part of the excitement (although it is important not to cause offence nor fall foul of the law).

Making love in a field, wood or park can provide a romantic sense of returning to nature and can also rekindle memories of courtship. Camping creates an environment which is slightly more private and very intimate, if potentially uncomfortable.

It may be for the same reason – the memories of courtship – that parked cars enjoy such enduring popularity for lovemaking, although for some the possibility of being watched (colloquially known as 'dogging') can provide a major source of excitement. Surveys suggest that in the USA, more than 60% of women and men, even with their own homes, still like making love in the car.

In terms of other public places, it seems that every possibility has been at least attempted. People have made love on trains and buses, on aeroplanes (becoming members of the Mile High Club), at the cinema, theatre and opera, in lifts, libraries, restaurants and fairground rides. Some have suffered the consequences of getting caught, but most have mainly had uniquely thrilling and memorable experiences.

Indoors

Any kind of accommodation can offer a variety of alternative locations for lovemaking. If sex is confined to a single room, different pieces of furniture can provide variation (see Sex Positions: Sitting and Standing) and other rooms may be available as long as other residents or family members are absent and there is privacy from neighbours and passers-by.

Dressing and Undressing

Throughout history clothes have been used to express sexuality. From codpieces to crinolines, changing fashions have drawn attention to different parts of the body as sources of sexual attraction. However, we rarely have the opportunity to make the most of the sexual potential our clothing offers. Very often, the place to do this is within the context of a sexual relationship.

Dressing for Sex

Surveys suggest that while most people make love naked, many men and women find certain ways of dressing for lovemaking arousing. They may be aroused by the image of the clothing, or by the teasing element of not being able to see the whole body naked straight away. Some like the idea of dressing up as a prelude to naked lovemaking while others like certain types of clothing to be worn throughout. In particular, many

Dressing for sex can be an opportunity for expressing fantasies or experimenting with role-playing games

people can find their partners more attractive partly dressed than completely naked.

The item of clothing most commonly worn while making love is underwear. The clichéd example of stockings and suspenders for women seems to enjoy an enduring popularity, and underwear designed specifically for sex – such as crotchless knickers and nipple-less bras – is still widely sold in sex boutiques. Even edible substances, from liquorice to flavoured gelatine, have been used to make underwear.

Dressing for sex can also mean indulging fetishes. Materials such as leather and rubber have long been seen as slightly risqué, and many people are aroused by the feeling of these or other materials against the skin.

Special materials, such as leather, rubber and fake fur, are widely available – including for underwear. Specialist shops produce leather and rubber goods to individual specifications

Brevity is the soul of lingerie.
DOROTHY PARKER

Costumes are also popular, and many people enjoy using these in role-playing games. These may involve one partner dressing as an authority figure such as a doctor or nurse, a police or army officer, or a nun or a priest. Alternatively they may be more fanciful, with exotic costumes or period dress. This can be one way of fulfilling sexual fantasies with a relationship.

Undressing in Style

The actual process of removing clothing can also be an exciting part of lovemaking, and one that is too often hurried, rather than enjoyed and explored.

- **Who undresses whom?** People either undress themselves or each other, both together or one at a time. One person may watch the other undress; one may strip for the other. Some people like to undress together in front of a mirror. One can remain partly or fully dressed while the other is naked.

- **What do you take off?** Rather than removing all your clothes at once, they can be removed gradually as a 'strip-routine' or as lovemaking develops. Some articles can be left on throughout.

- **Quickly or slowly?** Hurried, frenzied stripping suggests eagerness and passion, but slow undressing, continuing to touch each other in the process, can be seductive and sensuous.

- **Lights on or off?** Seeing a partner's body, face or genitals during lovemaking is important for many people. However, seeing each other's bodies as more is gradually revealed can be highly arousing, especially the first time; on the other hand, when lovers see each other less clearly or not at all, the focus is more on the feel of the clothing and skin which can also be very erotic.

- **What about underwear?** The variety of styles and fabrics available for underwear provides choices; in the end it is a question of working out what the wearer finds comfortable and what both people find arousing. It has been said that many people feel socks should not be left until last, although high-heeled shoes may be kept on!

> The Duke returned from the wars today and did pleasure me in his top-boots
> **SARAH, FIRST DUCHESS OF MALBOROUGH (1769)**

> No woman so naked as the one you can see to be naked underneath her clothes
> **MICHAEL FRAYN**

Sex and Food

Making love and eating are among life's greatest pleasures. They are natural, instinctive activities, but as humans we can also enjoy them as highly sensuous experiences. It is also possible to combine them, experimenting with different kinds of food and different ways of eating them.

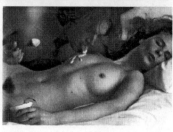

Food before sex, and during, and after...

Food has long been seen as a preamble, or accompaniment, to sex. A dinner date can create an opportunity to get to know a person as part of developing intimacy and can add romance at any stage of a relationship.

Edible sex aids are widely available, explicitly underlining the link between sex and food. This chocolate-flavoured body paint is sold in department stores throughout the UK

However, sex and food can be mixed in any number of ways; whether in a formal dinner in a restaurant or a take-away on the back seat of a bus, a naked picnic in the bedroom or strawberries and cream in the bath, eating together or off each other can be both erotic and intimate.

Types of food

The kinds of food eaten can add to the enjoyment. While large amounts of rich or heavy foods may not be a good idea before lovemaking, foods with a variety of different flavours, textures and smells can stimulate the senses. Many foods are reputed to have aphrodisiac qualities. While none has been conclusively proven to be effective, many people do claim certain foods to be so – experimenting with them can be exciting. Some foods are seen as explicitly sexual, such as asparagus or oysters. It is more likely that the association with the look, feel or smell of human sexual organs gives them their aphrodisiac status, rather than any inherent properties.

Feeding each other

Feeding each other can be almost instinctive in a close, loving relationship. It is a natural gesture of affection and intimacy – mouth-to-mouth kissing very probably originates from primates feeding their young from their own mouths. Many people feel a strong urge to nurture their loved ones: to feed one another can be seen as an extension of preparing food together or for each other. With carefully-chosen foods, this can be sensuous as well as affectionate.

Proserpine (detail), by Dante Gabriel Rossetti

Aphrodisiacs

The term aphrodisiac is used to describe anything said to increase sexual desire or performance. The search for effective aphrodisiacs has been going on for centuries. People have experimented with everything from books and pictures, to all kinds of magic and ritual, but probably most common of all are foods, drinks, plants and chemical substances.

Many of the substances that have been long used as aphrodisiacs have never been scientifically proven to be effective. In spite of this, they remain popular. This may be due to a certain novelty value, or a sense of adventure associated with reputed aphrodisiacs. The placebo effect – where the substances seem to work for no other reason than that people believe they will – can also be very powerful. Similarly, taking a supposed aphrodisiac can give people an excuse to lose their inhibitions and express their sexual nature more openly.

The dangers associated with losing inhibitions lie in regretting actions after the event, forgetting to follow the safer sex guidelines or becoming involved in bondage or similar practices without taking the necessary precautions. Some sexual practices require considerable care and attention.

Aphrodisiac foods

Food has always been associated with sex, not least for the reputed aphrodisiac qualities of foods. The types of food linked with sex vary, for reasons ranging from those with some scientific basis to those that can only be described as superstitious or anecdotal.

Certain foods may have been linked to sexuality by visual association, on account of their similarity to the sexual organs of either gender. Asparagus and the roots of ginseng and mandrake can be seen as phallic while oysters, mussels and clams have been likened to the female genitalia.

Edible plants

Chillies, onions, fennel, garlic and other spicy foods are often connected with sexual passion and with machismo. A number of plants generally used as tonics are also perceived as sexual stimulants. Several of these have been shown to contain hormones or chemical stimulants, including hops, pollen and honey, cocoa, liquorice water, and parts of plants, such as sarsaparilla in South America and hydrocotyle asiatica in the East.

Ginseng in particular can stimulate the flow of hormones and many people report aphrodisiac effects soon after having taken a dose. Guarana is made from the ground seeds of a plant from the Amazon basin and is sold as a stimulant in the form of powders, tablets, chewing gum and fizzy drinks. Love bombs containing herbs and spices from Brazil are combined with ginseng and royal jelly (from queen bees). Chocolate, one of the traditional gifts from lovers to people courting, is thought to contain stimulants similar to those produced in the brain by people who describe themselves as being 'in love'. Liquorice, fennel and ginger have all been used in commercial preparations sold as aphrodisiacs. Plants rich in certain vitamins, including B6, C, D and E, are also eaten as sexual stimulants and to maintain potency and fertility.

Animal products

The life-sustaining properties of blood have long been recognised and linked to sexual potency. Various sexual practices involving blood may have contributed to this connection, as well as the sexual connotations of myths related to vampires.

The sexual organs of animals have also been eaten as aphrodisiacs, in particular those of the males of various large species. Bulls' testes, known as 'prairie oysters', and sheep's testes known as 'mountain oysters', are considered delicacies and are often believed to have aphrodisiac properties. While they do contain male hormones, in practice cooking and/or the body's digestive fluids would probably destroy these.

While morally abhorrent to many, extracts from the testes, penises, horns and tusks of other animals have also been used, including rare and protected species such as tigers and rhino. Tiger and deer penises may be bought dried for use as aphrodisiacs in many parts of China. As a general rule, the more rare and difficult to catch the species is, all the more highly are its aphrodisiac properties rated.

The use of powdered horns and tusks of various animals are probably considered to be male aphrodisiacs only on account of their phallic appearance.

Seafood of all kinds has been associated with sexuality, perhaps because of its sensuous textures and links to sexual aromas. The fact that oysters are generally eaten alive may have led to their being attributed with life-giving properties. This may also be true of the custom of eating fish eggs (roe) – literally a source of life – as caviar. Again, the relative rarity of both adds to the excitement.

Sex and Drugs

Substances which produce altered states of mind have been part of sexual experimentation throughout the ages. However, these drugs can be extremely dangerous to a person's health. In some countries, many are illegal while others may only be available on medical prescription. There is rarely any control over the purity or strength of such drugs if they are obtained illegally, which increases the risk of side effects, addiction and overdose. However, as aware of the risks as people are, they continue to use them in the hope of altering or enhancing sexual experience.

Alcohol

In the past, some of the traditional love potions were in fact alcoholic drinks. Many of these are now made commercially as Avocaat, Chartreuse, Drambuie, Sloe Gin, Vermouth and other brands. Today, the West favours wine and champagne, while in China men may drink combinations, such as ginseng brandy.

Alcohol, in moderation, can help to ease shyness and lessen inhibitions. It can also heighten sensations of warmth and affection, making people more open to advances.

There is, however, a negative side. Alcohol can act as a depressant; large quantities can make people tiresome, aggressive or violent and reduce physical and mental dexterity. Alcohol can also affect a man's ability to have and maintain an erection. It is also addictive and can be expensive. Prolonged and heavy use can cause long term health problems, including liver problems and increased risk of cancer.

> I wish I could drink like a lady:
> I can take one or two at the most,
> Three and I'm under the table;
> Four and I'm under the host.
> **DOROTHY PARKER**

Naturally-occurring drugs

Cannabis (marijuana)
The plants from which cannabis (and opium) are extracted have probably been cultivated for longer than any other. Like alcohol, cannabis may be used to overcome inhibitions, make the user feel sexier, and for relaxation. It can also increase awareness and sensitivity of the skin and organs. In women, it can increase the likelihood of orgasm. It can make sex more lethargic and leisurely, or make it seem to last longer through its effects on the perception of time. The effects vary greatly from one strain of the drug to another.

Cocaine and Crack
Originally used as a local anaesthetic, cocaine is derived from the leaves of the coca plant Erthroxylon coca. It has been a popular recreational drug for centuries. It also has a reputation as an aphrodisiac: the feelings of exhilaration that it creates may increase people's sense of desirability. For some people it reduces inhibitions and increases libido, and may produce enhanced feelings of empathy and eroticism. Whilst promoting these feelings, it can either boost a man's ability to have an erection or severely reduce it - and has similarly varied effects on women's sexual capacity. Crack is a refined form of cocaine whose effects are more intense but do not last as long; it is also dangerously addictive.

GHB
GHB (gamma-hydroxy-butyrate) can be found in over-ripe guava fruit but also occurs naturally in humans as a neurotransmitter. It has been linked with the production of androgenic hormones, which can boost the development of body muscle and enhance the sex drive. It is available in many sex shops.

Magic (psilocybe) Mushrooms
Mushrooms of the genus Psilocybe grow wild in some countries but can sometimes be cultivated. They are similar in appearance to some poisonous mushrooms but contain the hallucinogenic chemical psilocybin. Their effects are similarly psychedelic to those of mescaline and LSD but, usually, less intense.

Mescaline
Mescaline is derived from the peyote cactus Lophophora williamsii and the San Pedro cactus Trichocereus pachanoi. It is a psychedelic drug with similar effects to LSD and psilocybe mushrooms (above). Native American Indians have used it for centuries in rituals and to add a new level to sexual experience. Mescaline is rarely available in its pure form.

Opium
Opium is derived from the Opium poppy, Papaver somniferum. Its active ingredient is morphine, from which heroin (diamorphine) is refined. Opium

is probably best known for its use in Chinese opium dens where opium and prostitutes were both provided; they were known as fume and flower dens where the fumes were the opium smoke and the flowers the prostitutes' vaginas. Opium, and heroin in particular, can be extremely dangerous and highly addictive. Accidental overdoses are not uncommon.

Spanish Fly and Yohimbine

Yohimbine is derived from the bark of the tree Corynanthe yohimbe. Spanish fly is available as a powder made from dried, ground cantharis, mylabris or lytta beetles. Both function by causing dilation of the blood vessels which can result in prolonged erections as well as irritation of the skin and mucous membranes (when taken orally, this effect is focused on the bladder, the urethra and the genital area). Both have been described as aphrodisiacs, but their effects can be painful as well as dangerous. The amount which is sufficient to create sexual arousal can be fatal.

Synthetic drugs

Amphetamines

Amphetamines, also known as speed, are sometimes taken to boost stamina for sex, although they can make it difficult to achieve and maintain an erection.

Amyl Nitrite

Amyl nitrite, also known as poppers or amyl, speeds up the cardiovascular system and may intensify sexual experience when sniffed just before orgasm, although this does involve interrupting sex play at the height of arousal.

Barbiturates and other Anti-Depressants

These drugs can lower inhibitions, but they also reduce sensory perception. Despite having been commonly available on prescription, barbiturates in particular are now recognised as dangerously addictive. Newer designer drugs, such as Prozac, are increasingly being offered. Many of the new SSRI anti-depressants are also sexual depressants and so can be used in the treatment of premature ejaculation.

Ecstasy

Ecstasy, or E, is methylene dioxymethamphetamine (MDMA), a chemical originally used as a diet pill. It was later rediscovered as a recreational drug, potentially enhancing sexual sensation and desire, with feelings of intense happiness and affection. The drug can however be highly dangerous, especially in impure forms.

Ketamine

Ketamine is also known as K, Special K and Vitamin K. K is an anaesthetic and is sometimes referred to as a horse tranquilliser. It is often used at dance clubs or during sex. Ketamine can come as a powder or a liquid that's dried to make a powder. It can then be snorted (known as a bump) or added to drinks (not alcohol) or mixed with cannabis or tobacco and smoked. It can also be mixed with water and injected or taken in pill form. Although ketamine can make the taker feel horny, it can make it difficult to get a hard-on or reach orgasm. Ketamine can lower inhibitions, which might lead to unsafe sex. As the drug subdues the feeling of pain, rough sex can lead to damage or cuts and bleeding that aren't noticed. This may mean more risk of HIV, hepatitis C and other infections being passed on.

LSD

LSD, also known as Acid, is lysergic acid diethylamide, a psychedelic compound which produces hallucinations (either blissful or horrific), enhances sensory perception and intensifies moods. It can make sex seem more pleasurable and experimental and increase feelings of closeness. Acid is physically – but not psychologically – harmless and non-addictive, though it may be dangerous for people with certain mental illnesses.

Methamphetamine

Methamphetamine, also called meth or ice, is a psycho-stimulant and sympathomimetic drug. Methamphetamine enters the brain and triggers a cascading release of norepinephrine, dopamine and serotonin. Since it stimulates the mesolimbic reward pathway, causing euphoria and excitement, it is prone to abuse and addiction.

Drugs for Erectile Dysfunction

There are currently several medications on the market that were developed for the condition of erectile dysfunction and that are also recreationally used for sexual enhancement (Viagra, Cialis, Levitra etc.).

Although there is no evidence that these pills actually increase sexual desire, it is believed that there is a psychological impact that produces a greater sense of confidence and psychological arousal alongside the improved ability for physical arousal.

Natural Mood Enhancers

One of the best and safest ways to boost or maintain sexual potency and libido in the long term is through good basic health. Regular exercise can help to increase sexual desire and enjoyment.

Yoga, Tai Chi Chuan, Chi-Kung, martial arts and dancing are particularly thought to enhance sexuality. A balanced diet and sufficient sleep are also important, while stress and anxiety often have negative effects. Reliance on any drug, including even those that are in common daily use such as caffeine, nicotine and alcohol, may have a detrimental effect on sexual potency.

Is this woman being exploited?
Or is she making a living and
supplying a market?

Pornography and Erotica

Pornography originally meant writing about prostitutes: the word is derived from the Greek words
'porne', a prostitute, and 'graphos', to write. The term
later came to refer to any form of image or text designed to be sexually stimulating. The way this kind
of material has developed has led to strong negative
connotations with the term pornographic, and to the
increasing use of the word erotica when referring to
sexually-stimulating material that is considered neither obscene nor offensive.

Use of pornography

Pornography, in the sense of sexually-stimulating
material, plays a role in many people's sex lives. It is
used by individuals and couples alike. Couples may watch it together or sepa-
rately in order to trigger sexual arousal and as part of building their fantasy
lives. It can add excitement to an established relationship or aid seduction
in a new one. Those who are not in a relationship equally use it to help with
gaining sexual relief, and it can even be a substitute for people who might
have difficulty with forming relationships.

It can function in a number of ways:

Pornography as an aphrodisiac

Erotic images are widely used as sexual stimuli. From the
ancient traditions of *The Bridal Roll* in Japan, pillow books
in China, or Vatsyayana's *Kama Sutra* in the Hindu world,
to the erotic images we can see on television, in films or
on the internet today, the power of the image has been
used to directly to arouse but has a secondary function in
educating and informing.

Pornography and fantasy

Pornography and sexual fantasy are implicitly linked, and can fulfil several of
the same roles. Both can function as aphrodisiacs and are associated with the
unobtainable or unusual. There is often a great demand in pornography for
that which is not considered acceptable in a society or within the context of
a relationship. Whether it is fetish, same sex or multiple partners material,
fantasy pornography can provide it.

Pornography for educational and group interest

A number of sex publications and, increasingly, internet sites deal with specific sexual tastes, enabling people to discover different forms of sexual activity and to exchange ideas. Some are made for interest and information, while others are more for titillation. Some are even used as vehicles for campaigns for greater sexual freedom under the law.

Pornography and society

While it is clear that pornography has a valid place in many people's sex lives, it has been a contentious issue for centuries. People have long reacted against pornography, believing that it has some capacity 'to deprave or corrupt', as the law in the UK describes its effects when it tips into the illegal. While some pornography is quite clearly illegal (for example child pornography), much of it is more ambiguous and it can be hard to agree where the line should be drawn - for one person seeing a woman's breasts will be obscene, for another an image of group sex will be perfectly acceptable. Notions of obscenity are as varied as notions of attractiveness: neither can be generalised.

The main criticisms of modern pornography are that many see it as sexist, exploitative and degrading, although women who work in the sex industry tend to deny this. In many cases this is true. Certainly the porn market continues to be dominated by men and orientated to a primarily male market. However, many women respond as strongly as some men, but sometimes to different kinds of stimuli. The demand for pornography specifically aimed at women is growing fast. Equally, there are many men and women who profess to have no interest at all in pornography.

As well as its potential to 'deprave and corrupt', another criticism is that pornography can incite sexual crimes. However, there is no substantial evidence to support this. If anything, repressing pornography may have a negative effect. Studies carried out in Germany, Denmark and Sweden have shown that, after the legalisation of pornography, such indicators as the incidence of sexual assault either increased less than non-sexual assault or did not increase at all.

The internet has made access to pornography vastly easier for most people, and thus more commonplace and harder to control. Some believe this is a positive sign for sexual liberation; some see it as a dangerous scourge. Either way, sexually-explicit images and writings are an important part of human sexuality and will remain a part of popular culture for the foreseeable future.

Sex Toys and Aids

In many countries, sex aids are achieving a major change of image. No longer only to be found in sex shops, and now sold to an increasing number of women, as well as men (with the development of new masturbatory devices for them, such as the 'Fleshlight'), they are being used more and more widely to increase pleasure, add excitement and combat sexual problems.

In ancient times, olive oil was used as a lubricant, condoms were made from goats' bladders and dildos were chiselled out of ivory, bone and stone. In the Renaissance, Italians enjoyed the delights of elaborately carved marble diletti. Lubricants, condoms, dildos, vibrators and any number of exotic sex-enhancing devices, have all developed in leaps and bounds, particularly over the last decade or so.

Precautions

Sex aids should not be shared without thorough cleaning. Sexually-transmitted infections and diseases can be passed on by sex aids just as they can be conveyed through genital contact. Condoms can be used to cover vibrators and dildos and keep them hygienic.

Any kind of sex aid which is used in or around the anus should be thoroughly cleaned before coming in to contact with the mouth, urethra or vagina. Bacteria which exist normally and healthily in the rectum can cause infections in other parts of the body.

Objects can be drawn in to the vagina or anus and become lodged inside, requiring medical attention and removal. Vibrators and dildos made for this purpose are usually constructed to avoid these problems (e.g. anal ones have large bases, so that they can't be drawn inside).

Many padded, textured and tickler condoms are actually not safe to use as contraceptives or for safer sex, so check the notices. Only condoms specifically labeled as contraceptives should be considered as reliable for that. Manufacturers of contraceptive condoms usually also make ribbed as well as flavoured varieties.

Any oil-based lubricant can damage the latex rubber of a condom or diaphragm and make it split. Use only water or silicone based lubricants with latex rubber contraceptives.

Condoms

While condoms are most commonly used as contraceptives and as part of safer sex practices, they can also be used as sex aids.

One of the most common concerns about condoms is that of reduced sensitivity. Male condoms are available in a wide range of textures, colours and flavours. Flavoured condoms are sometimes used by people to make the experience of oral sex more interesting, desirable or playful.

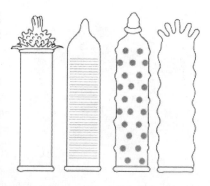

Some condoms are produced directly for pleasure. There are condoms made with padding, ribbing or extensions, to make the penis seem larger or to create strong or different sensations in the vagina. The outer ring of the female condom may also provide some clitoral stimulation during intercourse. Padded condoms can help to boost a man's confidence if he is concerned about penis size, though in reality the difference is likely to barely be felt – or may not be felt at all – by his partner.

Ticklers – textured condoms or ones with shapes at the tip – can provide some extra stimulation to the nerve endings at the opening of the vagina, the vulva and perhaps the cervix, although this is unlikely given that there are few nerve endings deep within the vagina.

Dildos

Dildos are objects that can be used for penetrative sex. They are probably the oldest form of sex aid, having featured in ancient Greek and Babylonian art and in the Bible.

They are usually realistic in design, and are made in many shapes, sizes, materials and colours. Some are curved to stimulate the G-spot. Some have a bulb on the end, sometimes in the form of testicles, which can be filled with liquid and squeezed to imitate ejaculation. Most are slightly exaggerated in size but much larger ones are also available. Double-headed dildos are also made.

Dildos can be used by both men and women and can add fun to love-making and prolong it, and may be used as a form of safer sex.

'Stay longer' creams and sprays

These products contain a small amount of local anaesthetic, the idea being to reduce penile sensitivity and delay orgasm and ejaculation. In some men they are successful, but with the inevitable loss of some sensation. These are some of the more popular sex aids sold at sex shops, although, they are not recommended. Ejaculatory control can be developed more effectively by increasing awareness of sensations in the penis.

Arab straps, cock and ball straps, cock rings, gates of hell

These are all devices used to help maintain a man's erection. They are made up of rings of metal, leather or rubber, which may be held together with leather straps or rubber bands. Tightly fastened to the penis, and sometimes the testicles, in the course of arousal, they constrict the blood flow out of the penile tissue, thereby maintaining the erection.

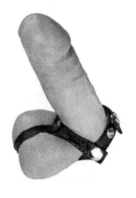

They can be stimulating both for the wearer and their partner, providing extra friction against the sides of the vagina or rectum. Some people find their appearance arousing. Some men just use an elastic band.

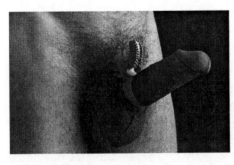

Clitoral stimulators

These are rings made of latex, rubber or plastic which fit around the base of the penis, with some form of projection which is designed to stimulate the clitoris during vaginal intercourse. There are many different designs (for ones including a vibrating mechanism, see penis vibrators, in '...for him' below).

Controlling the amount of pressure on the clitoris can be difficult, as can keeping the projection from twisting around to face the wrong direction. However, many people enjoy using them and they can also help maintain the man's erection by additionally functioning as a cock ring.

Love balls

Love balls, also known as love eggs or Ben-wa-balls, consist of two hollow balls connected by a cord. They contain smaller, weighted balls which are free to move around inside them.

They are inserted into the vagina; the weights inside cause them to move around as the woman moves. They can be used during love-making or for keeping the woman in a state of arousal at other times.

Some women find them highly arousing while, for others, they may have no effect at all other than causing mild discomfort. They can make a slight noise. They can be good for exercising the pelvic floor muscles. They should not be used in the rectum.

Thai beads

Thai beads consist of a number of plastic beads either on a string or flexible rod. They are inserted into the rectum and moved in and out during intercourse or pulled out quickly or slowly at orgasm.

Butt-plugs and anal vibrators

Latex attachments for anal stimulation are available for ordinary vibrators, but there are also dildos and vibrators designed specifically for this purpose.

They are not usually made to look like a penis and often have a longer or bigger hand grip than vaginal vibrators to prevent them from becoming lodged or drawn up inside the rectum.

They should not be used too roughly or without lubrication as the anus and the walls of the rectum are very delicate.

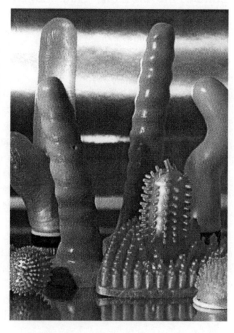

Vibrators

Sex aids, or sex toys, can add lots of fun and variety to people's sex life, even to the point of being the only way some women can achieve orgasm. As someone quipped: 'What man can go at 500 revs per minute?'

Statistics suggest that around half of all women in the Western world between the ages of 18 and 60 regularly use sex toys and, of those who do, a remarkable 78% do so within their relationship. Women who use vibrators tend to experience more frequent and stronger orgasms, have greater sexual confidence and report deeper satisfaction with their partners than women who don't.

Curiosity and an instinctive desire to enjoy greater physical pleasure has meant that people have looked for new ways to enhance sexual experience. By the Victorian era, sexual indulgence was being suppressed and punished. One flip-side, though, was an illness known as hysteria, literally: "womb disease". It was 'cured' by sympathetic doctors, who would offer relief from its symptoms of rapid heart rate, pelvic heaviness and vaginal lubrication, by manually bringing the patient to orgasm. Then in 1883, a British doctor, Joseph Mortimer Granville, patented the first electromechanical vaginal and clitoral massaging device, a steam-driven monster, and the vibrator was born.

Vibrators are probably the most common sex aid. Powered by batteries (earlier ones by mains electricity), they vibrate rhythmically to give sensual pleasure. There are several basic forms. Most vibrators are basically dildos with battery-powered moving parts. Again they come in various shapes, sizes and textures. Some are smooth with a hard plastic or metallic finish, while others are covered with realistic flesh-like latex and are made to look like a penis. Those which are covered in latex are also less cold to the touch and tend to be less noisy.

Shapes include those that are not unlike electric toothbrushes, the butterfly which is an oblong pad which fits against the vulva and the Magic Wand, a body massager with a great deal of power. There are also new designer varieties that look like futuristic phones.

Women and men can use vibrators, together or alone, on any part of the body. They can produce interesting sensations when pressed to secondary erogenous zones such as earlobes, nipples, lower back, thighs and above the genital area. However, they are most commonly used by women around the inner and outer labia and on the clitoral hood or clitoris itself. For a man a vibrator may be pressed against the shaft of the penis, or the tip of the vibrator may be used on the glans of the penis or around the scrotum and anus. They should not be used in the bath or shower unless they are clearly labelled as waterproof.

...for women

One of the more popular vibrators, the Rabbit, which rotates and provides clitoral and vaginal stimulation simultaneously, is one of the world's best-selling sex toys. It is known variously as the Jack Rabbit, the Rampant Rabbit and the Jessica Rabbit. An unknown Japanese designer in the Eighties combined the range of vibrations available through the main shaft of a regular vibrator with fluttering ears for simultaneous clitoral stimulation. It shot to fame when Charlotte in the TV series 'Sex and the City' developed a dependency on hers.

Direct stimulation of the clitoris can be too powerful, or even painful for some and so many women begin only by using the bunny ears on their clitorises. The Rabbit has a revolving shaft - often filled with tiny balls - which can usually be switched to go in either direction. Either the main head or the fluttering ears can be used on the clitoris and outside genital area. The shaft can be inserted inside the vagina, though good lubrication is required for this.

...for men

There are two types of vibrator made specifically for use on the penis. One is the form of a ring which fits around the base of the penis with an attachment which vibrates against the shaft – creating interesting sensations for the man and acting as a clitoral stimulator, during intercourse, for the woman. Others are substitute vaginas, made as latex or rubber tubes with or without a vibrating mechanism.

A major breakthrough came with special penile sleeves used as masturbation devices, the most notable one being the Fleshlight. It began life in 1998 when a former US police officer, who was looking for a way to deal with a period of enforced abstinence due to his wife's pregnancy, patented a "device for discreet sperm collection". He devised  the creation of a latex version of the vaginal tunnel – disguised, as its name suggests, as a flashlight. Two million dollars of product development brought it to market and the Fleshlight is now the world's number one best-selling sex toy for men.

Other versions are fitted into a model of a woman's head to simulate oral sex and sometimes they can be made part of an entire plastic torso or sex doll.

...for both

The revolutionary design of the We-Vibe has led to it being hailed as the first sex toy truly created for couples. Its revolutionary design is devised for it to be worn by the woman comfortably while having penetrative sex. Since its debut its been a constant best-seller.

The dual motor design provides both external clitoral as well as internal G-spot stimulation. The supple shape, crafted in high-quality silicone, conforms to a woman's body. One end of the C-shaped We-Vibe fits inside the vagina to massage and vibrate against the G-spot, while the other end cups and surrounds the clitoris. Together, these two ends provide enough tension to stay in place during sex. The slim connector leaves plenty of room for penetration, and for the man to feel the vibrations too.

The We-Vibe has also been claimed to be useful for other forms of sexual exploration including foreplay and solo sex, though it is not recommended for anal use. New generations of this innovative vibrator include an intuitive push-button control to switch between two intensities and seven pulsing patterns. The device comes with a remote control, which can be operated by either partner during love making. The manufactures claim that the We-Vibe is fairly quiet in operation, environmentally-friendly, cruelty-free, carbon neutral and rechargeable.

Some reviewers, though, have found the We-Vibe less than ideal in practice. Though most have found it effective for solo sex, in penetrative sex it could feel "weird and sometimes even painful." Some women have complained that it feels odd to have two things - the We-Vibe and a penis - inside of them at once and men have equally found the device intrusive.

Trends in sex toys

Back in the 1990s, sex toy retailer Ann Summers was launched on the UK high street and they sold one million vibrators in the first year alone. Twenty years later, luxury designer brands such as Coco de Mer, Shiri Zinn and Kiki Montparnasse service the new top end market. Their products are now available in many pharmacies, alongside condoms.

Today, the global sex toy industry is valued at over $15 billion, with much of its recent growth due to internet availability, which offers convenient anonymity to both men and women. At the click of a mouse, shoppers can venture into a virtual store they may not wish to be seen in in real life. It is discreet, reliable and safe to make purchases at such reputable website shops as www.loversguide.com.

For modern sex toys, form follows function and new technologies are continually driving innovation. Many new vibrators are sleek, body contoured, designer toys. There's the OhMiBod vibrator which uses an iPod playlist to create corresponding beat-driven vibrations. And there's the double-bullet cock ring which activates every time a call or text message is received.

Newer creations include virtual devices that can allow a person to wear a sensory suit and have "virtual sex" with a live person over the internet. There is no telling how creative sexual aids will become in the future.

Bodily enhancers

Penis extenders

Men have long been interested in various ways to lengthen their penises despite studies finding that that most men seeking size enhancement are within the normal size range and overestimated the average penis size. Normal is anything greater than 1.6 inches (4 cm) flaccid and than 3 inches (7.5  cm) in a stretched or erect state. As for the average penis size, though studies vary, most put this at around 3.5 inches (9 cm) flaccid, 4.5 inches (12.5 cm) stretched and 5.9 inches (15 cm) erect.

Many men who are concerned with their penis's small stature suffer from "dysmorphophobia", a condition where people see some imaginary flaw in physical appearance as real — in this case a false perception of penis inadequacy, the researchers say, even though few have actually suffered from the condition known as 'micropenis', a penis that is too small to copulate or pleasure their partner.

Several nonsurgical methods have been claimed to be effective in penile extension, such as penile traction gadgets, vacuum devices, penoscrotal rings and even "physical exercises" (hand stretching of the penis, also known as jelqing).

Vacuum devices used to be the most popular. They consist of a clear plastic cylinder with an aperture at one end that is placed over the penile shaft. At the other end of the cylinder is a pump mechanism that is used to generate negative pressure within the cylinder. There are a number of medical equipment companies that have specially-designed devices which are carefully constructed so that a limited amount of pressure is allowed to develop. This is to reduce the likelihood of pressure-induced penile injury. As a penile extension device, studies give it a failing mark, showing no significant penile elongation after six months of therapy. However researchers of that study noted a placebo effect in providing psychological satisfaction for some men. It's use is much more effective in assisting men with erectile dysfunction (ED) in achieving an erection and in the USA the FDA has approved it for such use there.

Penile-lengthening exercises also had no science backing up their effectiveness. Jelqing (also known as milking) is an exercise designed to force more blood through the penis, increasing the internal pressure and apparently creating micro-tears in the internal structure of erectile tissue. The exercise consists of applying an OK style thumb and forefinger grip encircling the base of a lubricated and partially erect penis, restricting blood flow, and pulling this grip forward toward the glans (head). Once one hand has reached the glans the same grip and motion is applied with the second hand. This process is repeated for a number of strokes in a continuous milking motion. The claims for this technique to increase length or girth have not been verified.

However, a few well-conducted studies on penile extenders, which use mechanical traction to progressively elongate the penis, did show that these devices can produce an effective and durable lengthening of the penis. For instance, one study showed that an extender called 'Andropenis' could add 0.7 inches (1.8 centimeters) on average to the penis given four months of use for around four to six hours a day. Another, called the Golden Erect extender, was shown to increase penis length in participants of a study published in the Journal of Sexual Medicine in 2010.

Breast developers

Breast developers are intended to function by stimulating growth of the breasts by massage, water jets or with the use of special 'expansion' bras or vacuum pumps. The bras and pumps are external tissue expander devices on the theory that when body tissue is put under sustained tension to expand, it responds with growth. As this is induced from outside of the body, it does not involve surgery (such as the use of implants) or drugs.

The user has to activate the pump or wear the bra-like device for many hours a day, over several months. Testers of these devices tend to report that, while the sensations created can be arousing, no permanent change to breast size is achieved. As with the majority of penis developers, these are usually more of a gimmick than a serious enhancement procedure. Though physicians have long used tissue expansion techniques with the intent to increase tissue growth in patients for various procedures, there is little direct research or evidence that this is effective in increasing the size or fullness of the breast.

Body Decoration

Humans have always adorned their bodies for purposes ranging from tribal identification to ritual celebration. Body decoration has many links with the expression of sexuality, where it can function as a specific sexual signal, a means of boosting attractiveness, or a way of enhancing sexual pleasure.

Make-up

Make-up has been used for centuries by members of both sexes, but particularly women. It is mainly used on the face, to draw attention to particular features or to present the face in a more attractive or alluring way, as well as to conceal whatever might be considered a defect. It can be used on the body in the same way.

There are many psychological theories about why people use make-up. It is used to draw attention to parts of the face (and body) that we wish to emphasise, such as the eyes and mouth, or to make other, less attractive features, such as the nose, less prominent. Others suggest it is based on the faces of babies – eyes and mouth made to appear large, whilst playing down the nose.

However, it is more widely believed that make-up was originally used to simulate the effects of sexual arousal, making the eyes look larger and darker, the lips redder (red labia in the animal kingdom are a signal of sexual preparedness), and the skin more flushed.

Women's magazines are full of advice on the most common form of body decoration – make-up

Body make-up can create the same effect. In India, henna has been used for centuries to redden nostrils, earlobes, fingertips and toes, all of which darken due to the increased blood flow during arousal. Rouge has been used on the nipples in some cultures. Nowadays red nail varnish for finger and toe nails is quite common, and rouge or blusher can be used lightly over the breasts, shoulders or any other part of the body.

FACT
In ancient Rome, prostitutes painted their lips bright red as an explicit signal that they would perform oral sex.

Body painting

Body painting probably began in prehistoric times and was used for tribal identification and ritualistic purposes. It survives as a cultural practice primarily among tribal peoples in Africa, America and Australia. In other cultures it is enjoyed by many for sexual stimulation.

As well as conventional make-up, theatrical make-up and special non-toxic body paints are available. The paint can be used to decorate the body and to emphasise its contours. Particular attention is usually paid to the most sensitive, erogenous or expressive areas, such as the hands, feet, face, ears, nipples and genitals. Actually applying the body paint, whether with a brush or with fingertips or hands, can be a sensuous experience for both partners. Only non-toxic substances should be applied to the skin, and care should be taken to allow the skin to breathe by not covering the entire body.

Body hair

Attitudes to body hair vary enormously from one cultural group to another. In some groups from southern Africa, to India and Pakistan, both men and women are expected to remove all body hair.

In others, the sight of pubic hair is considered so explicitly erotic that it features prominently in pornography, as in Japan. In many Western cultures, male body hair has long been seen as acceptable, while women have been expected to remove some or all of it. Some see hairless women as more feminine and some see hairy women as more masculine; others find hairless women sexual for being young-looking and some see hairy women as sexily more mature. This is echoed in images of men and women in Western art. More recently, with greater liberation among both women and men, people have begun to ignore society's dictates and follow their own preferences.

> **FACT**
> Among the Ila Bantu people of Zambia a bride is expected to pluck out all the facial and pubic hair of her new husband the morning after the consummation of their marriage.

The appearance or the feel of either skin or body hair can be arousing, as can any change in the way body hair is tended. It can be bleached, dyed, trimmed, shaped or removed completely to reveal areas of skin that are never normally seen. Many people enjoy the actual process of shaving their own or their partner's body hair. Shaving can enhance the sensitivity of the skin.

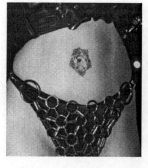

Tattooing and body piercing

Many people choose to decorate their bodies more permanently. While for some the mere idea of marking or piercing the body may be unacceptable, practices such as tattooing and piercing are becoming increasingly popular. The motivation behind these practices may or may not be sexual. They can lead to a more positive body image, and a sense of personal empowerment, in some people, and many find the appearance or the experience of tattooing or piercing arousing in itself. In recent years these practices have also become increasingly fashionable.

Both tattooing and body piercing can be enjoyed simply as adornment or specifically for sexual pleasure. They can be sexually arousing in various ways. Many people are aroused simply by the fact that they are very aware that they, and/or their partner, has a part of their body pierced or tattooed, particularly if this is on an intimate part not seen by anyone else.

For others the enjoyment is more symbolic, to do with the choice of the image or words tattooed or if the ring used for piercing is taken as a sign of commitment. Both practices can involve a certain amount of pain, and this too can be seen as symbolic, harking back to the origins of such practices as initiation rites and proof of adulthood or social status. Body piercing adds another dimension in that manipulating or gently pulling on the rings or rods that have then been inserted can be highly arousing.

Neither practice need be dangerous if carried out hygienically by a reliable professional, although in some countries both are illegal, particularly if carried out for sexual purposes.

More than half of those who have tattoos have them on or near erogenous zones

Designs may consist of words, pictures or both and tend to be intensely personal. The areas considered most obvious are the arms, chest and back. However, designs in hidden places, where only lovers will find them, are also popular, and tattoos on the genital area are not uncommon. The shaft of the penis is relatively easy and not too painful to tattoo, as is the skin of the thighs and abdomen surrounding the pubic area. The glans of the penis and the female labia are more painful and difficult to tattoo, so simpler designs may be required. Most reputable tattoo artists will not put designs on the face or palms of clients.

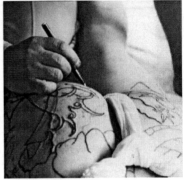

Tattooing

Any area of skin can be tattooed, with virtually any design, 'painted' on by pricking ink into the skin with a needle. A special tattooing machine with a sterile vibrating needle is usually used. The practice of tattooing is in fact ancient and has existed in many different cultures. It has developed to the point where it is widely considered an art form.

The oldest verified colour tattoos were found on a 5,300-year-old Stone Age man in Italy and a 4,200-year-old Egyptian priestess

Body piercing

Like tattooing, body piercing is an ancient custom that has become more widely acceptable and even fashionable in some cultures, particularly over the past 30 years.

Ornamental body piercing has been carried out for centuries in cultures originating in Asia, North, South and Central America, Africa and Oceania. In the West, only ear piercing is a well-established and widely-accepted practice. However, noses, eyebrows, cheeks, lower lips, tongues, nipples, navels and sexual organs can all be pierced. Women can pierce the clitoris or the clitoral hood vertically or horizontally, and the inner and outer labia. Men can pierce various parts of the foreskin, the glans and the base of the penis, as well as the scrotum and the perineum.

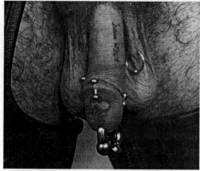

Genital jewellery – used by some people to embellish their genitals and enhance their sex play. Genital piercing is becoming increasingly common

Male genital piercing

A number of specific terms are used for certain types of male genital piercing. The most common kind is the Prince Albert or dress ring, which refers to a ring which passes through the glans, into the urethra just below the frenulum and out through the tip of the penis, curving round underneath. It was originally used by Victorian men to hold the penis flat inside one leg of the tight trousers which were fashionable at that time. The ampallang is a rod which passes horizontally through the glans; the apadravya passes through vertically. A dydo pierces the rim at the edge of the glans: several of these are usually used together. The term hafada refers to the piercing of the scrotum, while the guiche is a ring in the perineum.

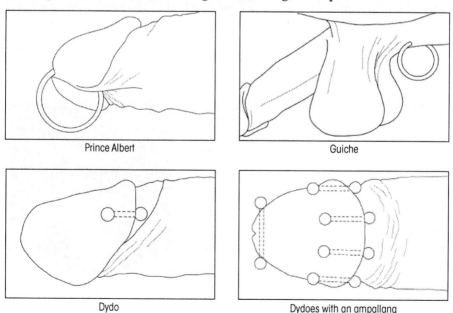

Prince Albert

Guiche

Dydo

Dydoes with an ampallang

Cicatrisation or scarification

Cicatrisation is the practice of scarring the skin for ritualistic or sexual purposes (French: cicatrice, scar). Evidence of cicatrisation has been found on Egyptian mummies of priestesses from more than 4,000 years ago. The practice was common in parts of Africa until the early 20th century, where it was used as a fertility rite for women and as a rite of passage for women and men. The resulting scars were seen as proof of inner beauty and strength of character as well as physical strength and health. They could also indicate social status.

Cutting has also been used in some cultures as a form of emotional or psychological healing. It has been said to make a person feel more in touch with their body and their humanity and to give a strong sense of personal empowerment.

Like tattooing, cicatrisation has also developed as an art form. It requires specialised knowledge as to where and how deeply the skin can be cut safely, and how to prevent infection. However, it is said to be less painful than tattooing and is becoming increasingly popular.

Branding

Branding is the practice of burning a mark or symbol into a person's skin, traditionally for tribal, political or religious identification, but also as part of sadomasochistic sexual practices and for body decoration.

Designs usually consist of simple lines and curves, on any relatively flat part of the body. The branding is permanent, and like cicatrisation requires specialist knowledge by the person carrying out the procedure.

Bondage and Discipline (BD)

Bondage, discipline, submission and pain are rarely discussed publicly and, when they are, tend to receive bad press, for the notion of deviancy is frequently involved. However, they are forms of sexual expression that are enjoyed by many people and are increasingly gaining more public forums (such as 'Torture Garden' events, in the UK).

All of these practices are deeply rooted in the human psyche. Aggression, domination and dependency, along with the sexual urge, are amongst the most basic human motivations in interpersonal relationships. These forms of motivation are linked with sex in that they, too, tend to be repressed. In many societies they are either seen as inappropriate except in specific situations, or considered appropriate only to one gender or the other.

The experiences of pain and resisting restraint result in a raised pulse rate, increased adrenaline and feelings of euphoria, all of which are also produced by sexual arousal.

These kinds of activity can be practised at many different levels, according to the personal pain thresholds of those involved. Engaging in such activity should never mean forcing an unwilling person to comply with one's desires. However, when there is genuine consent and understanding, they can become a positive expression of desire and affection. For a guide to details and precautions see Rules of the Game.

Bondage

Bondage means restricting a person's movement for sexual pleasure. Its most common use is to increase excitement for both partners by a willing defining between them of active and passive roles.

Active and passive roles, naturally play a part in all sexual relationships. These can be expressed in the simplest ways, such as who is on top, or who is giving or receiving oral sex. The notion of giving and receiving can build a strong sense of security in any sexual relationship. That each partner is capable of giving a selfless demonstration of affection or desire, focusing particularly on his or her partner's pleasure, can reinforce the relationship.

Sex games and lovemaking linked to bondage generally involve one partner being tied up by the other, who then devotes him- or her- self to arousing, stimulating and teasing the tied partner and, usually ultimately, bringing them to orgasm. They can give or withhold sexual pleasures as, and for as long as, they choose. This can be highly arousing for both partners. The tied partner, unable to move, can be relieved of any sense of responsibility, guilt or inhibition, and this may increase arousal.

Bondage can also be used as a part of submissive/dominant practices and games involving pain. Alternatively it can be used for physical support for certain positions and practices.

Bondage can include dressing up, costumes, role-playing games and any form of fetishism

The most common bondage uses ropes or handcuffs but many people simply use fabric or clothing such as ties, scarves, and/or hosiery to tie a partner up or to tie them to a bed or chair - though this is not always recommended because these fabrics may not easily untie and can pinch and cut off blood circulation.

A certain amount of freedom of movement may remain, but the accepted or actuality is that the restrained partner is sufficiently immobilised to enable the other to take a dominant role. Full-scale, purpose-made equipment is also available from specialist suppliers, some of whom will make to order. This equipment can range from leather collars and cuffs to full body harnesses, chastity belts and chains. It often includes objects and materials to which the people involved have some kind of fetishistic attachment, such as fur, leather, rubber, vinyl, shoes, gloves and so on. In some cases people construct their own dungeon rooms or find fully-equipped ones that are available for hire by those who may not have the necessary equipment.

Sub-Dom/S&M

The wish to dominate and to submit, to control and to be controlled, is present in most people's psyche: sometimes the non-fulfilment of either need in one area of a person's life can be compensated for in another, such as in his or her sex life. The popularity of submissive sexual practices recently exposed among high ranking politicians and powerful businessmen in some countries has been attributed to this concept, since they provide a complete removal of responsibility for decision-

making. Likewise those who are frustrated in their daily lives may find that dominant sexual practices boost their self-esteem.

Domination and submission in sexual relationships can take many different forms. They are often part of role-playing games and fantasy: one of the most popular forms is taking the roles of master and slave. Exactly how control is manifested tends to be a very personal matter. Some of the more common, or well-recognised forms are:

- Bondage
- Humiliation and degradation: insulting a partner, forcing him or her to do something menial or embarrassing, or using some form of defilement
- Infantilism: in this sense, being dressed and/or treated as an infant or child
- Coitus à cheval: in this sense, wearing a bridle-like harness and being ridden or 'trained' as a horse
- Defilement: the use of dirt, urine or faeces to humiliate
- Symbolic dress: including uniforms, lingerie, cross-dressing and furry creature costumes ('furverts')
- Flagellation
- Pain

Illustration for the Earl of Lavender
by Aubrey Beardsley (1896)

Pain

The experience of pain can be close to the experience of sexual arousal. Slapping the skin causes it become flushed and swollen, which is what happens to the sexual organs when they become engorged with blood. For many people the two are implicitly linked. Spanking, in particular, is popular using the hand or canes, whips, paddles, tawses and the like.

The terms most commonly used to describe this kind of behaviour are sadism (named after the Marquis de Sade, 1740-1814) for those who enjoy inflicting the pain on others, and masochism (named after Leopold von Sacher-Masoch, 1836-1895) for those who enjoy experiencing the pain.

Sexual practices involving pain are referred to as sadomasochistic or S&M – and, if they involve bondage, BDSM. The term is a conflation of the initial letters of bondage and discipline, with dominance and submission and sadism and masochism.

> I'm bringing back the birch, but only between consenting adults.
> **GORE VIDAL**

There is however a distinction to be drawn between BDSM sex involving consenting partners, and sex play which involves physical pain and injury against a person's wishes. Consensual BDSM is negotiated in advance and can be stopped at any time by either partner by using a safe word such as 'red' ('no' is not used, as it may mean the opposite).

Rules of the game

- All activities must be Safe, Sane and Consensual
- Agreement should be reached in advance of any activities which either partner wishes to avoid
- There should be an agreed safe word or release signal which will be honoured instantly
- Only knots that are easy to undo should be used
- Breathing should not be restricted
- Nobody should be left tied up without supervision

Group Sex

Sex with more than one partner has probably always been part of human sexuality, although the way it has been viewed by society has varied greatly from one set of cultural norms to another and throughout time. Sexual freedom appears to have

reached a highpoint in the late 1960s and early 1970s in Western society. Open relationships and sexual freedom were more common before the discovery of HIV and the ensuing AIDS panic. Now, with safer sex practices and increasing social acceptance of different forms of sexual expression, group sex in general and partner swapping in particular are enjoying something of a revival.

The attraction of group sex

Many people are aroused by the sight and sounds of other people having sex (hence the allure of porn films). But to be actually present while people have sex, to see, hear and smell them and even to be actively involved, can be intensely erotic.

At the same time it can also be instructive to see how other people have sex: singles and couples alike can find the experience rewarding. It can provide a

secure environment for experimentation with different kinds of sexuality and sexual expression. For established couples, group sex can add variety and boost each person's sense of his or her own attractiveness, without threatening the relationship. For others, at the heart of the attraction is the novelty and thrill of doing something which in many cultures is considered taboo.

Group practices

Group sex can take place with friends, acquaintances or complete strangers; the opportunity can be arrived at through advertisements placed by couples or singles, at parties, clubs or through group sex houses. Group sex houses usually have a strict code of behaviour pertaining to how individuals and couples are approached, or refused, for sex, what activities can take place and what safer sex practices are enforced. The idea is to create a secure environment for free sexual expression.

Some people enjoy having more than one partner or making love with more than one person at a time. Others like performing for an audience. Any number of different people, positions and sexual practices may be involved. Certain terms are sometimes used for specific kinds of group sex: a rainbow and

Erotic Relief Carvings, Laksamana Temple, Khajuraho, India

daisy chain are terms first introduced in the 1960s for – respectively – a group of different people each performing oral sex on a person with different coloured lipstick and a string of people each having sex with the person in front of them. The term 'gang bang' refers to a succession of people having intercourse with one person, usually a group of men with one woman (although this term may also be used to refer to a group rape).

Swinging in the 1890s - Group sex and swinging have been part of human sexuality in all cultures and throughout time

Swinging

Swinging is the term used for couples having sex play in groups, in front of each other or with new partners, with mutual consent and usually together at the same venue.

One of the older terms for this kind of activity was wife-swapping, which originated in Victorian times when husbands swapped keys to go to one another's homes in the evening. Today these practices can be arranged through swinging clubs or conferences, swinging parties or advertisements in specialist magazines; alternatively wife-swapping may occur between friends. Group sex and/or lesbian activity may be involved, although male gay sex is sometimes ruled to be out of bounds.

The objections to swinging and group sex are moral, emotional and medical. The morality is very much a personal – and sometimes a religious – issue. The emotional side is more complex. Swinging as a couple requires a very strong commitment to one another and solid management of jealousy. If a relationship is unstable, swinging often does more harm than good, but experienced swingers say that they find that it can strengthen their relationships. Swinging is about sharing exploration and novelty, rather than having such experiences without a partner's knowledge. Safer sex guidelines should be followed to reduce medical risks. In some countries there are legal restrictions on group and/or homosexual sex.

Exhibitionism and Voyeurism

Sexual display and visual stimulation play a part in most people's sex lives. They are a natural and instinctive form of sexual communication, both in the process of attracting a mate and within an established relationship. This aspect of sexuality is more prominent in some people than others and in some it can become compulsive. In certain cultures, if done in public, this may conflict with the norms of sexual and social behaviour and carry legal penalties.

Exhibitionism can be understood broadly as deriving sexual pleasure from displaying oneself. Voyeurism involves watching other people in order to become sexually aroused.

The desire to watch other people without their knowledge is also more common among men, although it has been reported among women. It may involve watching a person undress, spying on sunbathers or watching a

The Swing, by Jean Honore Fragonard (c.1767). Showing and looking, in one form or another, are arousing for most people. In this case, both girl and boy seem equally aware – and equally enjoying themselves

person or couple engaged in any form of sexual activity. The fact that in many cultures this is a taboo, and in many illegal, may only add to the attraction.

Forms of exhibitionism and voyeurism in the West...

...in daily life

Most people engage in some mild form of exhibitionism and/or voyeurism as part of daily life, in open or subtle forms of sexual display. These include, primarily, body language, (un)clothing and other forms of body decoration, most of which have some sexual origin.

...in a relationship

This occurs on a more open and conscious level in the context of a sexual relationship. While men tend to be more responsive to visual stimulation than women, many people of both sexes are excited by the sight of themselves sexually aroused, or their partner aroused. Many people enjoy watching themselves making love with their partner in front of a mirror or watching their partner masturbate. Others are aroused by the thought of being watched. The two sides are closely linked: some couples get a thrill out of making home videos of each other and their lovemaking, and enjoy performing for the camera and watching the results.

…in public

Many people are aroused by the risk of making love in public. Others actually seek out the sight and sounds of other people having sex, and some enjoy being watched or thinking they may be watched. This includes having sex in public places such as parks and in naturist/nudist colonies (although many naturist resorts and colonies do not officially allow this). Having sex in cars in car parks, so that others may watch and so, usually, with the lights on, is known as dogging; watching and being watched in such situations is implicitly consensual.

The exhibitionism and voyeurism of pornography and sex shows are different, but here too the practices are acknowledged and consensual. Whether or not the 'performers' are there out of choice and for pleasure, their customers are paying to see what can range from suggestive photographs or a sophisticated striptease to an explicit display of full-on sexual intercourse.

…in secret

Lastly there are those who watch other people or expose themselves to strangers without anyone's consent; it is these people that the words exhibitionist or voyeur are most commonly used, as well as other more disparaging terms like 'flasher' and 'peeping Tom'.

Those who expose themselves to others are, on the whole, male, and they tend to have little self-confidence, especially with regard to sex. Their intention is not to hurt but to shock: the pleasure derived from the experience is based on the shocked or horrified reaction of their victim. Being approached by a flasher may be alarming, but they are rarely involved in more serious sexual crimes.

Prostitution

Prostitution is often called 'the oldest profession in the world'. It seems to have existed in almost all cultures in one form or another. However, this is one sexual practice that is scorned in some cultures, illegal in many and highly esteemed in others.

The reasons for prostitution to remain so popular are varied, from the basic one of providing sexual relief for those who don't have a partner (or an unresponsive one), through offering varied sexual expression, relief from boredom and loneliness and as an activity for fun. In cultures where monogamy is the rule, it can be an outlet for alternative sexual cravings.

As the instinct for producing healthy offspring and ensuring their survival tends to overrule other considerations, so, in the wider animal kingdom, few species are naturally entirely monogamous. Humans, and male humans in particular, are by nature promiscuous, having a basic drive to spread their DNA, and most are interested in a reasonably wide variety of sexual experiences. This is not always acknowledged, even in the West, where much store is set on the appearance of faithful marriages.

The professional relationship

Prostitutes can be female or male, adult or child, professional or amateur. A prostitute is described as professional if she (or he) makes their living from charging for sexual services. The majority do not work as prostitutes from choice: money is the main objective.

In many ways the relationship between prostitute and client is a business relationship like any other (and it is often this lack of any emotional involvement that many clients prefer). The activities involved are usually negotiated and paid for in advance, with any further activities requested paid for before they are performed.

More importantly, the relationship is founded on mutual consideration and respect; once this is established the prostitute can take pride in providing services to the client's satisfaction. Consideration and reassurance between the parties are particularly important in those societies where prostitution is illegal or taboo.

What is prostitution?

Prostitution is selling sexual services, usually for money, although its forms may be as varied as any other sexual practices. It can provide sexual healing and sexual freedom, as well as straightforward sexual satisfaction. It caters to people who are single and people whose relationships do not satisfy their sexual needs; it can provide satisfaction for those who feel unable or unwilling to form a relationship.

Where necessary, it can also provide sexual experiences for people with special psychological or physical needs or disabilities. The term sex worker is now frequently substituted for the term prostitute.

Prostitutes generally cater to a wide range of sexual preferences, although in each cultural group the sexual acts most commonly requested are those which are often considered taboo. The same pattern may be seen in the demand for particular types of pornography or eroticism. Many people find release for their more far-fetched fantasies through prostitution.

Prostitution and society

In many countries laws against prostitution have driven the profession underground. Such laws have also made it potentially more risky for both prostitute and client and harder to monitor in terms of health and hygiene.

Prostitution may occur through street soliciting or legal or illegal brothels in any number of guises. Massage parlours, saunas, escort agencies or sex shows are all common fronts for prostitution and/or brothels (although, on the other hand, many such businesses do not involve prostitution).

Procurers or pimps may find work for prostitutes, taking a cut of their earnings and sometimes offering a degree of security or protection in exchange. However, it is still potentially dangerous work, which is not aided by the social stigma attached, although support and self-help groups are now becoming more common.

A red light district – one of the most common ways in which prostitutes and their clients meet, but also potentially dangerous

Recent changes in prostitution

By the millennium, the number of male prostitutes had increased significantly. The largest proportion of male prostitutes service male customers. Some may be transvestites, impersonating women very adeptly, or transgender individuals.

There is a market for underage sexual partners as well. Many of the children drawn into prostitution are runaways who have no other source of income and the recent increase in child prostitution is of great concern. Child prostitution exists all over the world but trends show that the consumers tend to be from first world countries, and the suppliers mainly come from developing countries. This partly explains the fact that so-called *sex tourism* has generated a vast market for prostitution in certain countries, especially in the large cities of Bangkok and Calcutta.

Attitudes towards adult prostitution in general have become more liberal. There are some who hold that eliminating prostitution would only breed more forms of perversion and immorality, and that prostitution actually serves to reduce the instances of illegitimacy, abortion, rape and attacks on children. Contrary to previous belief, prostitution is not commonly linked to organised crime and in the West public health officials indicate that prostitutes are responsible for only a small percentage of sexually-transmitted diseases.

Strong arguments have been made in favour of legalised prostitution, on the grounds that decriminalisation would free the police and courts from dealing with a so-called 'victimless crime', allowing more time to concentrate on more serious cases. However, the recognition of HIV and AIDS and the number of reports on the prevalence of HIV among prostitutes and their customers has generated new concerns and fears about prostitution.

Prostitution and the law

In Britain, it is not prostitution that is illegal, but the practice of soliciting for the purpose of prostitution, as is living on 'immoral earnings'. It is also illegal to procure clients to, or to take part in the management of, or to commit premises to be used as, a brothel. Recent new legislation has resulted in the police being much tougher on street walkers, which in effect has pushed prostitution underground and given rise to many new guises for prostitutes, including such titles as masseuses and escorts. Brothels are now more commonly known as 'massage parlours'.

America is one of the few countries in which prostitution remains to all intents and purposes illegal (the State of Nevada, home to Las Vegas, is an exception). In most other countries the laws concerning prostitution are aimed at controlling its socially-damaging consequences, restricting the numbers of those who would try to exploit prostitutes and at reducing public soliciting.

Sex and Technology

Technology has allowed sex to come into our homes, in a way that is accessible, affordable and anonymous. The internet, along with smart phones and pay-per-view, encrypted television, offers the opportunity to experience a diversity of sexual options instantly. It has also opened up a variety of new possibilities for meeting others for dating and sexual encounters, both virtually and in person.

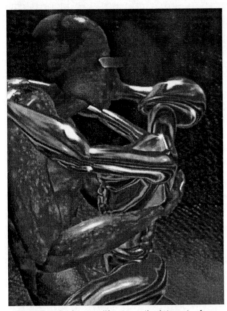

Sexual web sites proliferate on the Internet – from commercial erotica through to user discussion groups

Sex on the internet

The internet, e-mail, instant messaging (IM), and texting (in this context better known as 'sexting') all offer a vast range of sexual possibilities. As technology develops and the number of users grows, these possibilities continue to expand.

Currently, the widest sexual use of the internet is for access to pornography. Among the most popular sites are those that provide pornographic moving and still images – and even real-time encounters where women and men will perform to the wishes of the online audience. In theory, all of this activity has a valuable role to play, enabling people to explore their sexuality in new ways and in private. It makes sexually-explicit material easily available to those who want to access it discreetly. In addition, the on-line sex shops provide easy access to sex toys and apparel (see www.loversguide.com).

On the other hand, there is growing concern over this ease allowing access by minors and the ability to get around the controls that are currently in place. There are those who believe that all these materials are offensive or even dangerous. This is particularly so when pornography involves, or is accessible to, children. For this reason, several countries have taken measures to monitor the internet. Civil rights groups oppose this, however, considering it a violation of privacy.

The internet is widely used for making contact with other people, offering opportunities such as chat rooms, online dating and computer sex. People are able to communicate through user networks or bulletin boards set up specifically for sexual communication. These are frequently used for exchanging ideas, experiences or fantasies, or for looking for sexual partners. These internet services cater to singles, couples and all forms of sexuality and sexual preferences.

Virtual reality sex

The term virtual reality refers to the most realistic computer simulations. There are two sides to virtual reality sex. Firstly there is the idea of interactive computer software, in three-dimensional format, on screen. This has been referred to as teledildonics. And there is the much-publicised idea – particularly in science fiction films and books – of the virtual reality suit. This would be a complete 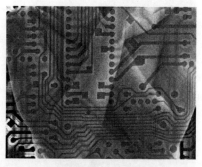 body suit to make possible lifelike simulation of sex, in three dimensions and involving all the senses. It seems inevitable that computer programming and technology will eventually turn even this idea into reality.

Internet (online) dating

The internet abounds with affordable and easy–to-navigate dating and meet-up websites such as www.match.com, www.singles.net, and www.datehookup.com. No need to get dressed up and head off to the local bar; these days it is easier – and more reliable in terms of matching needs and wants - to meet people from the privacy of one's own computer.

Internet sites allow individuals, couples and groups to communicate, with the intention of sharing personal, romantic and even sexual relationships. These days, it is very common for people to meet their future long-term partners on dating sites, as well as to get together with no-strings sexual partners. There are even websites for married people looking to have discreet affairs.

Phone Sex

Cell, and smart-, phones have made it easier than ever to find sexual partners in an instant. With a simple push of a button, or touch of a screen, a suitable sexual encounter can be arranged quickly and discreetly. There are several apps dedicated to helping find sexually-available partners. Cell phones are also used for sexting: the act of sending sexually explicit messages or photographs from one phone to another. Sexting that involves minors has led to a legal grey area for countries that have strict anti-child pornography laws, such as the United States. There are cases where teenagers who have texted sexually graphic photos of themselves have been charged with distribution of child pornography and those who have received them have been charged with possession of child pornography.

Fantasy

The most powerful human sex organ is the brain. Sex has been described as: 'ten per cent friction and ninety per cent fantasy'. The capacity to use imagination is something that sets human beings apart from other mammals and is particularly important in the context of sexuality.

Most people fantasise, whether only occasionally or frequently, although the forms and subjects of those fantasies are so many and varied that the term may mean different things to different people. Fantasy reflects every aspect of a person's sexual psyche but potentially without any of the personal or social constraints which might be experienced in reality. Fantasy can be the truest form of sexual expression and has an important part to play in many people's lives.

More than 70% of men and women are reported to use fantasies while having sex

What is fantasy?

Sexual fantasy is the sexual use of the imagination. It means imagining situations, experiences, people or sensations for the purposes of sexual arousal. It can take the form of a long sequence of events or story, or it may simply consist of isolated sensations or images. It can be conscious day-dreaming where the mind directs events, or the dreaming during sleep which is beyond any conscious control. It can last for several hours or a few brief moments.

Fantasy may or may not involve more tangible forms of stimulation. People may fantasise while masturbating, while making love with a partner, or while doing something completely unconnected such as working or travelling. The thought may be dismissed or, in a psycho-physiological merging, it may be carried through to orgasm.

Fantasies are usually personal and private, remaining in the imagination of the individual, and many people prefer to keep their fantasies to themselves. However, they can also be shared, or acted out. Sharing a fantasy with a partner can add excitement to lovemaking, though care should be exercised, as some people feel can feel alarmed or even insulted by the nature of their partner's fantasies.

Sharing a fantasy should be handled sensitively and, where appropriate, with a clear distinction between what appears to be desired in fantasy and what is desired in reality. The decision to act out a fantasy can be a difficult one, as the actual experience may be disappointing when compared to the imagined one. On the other hand, it can be the springboard to a thrilling way of exploring sexuality and experimenting with sexual practices.

Why do people fantasise?

A number of negative assumptions are sometimes made about sexual fantasy. Having them has been said to imply that the person's real sex life is disappointing, or that they are not in love with, or committed to, their partner. However, this is usually far from the truth. Surveys suggest that people who consider themselves and their partners to be good lovers are more likely to admit to having a strong fantasy life. If anything, the extent to which fantasy is used strongly correlates with the strength of a person's libido. Equally, research suggests that there is no connection between use of fantasy and infidelity. Fantasy can take many different forms and serve many legitimate purposes, indeed, it could also be considered the safest form of sex.

During lovemaking

Fantasy can boost arousal at any stage of lovemaking. It can prepare the way for sex, arousing people before lovemaking even begins, or it can add excitement during sex. It can even help to bring on climax; this can be a key factor in enabling both partners to reach orgasm. It can also help to solve arousal or orgasm problems and so is often encouraged by sex therapists for clients to use it to aid in every aspect of sexual expression, arousal and climax.

Emotional release

Fantasy is often used as an aid to sexual release, and as a substitute for sexual activity in reality. Many people, particularly women, are able to reach a high levels of sexual arousal through fantasy, some even reaching orgasm through fantasy alone. As with pornography, using sexual fantasy is often associated with masturbation but it can be just as important as an aid in fulfilling intercourse.

A sense of guilt is one of the most common indicators of sexual inhibition; it is generally the product of longstanding negative attitudes to sex in the family or cultural group. Fantasy can ease this in two ways. Firstly, people can fantasise about activities with which they would not feel comfortable in reality (see below). Secondly, fantasies such as those in which the person is compelled to be involved in sexual acts, can remove the fantasiser's sense of responsibility: in the fantasy he or she has no choice, leaving them free from guilt and thus able to enjoy themselves freely. This is the source of many masochistic, submissive or so-called rape fantasies, which are quite distinct from desiring the use of force in reality. Equally, sadistic or dominant fantasies may be indulged in as a safe outlet for pent-up anger or aggression. Finally, of course, no one can know what goes on in the mind and imagination.

> Sex, or sexual fantasy, 'the Mills & Boon tendency' as I call it, is what leads some largely female selections committees to choose good-looking young men rather than outspoken middle-aged women.
> **TERESA GORMAN, UK MEMBER OF PARLIAMENT**

Experimentation

The world of fantasy provides the ultimate safe environment for sexual experimentation. All guilt, anxiety, embarrassment and fear of consequences are banished; this is the one instance where full, free sexual expression is possible. This may be the most common use of fantasy.

There are two distinct kinds of fantasy experimentation. The first is largely based in reality, and takes the form of a kind of sexual rehearsal. The person can try out a particular sexual practice - without actually doing it; they can then decide whether or not they feel they may want to try it in reality.

The second kind is based more in the unobtainable, and can include anything from sex with a favourite film star, say, to sex with one's partner on a desert island: this is fantasy as wish-fulfilment. However, this category can also include activities that the person would not desire in reality, which could range from extramarital sex to some of the more extreme practices such as sadomasochism or bestiality. Such fantasies are not uncommon and they should be considered to be harmless so long as they do not lead to any illegal or dangerous activities in reality.

Women and fantasy

What do women fantasise about?

The most popular female fantasies include:

- (Strange as it may seem:) Sex with usual partner
- Sex with a stranger
- Sex with a former lover
- Sex with another woman
- Sex with someone of a different race
- Sex in exotic or unusual locations
- Sex in imaginative or romantic circumstances
- Having sex in public and being watched
- Sex with two men or a man and a woman
- Group sex
- Watching a partner having sex with someone else
- Watching other couples having sex
- Working as a prostitute or a stripper
- Being 'forced' to have sex
- Being tied up for sex
- Being the dominant partner
- Sexual activity with an animal
- Using a male sex slave
- Having sex with an authority figure (teacher, officer...)
- Erotic dancing

How do women use fantasies?

Women's fantasies tend to have more to do with atmosphere and circumstances than men's; they are more likely to involve a story or a series of events leading up to sex. Women are more likely to

> In my sex fantasy, nobody ever loves me for my mind.
> **NORA EPHRON**

fantasise about their regular partner, albeit in different guises or situations. While men's fantasies tend to be more voyeuristic, women's are more exhibitionistic.

The process of sexual liberation is reflected in changes in women's fantasies, which have increasingly included dominant and assertive sexual practices. In many cases they have also become more overtly sexual and less romantic.

Where men tend to be more visual in what they find erotic, women tend to respond more to the written word; however the more romantic novels of the Harlequin/Mills & Boon ilk have recently been losing ground to much more explicit fiction. Surveys have shown that women's sexual fantasies have always tended to be more varied and imaginative than men's and this continues to be the case: 75% of women say that fantasy is an important and fulfilling part of their sex lives.

Men and fantasy
What do men fantasise about?

The most popular male fantasies include:

- Sex with a woman other than their usual partner, such as neighbour, colleague, friend, partner's best friend, past lover, stranger, celebrity
- Sex with someone of a different race
- Watching a woman masturbate
- Watching two women have sex, often usual partner with another woman
- Watching other couples having sex
- Sex with another man
- Sex with two women or man and a woman
- Group sex
- Watching other people having group sex
- 'Forcing' a woman to have sex
- 'Forcing' a woman to have oral sex
- Being made to have sex
- Sex in public place
- Sex with a virgin
- Anal sex with a woman
- Having a woman use a dildo to perform anal sex on him
- Having sex involving bondage

How do men use fantasies?

Men's fantasies tend to be more visual than women's, focusing on particular key images. They tend to concentrate more on the person or people involved, and the sexual acts being performed, rather than on the situation or atmosphere. Men's fantasy partners may include acquaintances or a regular partner, but are often influenced by images or sequences from internet porn sites. Voyeuristic fantasies are more common among men than women.

All kinds of sexual activity can feature in men's fantasies, from the simplest and most straightforward practices to the more extreme and bizarre end of the scale. Dominant and sadistic practices may feature as an outlet for aggression, while fantasies about submissive practices can be used to relieve a sense of obligation to fulfil a stereotypical masculine (active, dominant, aggressive) role.

> Fantasy love is much better than reality love. Never doing it is exciting. The most exciting attractions are between two opposites that never meet.
> **ANDY WARHOL**

SEX AND YOU

Relationships are important to most of us. It is likely that some relationships will be sexual ones and will vary according to sexual orientation, gender, upbringing and education about sex.

Many people are anxious about sex and relationships and would like to improve their interpersonal skills. This section of the Lovers' Guide Illustrated Encyclopedia invites you, the reader, to use the exercises here, together with the information gathered from the previous sections, to develop your own sexual profile. It is designed to advise, inform and help you get the best out of your relationships and sex life.

Overcoming Inhibitions

Inhibitions are feelings that can prevent you from enjoying sex to the full or, in extreme cases, even from becoming sexually aroused. Nearly always these inhibitions are caused by feelings of guilt or anxiety about sex instilled in the individual during their upbringing or by some traumatic sexual episode.

We know, or we quickly learn, what makes us uncomfortable and we learn to avoid those situations or activities. But sometimes this can become critical where people become set in patterns of attitudes and behaviour that can make them avoid sex or suppress sexual feelings altogether.

Letting yourself be sexual

If it is at all difficult for you to think of yourself as sexual, or to develop your sexual feelings, start by using fantasy. In your imagination, you can safely experiment with feelings and sexual activities that you might find threatening in reality. Let yourself go. Become totally involved and concentrate on all the sensations you feel. If you practise this when you are alone, and let your thoughts and feelings arouse you in masturbation, this may help you feel less self-conscious about expressing pleasure with a partner.

Reassess your attitudes

Take a fresh look at your attitudes towards sex, and perhaps towards pleasure too. People who are inhibited, or struggle in any way with personal sexual expression, often feel that any sensual pleasure for its own sake is wrong. This guilt or shame can block positive experiences for them and with their partners. Re-examining your sexual attitudes, values, education and experiences can open new doors to sexual acceptance.

Making yourself more receptive to pleasure, and happy to receive it, can provide opportunity to make your sex life much more enjoyable and to enjoy sex as a natural, legitimate and healthy source of pleasure.

Learn to like your body

Some people are embarrassed by their bodies simply because they have an image of how they would like to look and judge their body as failing to measure up.

The media is filled with images of what may be considered ideal beauty (especially for women, though, increasingly, for men, too) that are very unrealistic. Often, the original models have had their images altered and airbrushed to portray a perfection which even they do not possess. Such images can engender feelings of shame and inadequacy in the ordinary mortals about their own body image and have a negative impact on their sexual expression.

Everyone has to learn not just to accept but to appreciate their body as it is; only then will they be able to believe that anyone else can really like it, and love them.

Sexual Anxieties

Anxiety about sex is as destructive to enjoyment as inhibitions. People may be anxious because they lack correct information. Ignorance about your own body and lack of opportunity to compare it with anyone else's can make you believe that your genitals are odd, or ugly, or even abnormal.

Ignorance about sex itself means that first night nerves are common, and anxieties about sexual performance, or about whether you will please your partner, are almost universal. Often you can dispel sexual anxiety by telling a partner how you feel. Discussing your fears helps you to put them into perspective; it allows your partner to reassure you, and you to reassure him or her.

Fear of intimacy

When you are in a close sexual relationship, you should be able to tell your partner honestly what you want and how you feel without having to worry that you will be mocked or rejected. But to achieve this kind of intimacy demands trust and commitment.

If you have been hurt in past relationships it may take time before you risk getting close to anyone again. And if you were raised in a family where feelings and emotions were seldom shown and never talked about or, worse, were always negative, you may find it hard to develop an intimate relationship in adulthood. To do so will involve changing fundamental aspects of your outlook and behaviour.

Choosing the right partner

Do you have an image of an ideal partner in your head? Perhaps you have a list of 'must have' traits. If so, you are by no means alone, but does your wish-list blinker your outlook or leave you open-minded? The most common characteristics people want in their partners include honesty, intelligence, sense of humour, openness to new ideas, a strong sense of stability, good communication skills, common hobbies and interests, and a willingness to work on the relationship to make it succeed.

Though men and women might seek similar traits in a partner, research has demonstrated that each individual focuses on different qualities. Men typically may want a relationship that allows them some autonomy, whilst women tend to look for a stronger sense of connection.

To begin your quest to find the right partner, think about the traits and behaviours you prefer. Most people automatically think of superficial traits such as physical characteristics. Though these traits can be important, other traits are more important when it comes to having a healthy, long-term relationship. See Part 2 for greater detail regarding sexual attraction.

When you sense that you are growing closer (perhaps closer than may feel comfortable), try not to back off emotionally. Take care not to put a distance between you by provoking an argument, or remembering past grievances, or by focusing on your partner's least attractive features. These can simply be excuses for avoiding intimacy. Also, if you have a partner who is critical of you, it can be harder to think better of yourself.

A loving and supportive partner is important for most people – and particularly for anyone for whom lack of self-confidence is a problem.

Building intimacy

Set aside time each day to talk with your partner about what has happened to you. Discuss your worries or problems – and ask them to do the same. Try to talk about what matters to you both, and don't avoid sexual or emotional issues even if initially they make either of you feel uncomfortable.

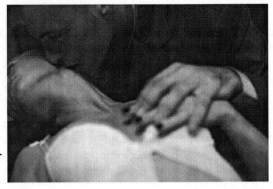

Spend time together on leisure activities as well as in sexual encounters. And when intimacy builds up, don't back off or let excuses such as pressure of work or other commitments keep you apart.

Learning to show your feelings

Affection needs to be demonstrated as much and as often as possible. Touching your partner in an affectionate or loving way is one of the easiest ways of showing it. You don't even need to say the words – 'I love you' – that people who fear emotional intimacy and commitment can find so difficult (though it helps if you can do this, too).

Make a point of touching just for emotional warmth and when there is no question of this being interpreted as an immediate sexual invitation. The lesson you are trying to learn is that physical affection can be built into the fabric of a whole relationship, and should not be confined only to its sexual moments. Though, when you are making love, spend time on loving foreplay, for example, kissing, touching and fondling.

Giving up your emotional independence

The more self-contained you are, the more you may shut your partner out of the important areas of your life. Giving your partner a chance to do something for you occasionally can allow them to express their feelings for you. Ask for help, or advice, or a shoulder to cry on. Don't be afraid to show your vulnerability.

It is important for you to learn to show your partner that you have needs, and to allow them to try to meet them. Of course you are running an emotional risk by doing this, by putting yourself into someone else's hands. But the rewards in your sexual and emotional life should be correspondingly great.

Improving Your Self Esteem

A poor self-image can have a significant effect on the way you behave towards other people – a fear of being rejected can make you shy or over-eager to please in social situations, and insecurity can induce jealousy, which may damage your relationships.

It also affects the way other people behave towards you. By and large, other people will tend to accept you at your own valuation. Your self-esteem has a direct bearing on your confidence – and so to your own ability to attract and keep friends and sexual partners. When you have a healthy sense of self, you feel you are worthy of being appreciated by friends and loved by a partner or partners.

Causes of low self esteem

Most of the causes of low self-esteem stem from the way we were treated in childhood, though also, to some extent, with one's innate personality. Children accept their parents' view of them. Made to think they are good, loveable and successful, they will grow up believing this, and any later, unsuccessful or negative experiences will much less likely be strong enough to induce feelings of inadequacy.

However, even a self-confident person can suffer a temporary failure in self-esteem, such as a consequence of a break-up of an important relationship or a major setback at work, for example. When you have been dealt some major blow to your self-esteem, it is important to try to see it in perspective, as only confined to one part of your life, not the whole of it. Everyone suffers setbacks, but we all need to pick ourselves up and look forwards positively not backwards with bitterness.

Avoid affairs on the rebound

After any episode of damage to one's self-esteem, whether at work or in a relationship, it can be tempting to throw yourself headlong into an affair. This is certainly a quick way to soothe a bruised ego, and it may work for a while, but the risk is that rebound affairs seldom last long.

It is usually wiser to rely on the support of friends, and wait until your emotional equanimity is reasonably restored before seeking another lover. However, if in two or three months you still feel a lack of personal or sexual self-confidence, the problem may be a deeper one. In those circumstances, it may be important to seek out the aid of a qualified counsellor to help resolve any underlying issues.

Learning To Assert Yourself

Shyness is a label many people attach to themselves. Unfortunately, other people may see you as being unfriendly, stand-offish or, because you may not speak much, boring or uninteresting. Have faith in your own likeability. You may have to learn to be more assertive, to believe that you are a person worth knowing, with views and opinions that are worth listening to. Then others will believe it too.

Overcoming shyness

Shyness is an attitude of mind. This may sound simplistic, but the way to stop being shy is to change your attitude. You can start by thinking of yourself not as a shy person, but as someone who is only shy in situations in which most people would feel at least a little shy – in large social groups, for example, or when meeting attractive strangers. When talking to people, direct all your attention outwards towards being interested in them, not inwards towards worrying about yourself or what others think of you. It may help to become involved in some quite new situation with people who don't know you but with whom you have interests in common (a club, reading group, social meeting place or political party for instance). Here you can make a fresh beginning by starting out by believing in yourself as someone who is not shy at all.

Practise assertiveness

If you are shy and low in self-esteem you may have a tendency to go to any lengths to make sure people like you. But it can help to remember the adage that you can't please everyone all of the time. If you are the kind of person who feels constrained by fear of the risk of offending others, you are also likely to be the kind who makes little effort to ensure that your own wants and needs are met. It is a good idea to practise being more assertive in your daily life. You should then gradually find it easier to tell others – including sexual partners – what you want. Practise saying 'no' in situations where you would normally, but unwillingly, give in and say 'yes', for example. Learn how to ask people to do small favours for you. You should not be at all aggressive about this; you are simply stating your views and preferences and engaging other people in little acts of kindness to you – and for which you should reciprocate.

Building Self-Worth

When you have a poor self-image, you may believe that you are unlovable and may also believe that it can't be changed. Both of these notions are wrong. There is a lot you can do, not only to build up your own self-esteem, but also to begin to change the way other people see you.

Assessing your strengths and weaknesses

First, make two lists: your good points – character and personality as well as physical; and your bad ones – the things about yourself that you wish were different or could be improved.

Be specific. Don't be tempted to minimise your strengths. Don't just do this from a sexual point of view – if you play soccer well, or are a good cook, or musical, or paint, include these as positive capabilities, too. If there are talents you admire in others and feel would add to your self-confidence if you had them (learning to drive or play an instrument for instance), put these down.

If your list of weaknesses is by far the longest, you are probably being way too self-critical, as people with a poor self-image tend to be. You will no doubt be overlooking some of your good points as too trivial to include. It may be helpful to enlist a close friend or family member to help do this with you, because they may see qualities in you that you do not.

Analysing your strengths

Look at your list of strengths. Are you making the best use of the ones you've got? Do you try to put yourself in situations in which you know you can shine? If you have good eyes or a nice smile - do you know how best to use them? If you are tall, do you make sure your posture is good or do you slouch, round-shouldered?

Finally, look at the 'weakness list'. How many items on the list are things you can do nothing about (no-one can make themselves six inches taller, for example)? Delete these from your list and resolve never to think about them again. As for the rest, those you can change, make rectifying them the start of your self-improvement programme.

Improving your image

Start with your appearance. Don't be defeatist. Saying 'I never bother with the way I look' often covers the fear that even if you did bother it wouldn't make any difference. But appearance can be changed. A new and more flattering haircut or contact lenses instead of spectacles, or vice versa, would probably work wonders. There are endless ways to improve the way you look. When you are buying clothes, think about styles and colours you have never tried before but which could better suit the way you'd like to look.

Most importantly, get healthy. This means eating right, exercising and getting enough sleep. As you feel healthier you will begin to feel better about yourself. Also, begin to do things that give you a sense of self (e.g. hobby) or that builds self-confidence.

Make gradual changes

When you make changes, don't try to do too much too quickly. Introduce new looks and behaviours gradually, step by step, over a few months. This will ease you into the 'new you', make you less self-conscious about your newly developing image and give you and everyone else time to adjust to it. It may also take time to get used to other people's changing reactions to you.

When you have done what you feel is the best you can with yourself, learn to be proud of your progress and like yourself the way you have become, even if you feel you still fall short of some ideal. Let that go.

Making yourself more flexible

The more qualities you require for someone to be attractive to you, the less flexible your blueprint for a partner will be, and the less chance there may be that anyone will ever satisfy it. Instead, it is better to try to change your expectations and develop a less rigid blueprint.

The next time you meet someone you are interested in, don't worry too much about whether they match up to the whole list of what would be your ideal. Instead, concentrate on the things about them that appeal most to you.

You may find they have qualities that you wouldn't have listed in your blueprint, but which seem engaging to you in this person. Focus on these positive qualities as much as you can. Equally, there will be some qualities you will never be able to change in another person (as there will be some traits they will never change in you). But do their qualities outweigh their faults?

Many people are perfectly happy being single, but for those who are not, finding the right relationship can be a central concern of life. However, it is important to recognise that, while some people believe there is just one perfect partner (soul-mate) for them, there are in fact many people with whom you can fall in love and have rewarding and lasting relationships. Don't let 'perfect' be the enemy of 'good'.

If you are always wondering whether someone better might come along, that alone may prevent you from making the most of the relationships you do have. Even if you think of yourself as an ordinary person, you can be sure that there will be some people who will find you uniquely attractive. As an initial friendship develops, you may want to transform it into a sexual relationship.

The first date

The aim of your first date should be to begin to get to know each other and make the other person feel you like them, if you do, without making it too heavy and so frightening them off.

A casual date, which minimises any sexual overtones, may feel most comfortable – lunch or a drink after work perhaps. Don't be overly familiar on a first date, or try to be too intimate – and don't make the mistake of talking about previous partners.

The importance of timing

Choosing the right moment to advance a relationship and knowing when to hold back, can be crucial to sexual success. Moving too fast can put the other person under too much pressure too soon; then again, moving too slowly may cause them to lose interest.

If you get it wrong, it is often because you have ignored or misread the other person's signals. Body language plays a part (see the chapter on that and Sexual Attraction in Part 2).

If you find that you are looking into each other's eyes for longer and longer periods, this is a definite 'come-on' signal, indicating that it is time to move on to a more overtly sexual stage.

Start by taking the person's hand. If they don't draw away, move on to more intimate gestures such as hugging and then kissing.

FORMING RELATIONSHIPS

Taking too much for granted

If you are often rebuffed in response to your first sexual overtures, it may be because you are too readily taking it for granted that sex is on the agenda in any relationship. It isn't. You may need to spend a while getting to know each other first. And if the other person feels that they are free to choose, not under pressure, they will be less likely to reject you. Never, ever, make someone feel they are under any obligation to have sex with you. Nobody ever is.

Sexual good manners

When you are both ready to make it sexual, be sensitive – you will be nervous, no doubt, but so will they. If you are both clearly tense, suggest a bath, shower or massage together first. Tell them how desirable you find them, and never criticise their looks. This first time you might both prefer just to lie and explore each other's bodies and cuddle. If you do have intercourse, either discuss safer sex beforehand or simply ensure you have proper protection for when the time comes.

Minimal Dating Programme

For some people, even taking the first steps towards a sexual relationship is hard, because they doubt their ability to make any kind of close friendship or sexual relationship. If you are in this position, this minimal dating programme should help you establish a normal social, and then sexual, life by going through a series of gradual steps.

Step one: Practice dating

The first step is to set up a practice date that will cause you as little anxiety as possible. So it should be with someone you know and like, but don't find especially attractive, and don't care at all about the outcome or making a sexual impression on. Make it casual, with no romantic overtones – lunch, or a visit to a concert or film or exhibition. Asking them at fairly short notice makes it appear even less of a formal date – and will give you less time to be anxious about it too. Repeat this kind of date a few times until you feel little anxiety about it.

Step two: Dating someone who matters

The next step is to date someone you do find attractive and potentially of interest. To begin with, keep to the same platonic, neutral dating you practised in the first step. When you feel relaxed with your date, start to make it clear that you find them attractive. Don't rush things, but don't let them stand still either. Make each occasion a step more romantic, involving a little more affectionate physical contact. Taking their arm, holding their hand, a goodnight kiss – these are all recognised steps on the way towards a sexual relationship.

Step three: The final move

Once you feel you have become close to the person, and you think there is a real sexual spark between you, you – or they – can make the final move. Here, if it's you, then you have to take a risk, but don't hold back for fear of rejection. The only way you can succeed is by risking failure.

You also have to decide whether to be open and tell them of your sexual anxiety, or whether you simply go ahead and trust to luck. In fact you may find that because you've already established a close relationship, there is no failure. Even if things don't go well, it should be easier for you to talk about your situation, and enlist his or her help in trying again.

Step four: First times

First night nerves are probably universal. Whether it is love, lust or simply curiosity that has got you into this situation, it is an unusual person who doesn't feel at least a little tense or nervous – and finds their heart to be beating a little faster. It's best to be open with your partner – they'll probably be relieved that you are as  nervous as they are. If you're a virgin, or have less experience than your partner, then they can reassure you. Don't expect the first time to be a great experience – it seldom is, and sex improves with practice.

Talking about sex in general can be relatively easy, but talking about your personal sexual feelings and preferences can be difficult for almost everyone. It isn't only that it makes you feel vulnerable to reveal your intimate thoughts and feelings; because your sex life is a concern shared with your partner, you need to consider his or her feelings too.

Learning To Communicate

Learning to communicate the way you feel, to make suggestions or request changes, without making your partner feel hurt, rejected or criticised, is a real art. But, if you want a relationship that is able to grow and develop so that it can meet both your needs, it is a necessary skill for both partners to learn.

Talking about sex

However close you are, your partner cannot read your mind. There is no substitute for straight talking if you want to discover each other's sexual needs and preferences. Remember, if you are close enough to have sex, you should be close enough to talk about it. Paradoxically, though, it can often be easier to talk about sex with a new partner, when sex is very probably on both your minds, than in a longstanding one where habits can have set in.

So take advantage of any new relationship to set up a pattern of good communication from the start. At this stage you know little about each other, so it can seem natural to ask them what they like, and to tell them if there is any sexual activity you particularly like or dislike. Be as specific as you can. Then when you get to know each other better it will be easy to continue the same pattern. In a long-term relationship, use resources such as books or videos as triggers to aid the process of bringing up particular issues.

The right time to talk

Most people find it easiest to talk about sex when they are actually making love. It's easy to say 'I love what you're doing to me', or ask 'Am I pressing too hard/going too fast?' However, for couples in well-established relationships, who have never been in the habit of talking about sex, it can be hard suddenly to alter the pattern and start making comments – it may seem too much like an accusation that sex hasn't been great up until now. It may be easier to broach the subject of sex on more neutral ground – perhaps over a relaxing drink or meal.

Reassuring your partner

It always works best to 'accentuate the positive' and compliment what you like about what your partner does with you sexually rather than criticising what you dislike. Remember, everyone can be sensitive about their sexual performance, and anything that can be taken as a criticism probably will be. So try saying 'I love it when you stroke me just there', rather than 'Why can you never ever find the right place?'

If there is a really delicate matter to be raised – personal hygiene for example – try suggesting it's a problem you share. 'I haven't had time for a bath for a couple of days – I'm sure I must stink. Let's take a shower together.'

Don't expect too much self-disclosure too soon, or ask a question you wouldn't want to answer yourself, or one that you know would embarrass your partner.

Saying no, yes and maybe

At times, one of you will want sex and the other will not. It's important to find a way of saying no without hurting the other person. The secret is to make it clear that it is not the person who is being rejected, only the invitation, and only temporarily.

It is also okay to say 'yes' to sex. Managing inhibitions and taking risks in being sexually vulnerable can create greater intimacy. Even if you are not completely in the mood, you can say yes as a loving gift to your partner. It is also okay to say 'maybe' if you are not sure and need some time to think about it, and take time to get in the mood or prepare for sexual intimacy.

Dealing with anger

Anger and good sex are incompatible to creating loving intimacy. Two people who set out to live together have to learn to talk their problems out without letting anger get out of control and destroy their relationship.

- Say what has upset you at the time, don't let it fester and bring it up days or weeks later.
- It causes less resentment to say how your partner's behaviour makes you feel than for it to come out as a criticism of them as a person.
- In an argument, stick to the point at issue. Don't say '... and another thing' and bring up past grievances.
- Don't let yourself go out of control, or start an argument when you are blazingly angry. It is too easy to say wounding or destructive things that can't easily be forgiven or forgotten. Cool down a little first.
- Make up before you have sex.

Sustaining Relationships

No-one can predict with any degree of certainty whether a relationship will last. The most unpromising-looking partnerships often survive, while others, which

seem to have everything going for them, fail. What we can say is that a relationship works best when both partners satisfy most of each other's needs for much of the time, and that the most important ingredient for success is your own determination to make it work. Certain other factors also seem to be particularly important in determining a couple's chances of making a successful long-term partnership.

Timing

Don't commit to what could turn into a life-long relationship too young. No matter how much you feel you are in love, commitments made before the age of 19 are statistically the least likely to survive, simply because the two people involved will change as they mature and, typically, in doing so, will grow apart. It's also sensible not to assume you will get too much from a relationship so early on.

Though new relationship energy (NRE) can be very powerful, it probably takes at least several months to get to know the best and worst of each other. On the other hand, if commitment is postponed for longer than about two years, it may be a sign that you may never want to commit to that person (or them to you), or that one or both of you are not ready to lose your independence.

Similarity

It is probably easier for a couple who have similar interests and attitudes and want much the same sort of things out of life to live together without friction. It may help if you are both of similar intelligence and if there is not more than 10 years' age gap between you.

It's important to have the same feelings and attitudes towards sex, too. Sexual compatibility is not just a question of technique – that can be learned and developed. What matters is that sex should not be much more (or less) important to one partner than the other, that you are truly attracted and aroused by each other and that you have a similar sexual outlook.

Flexibility

Look for a partner who is flexible, receptive to new ideas or willing to try out new activities. Neither relationships nor individuals remain the same. Everything changes and a partner who is very inflexible and uncompromising may find it hard to adapt to the inevitable changes faced in any long-term partnership.

However, it is equally important not to assume that a partner will change, or that you can change them. The chances are that a partner who is jealous, moody, alcoholic or wildly extravagant will not change substantially under your influence. If you cannot put up with them as they are, you'd do well to steer clear of attempting to have a long-term involvement with them.

Emotional maturity

A stormy courtship is a bad sign. It will be difficult to have a fulfilling and happy relationship with a partner who is angry, domineering, aggressive or critical. On the whole, people change very little, and a pattern set in courtship quarrels is likely to continue. Be wary, too, of making a lasting commitment to someone who is very insecure or over-dependent, unless you are prepared for an unbalanced relationship in which you always have to be the supportive and reassuring partner.

Finally, for the vast majority of people, it is crucially important to have a partner who is capable of giving and accepting physical affection and emotional engagement.

Jealousy

Everyone who has ever been in a close relationship has probably experienced jealousy and recognises the pain that it can cause. It is one of the most power-ful and destructive of emotions. Jealousy is often assumed to be a sign of love. If you are insecure in your relationship, you may even try to make your partner jealous, as if this would some-how 'prove' he or she loved you. In fact, what jealousy really demonstrates is not love but a fear of loss or your inadequacy.

When is jealousy reasonable?

Sometimes jealousy is a reasonable response to a relationship under threat. How much you show is matter of judgment and control. It is reasonable to be jealous if a partner sets out to flirt with someone else in your presence, for example, or if you have solid grounds for thinking that they are involved with someone else.

Under these circumstances a flash of jealousy may serve a positive purpose. It can either act as a timely warning to a partner that his or her behaviour is going beyond the bounds of what you are prepared to tolerate, or force hurt and angry feelings into the open that need to be acknowledged if the relationship is not to be permanently damaged.

Unreasonable jealousy

Jealousy is not always justified. It is unreasonable to be jealous of lovers your partner had before you met, for example, or of old friends who have long been part of his or her life.

You cannot rewrite anyone's past and if you try to destroy it, or insist that all ties with the past are cut, your partner will inevitably feel resentful.

Jealousy that arises from your own feelings of insecurity can cause deep resentment too. Unless you have solid grounds for thinking a partner is cheating, it is a mistake to cross-examine them about what they do in your absence, or to look for clues to infidelity amongst his or her belongings.

Rebuilding trust

When you have once had good cause for jealousy, it is natural to worry that the same thing may happen again. It takes time, sensitivity and self-discipline to rebuild trust, and to repair the damage to self-esteem that is inevitable when you find a partner has, even temporarily, preferred someone else to you.

It's important that the 'wronged' partner tries to let his or her grievances go, and does not show a lack of trust by monitoring his or her partner's every move. It is equally important for the partner who has strayed to give the relationship priority and offer extra reassurance and affection.

Infidelity

Most affairs are with colleagues and close friends. Affairs that are based only on sexual attraction are usually self-limiting, lasting on average only a few months, and probably do least damage to a long-term relationship. More damaging is the affair that satisfies an emotional need to be more deeply loved or valued in the unfaithful partner.

Why do affairs begin?

Most people convince themselves that their affair was a spontaneous and irresistible case of 'falling in love'. In fact, it nearly always involves a conscious decision.

It may begin out of curiosity or a need for sexual excitement, or because their regular partner has a problem that makes sex difficult or unsatisfactory. An affair may be a morale booster, or entered into as revenge on an unfaithful partner, or a way of finding the ideal partner with whom (it is believed) a perfect love would be possible. It may have the relatively positive aim of precipitating a crisis in a relationship that needs a thorough overhaul.

Whatever the reason, there is always the risk that continuing the affair may seem to be an easier option than solving the problems in the relationship. Typically affairs do not offer relief, especially in the case of families with children, and affair relationships lose their energy in the same way all relationships can with time.

Running a successful affair

An affair probably causes least grief and gives most pleasure when it fulfils a simple sexual need for both partners, neither of whom makes additional demands on the other. But few relationships are as simple as this.

If you want to have a successful affair without jeopardising your primary relationship, you need to make a commitment to both, which means compartmentalising your life and your emotions. Don't neglect your partner or try to justify what you are doing by dwelling on their failings, even to yourself. Make the most of your time with your lover – most affairs have to be conducted with one eye on the clock, and grievances can build up quickly when there is little time to resolve them.

Whether to confess

Confession is bound to affect, and may destroy, a relationship. If you do confess, or are found out, your partner's reaction will depend partly on how long the affair has been going on. It is easier to understand and forgive a casual brief fling than to accept that they have to view a large part of your life together quite differently. It can take a long time to rebuild trust.

The unfaithful partner also runs the risk that the affair may be too successful, becoming more important to them than was ever intended so that they, too, have to re-examine their commitment to their partner.

Discovering a partner's infidelity

If you suspect your partner is having an affair, should you confront them? Before you do, be sure that you really want to know and have considered the implications. Remember that most affairs last only a few months at the most.

If you do confront, decide on your aim. If you are trying to save the relationship, however bitter you are, try to get your emotions under control first so that you do not say too many things that will be unforgivable or unforgettable.

You want to know why it happened, so give your partner the chance to tell you. Ask questions only if you want to know the answers. It will probably hurt more than help you to know, for example, the sexual details of the affair.

Working out a solution

Once an affair is out in the open it is essential that you both make time to talk about it. It will be tempting to want to give vent to your own feelings, and of course you must have the opportunity to do this. But it is actually more vital to the survival of the relationship that you understand why your partner went into the affair and how they feel now.

If they were looking for something in the affair that was missing in your own relationship you both need to recognize and acknowledge this, and work out what can be done to meet the need they evidently felt. Many couples who survive the discovery of an affair do so by emerging with a stronger mutual understanding.

Enriching Your Sex Life

What makes a good lover? Sexual happiness depends on more than technical ability. The good lover is confident in his or her own sexuality but, just as important, they have the ability to make their partner feel good about themselves – sexy and responsive.

The best sexual relationships are equal, so that neither partner has to feign enjoyment or enthusiasm and both have a real affection for each other that makes them able to satisfy each other's emotional as well as sexual needs. Finally, there is no substitute for sexual chemistry, which no-one can fully explain or understand.

Attraction and affection

Love-making should be sensual as well as sexual. Foreplay is important because it is the way both partners express their sensuality and delight in each other's bodies. Use touch to show affection as well as to ask for sex. For some, after sex, a partner's needs may have been satisfied but, for others, continued affection is often required.

Afterplay – a hug, a cuddle, and a few intimate words – may be as important as the foreplay or sex itself. Don't be afraid to show that you like sex. Sex should never be something that is 'done' by one partner to another, either performed or received as a duty. It is for your mutual pleasure.

Imagination and innovation

One way to keep a sexual relationship exciting is to explore a range of sexual activities. Use your imagination to introduce variety in to your sex life. A different time, or place, or position, or having music to make love to – if sex is beginning to feel boring there are innumerable ways to spice it up.

Make time for sex so that there is no need to rush. Pause every now and then and let your arousal wane, perhaps talk for a while, and then have the added pleasure of arousing each other all over again.

Sexual Boredom

Getting into a sexual rut is a major issues for many couples. Sex doesn't have to become boring if the couple involved is flexible enough to change and adapt as the years go by. The reality is that things inevitably change. The excitement and intensity that mark the early stages of a relationship give way to a calmer, less frenzied phase.

Passion diminishes, but long-term lovers who know each other's bodies, needs and preferences, and accept and trust each other, can more than compensate for anything that may have been lost.

Enjoying a life together

Sex is only part of a relationship and, if the relationship as a whole bores you, the chances are that sex will do so too. Try giving each other more attention, spending more time together, having more fun together and flirting with each other. Shared activities or new interests can give you engaging points of contact and something to talk about, perhaps even make you more stimulating and interesting for each other.

Try occasionally doing something nice for your partner, for no special reason except just to please them. It doesn't have to be anything spectacular – just something to make them feel that they enhance your life.

Breaking your sexual routine

Introducing change into a long established sexual routine is often difficult, but it is a good way of combating sexual boredom. However, when you suggest making changes, be careful not to make it seem as though you are criticising your partner.

If your partner views new ideas with suspicion, make the changes small and subtle at first. You might suggest simply that you leave the lights on instead of making love in the dark, or go to bed on a Sunday afternoon if yours has always been a bedtime-only sexual routine. Later you might want to make more dramatic changes, adding a new position or even a new activity to your sexual repertoire.

Valuing your relationship

One way of dealing with boredom is to look for new levels of excitement or new experiences you can share together. Another is to try to feel more positively about your present sex life and your present partner.

Start by looking at all the things you enjoy about having sex with your partner. When you are making love, concentrate on the physical sensations. Remember, these don't change – there is really nothing new out there.

All that really changes is your attitude towards sex with your partner. Even if you don't feel like sex, keep up the habit of affectionate contact, spontaneous hugs and kisses; don't withdraw physically from your partner. Above all, discuss your sex life with your partner and decide what is good and what might need changing.

Being open to change

Back at the time of one of the Kinsey reports in 1953, fewer than half the women interviewed had ever had sex in anything but the missionary position.

Couples are now generally much more innovative, but many people are still resistant to change, sometimes because they feel anything that isn't 'normal' (i.e. what they are used to) is wrong, or because they feel embarrassed about looking or feeling ridiculous should they try anything new.

Don't approach a new sexual activity as a challenge; it's meant to be a pleasure and if you don't both enjoy it, drop it but be positive that at least you tried it. And remember that most human sexual activity is reassuringly ordinary. Anything too wild or acrobatic is usually also way too uncomfortable to for most people to enjoy.

Accepting Sexual Reality

The early stages of a sexual relationship are magic – but they often have little to do with real life. No-one can live at that level of passion, excitement and intensity for long, and it is these very qualities that tend to fade the fastest. If this sexual high is what you continue to crave, then you are bound to be disillusioned.

Unless you are realistic enough to accept that intense passion is bound to fade, and learn to value the calmer waters of the next, less frenzied, stage, you may write off a perfectly good relationship as boring and keep jumping from one to another.

Don't reach for the unattainable

Sometimes disillusion sets in because you have a fantasy view of sex that could never live up to your expectations. The danger of these unrealistic expectations is that you may go from one relationship to another, each time convinced that each new one will prove to be the ultimate sexual experience and, each time as familiarity sets in, you will be disappointed. Instead, try to feel more positive about the way things actually are.

Living in the present

Learn to value your relationship as it is now. Try not to compare things as they are with past experiences. Comparisons are odious – and may be unfair. For instance, sex may not be as exciting now, but it is probably much more reliably enjoyable. As you mature sexually neither of you is as likely to suffer sexual or performance anxiety and it has been shown with women that orgasmic capability increases as they enter their thirties.

Keep in mind that with long term relationships each of you knows so much more of what the other likes and how best you can arouse and satisfy each other. And, even though your excitement and arousal levels may not be quite hitting the peak they used to, particularly for men, the lower levels probably allow you to significantly prolong your love-making.

Increase the pleasure

All truly satisfying sexual activity should ideally be a two-way process. Your partner's demonstrable pleasure in your lovemaking will be satisfying to you. And the more pleasure you give, and the more they enjoy sex with you, the more they will want to give pleasure to you.

Make use of the fact that you can intensify any physical sensation by focusing on it more. Everyone has experienced this with pain, but it works just as well with pleasure too. Learn (and help your partner) not to equate physical affection entirely with sex. It is a pleasure and a comfort in its own right, and helps keep your relationship alive. When you feel strong affection for someone, you will enjoy making love to them more.

There are many challenges that can affect a couple sexually. Major issues are likely to be achieving orgasm for women and erectile difficulties and premature ejaculation for men. But there can be long term issues of unresponsiveness by either partner or both and discrepancies in sex drive. This section also looks at the challenges introduced by ageing and disability.

Male and Female Sexual Problems

Unresponsiveness

It is quite possible to be intimate with an unresponsive partner, but it is almost certain not to be a fully satisfying experience for either party. Your partner is likely to view your sexual arousal as a direct response to them and proof that they are desirable. However, when a partner is not able to get aroused it may be for a variety of reasons, many that have nothing to do with how desirable their partner is or something lacking in the relationship.

Occasional unresponsiveness

Your sexual response is very much affected by circumstances. If you are on bad terms with your partner, for example, you won't readily respond sexually – and may feel used and very resentful if they want to have sex, say, to patch up a quarrel without having resolved the underlying issue properly first.

Sheer exhaustion can make you unresponsive; too many demands in other areas of your life can leave you with little energy or enthusiasm for sex. A busy couple, especially when they have children, may have to make sex a priority in their lives and plan for it if their sex life is not to disappear altogether. Some medications, alcohol, and even a lack of privacy or a fear of interruption can be contributing factors in unresponsiveness, too.

Long-term unresponsiveness

A few people have such a strong and permanent mental resistance to sex, or such deep physical problems, that make it makes it difficult for them to respond sexually to anyone. In such cases, professional therapy will probably be needed to overcome the problem.

Unresponsiveness, though, more often develops because of some long-standing problem or disappointment with sex in a relationship, which has resulted in one of the partners 'switching off' sexually. A programme of exercises designed to reawaken their sexual feelings may be helpful, provided they have the co-operation of a sympathetic partner. If they are to be successful it is important that there should be no unresolved issues between the partners, which may have contributed to the problem in the first place.

Learning to enjoy pleasure

Sexual responsiveness is impossible if you are blocking out all sexual feeling, however unconsciously. You have to learn to accept and enjoy these feelings and, to begin with, it is easier for you to do this if you are under no pressure to have sex. Avoid the genitals and intercourse at first to give you the chance to explore the sensual responses of your whole body. You and your partner simply take turns in focusing on what you feel and in enjoying the sensations. Ideally both of you should be naked, and you may want to have a warm bath or shower together first to relax you.

Try to practise this exercise, known as 'sensate focussing', for at least two weeks before moving on to the next stage. However, should sexual responsiveness develop faster than this then it may work out to let things take off instinctively. That aside, do beware of feeling pressurised into genital contact too easily, and be ready to retreat from it if either of you feel that you have moved too far too fast.

Genital pleasuring

When you and your partner feel completely comfortable with doing the previous exercise, move on to the next stage of the programme. This involves exploration and caressing of each other's genitals – but still no intercourse.

It is important for you to communicate as fully as possible with your partner and let them know when they touch you in a way which feels good. If you feel tense or anxious doing the exercise, erotic fantasies may help to distract you. Although orgasm isn't the aim of the exercise, if either of you do become highly aroused you can continue stimulation to orgasm.

Finally, if you wish, you can move on to having intercourse with your partner. Once again, experiment to discover the movements and positions that produce the most intense sensations before attempting to reach orgasm. It is important to share your feelings and emotions during each stage of these exercises.

Conflicting Sexual Tastes

Very often some new activity or approach to sex can give a real boost to a sexual relationship and, if you both enjoy it, it can strengthen the sexual bond between you. If your partner suggests a new sexual activity that you feel unenthusiastic about, try not to reject it out of hand. Don't think of it as something designed to test you, but as a possible new source of pleasure.

Do be guided by your own instinct, but recognise that it can be fine occasionally to do something you don't particularly like just to please your partner. But if you really dislike the idea of something, don't do it. And if you try something new and discover that you don't enjoy it, let your partner know how you feel.

Sexual Guidelines

The rules for any sexual activity should be:

- Do your best to try it but don't continue to do it unless you both enjoy it.
- Don't put pressure on each other to do anything that one of you finds distasteful.
- Don't do it if it is harmful.
- If relevant, practice safe sex measures to avoid infection.

Oral and anal sex

Oral and anal sex are among the most common areas where men's and women's desires conflict and so can be the most difficult activities for men and women to confront. The idea of anal intercourse, especially, tends to arouse strongly negative feelings. It can be painful, unless it is performed gently, sensitively and with plenty of lubricant. There is also a risk of infection then being carried by the penis to the vagina unless it is washed well in between times. With practice, however, this can be a very enjoyable experience for both partners.

Reluctance to try oral sex can also often be based in hygiene concerns; typically with odours and dealing with or consuming fluids. Men are often concerned with vaginal odours – though partners should like each other's tastes and smells, given a reasonable level of personal hygiene.

For women, greater acceptance of oral sex can come from having their partner agree to withdraw from her mouth before ejaculation and if only part of the penis is taken in to the mouth to avoid any fear of gagging or choking (this can best be controlled by the receiving partner keeping her hand on the shaft of the penis). Hygiene issues should be discussed as personal preferences may vary between partners.

Sex-Drive Discrepancy

Individual sexual needs vary widely – there is no such thing as a normal sex drive. Sex is not a competitive sport so it doesn't matter how often a couple make love. What does often matter, though, is when the needs of the individual partners do not match. If this is the case, it does not mean that one of you is over-sexed or that the other is under-sexed.

A man's sexual drive is at its height in his late teens and twenties. Women usually find their sexual needs increase as they grow sexually more experienced and confident, usually reaching a peak in their 30s. In everyone, sexual drive is likely to decrease somewhat with age.

Bridging a Sex-Drive Gap

If there is a substantial difference in a couple's sexual appetites, they will need to engage in various strategies to cope with this in order to minimise tensions in the relationship.

Masturbation is the most obvious and easiest solution to a sex drive gap.

When your partner suggests sex and you don't feel like it, don't reject the idea out of hand. Let your partner try to arouse you – stimulation can often trigger sexual appetite.

If you are the lower-drive partner, make the first move whenever you do feel like sex. Don't feel that this will only encourage your partner to make even more demands on you. Your initiative is more likely to make them feel they can back off a bit.

Use psychological stimulation – fantasy stimulated by erotic books, magazines, videos or material on the internet – to increase arousal. Never use sex as a weapon – either refusing it as punishment, or demanding it when you know your partner is not interested.

Male Sexual Problems

Erection Problems

Almost every man, at some time or another, has failed to get an erection when he wanted to, or lost it at a critical moment. This can happen because he is tired, has drunk too much, is on certain pharmaceutical drugs, is not in the mood, or has lost interest in sex or in his partner.

Very often, because erection is a reflexive psycho-physiological process over which a man has very little control, it can fail because anxiety interferes with the natural process. Nervousness of a new relationship, or guilt in an illicit one, can often induce 'performance anxiety'. Occasional failures are quite unimportant – unless they create an ongoing anxiety that then perpetuates the problem.

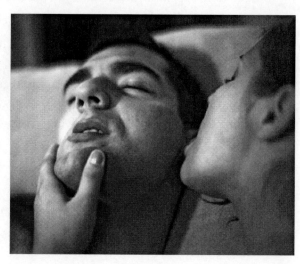

Coping with occasional erection failure

Things may improve if you resolve only to have sex when you feel in the right mood and really want to have it. Avoid casual encounters, at least until your sexual confidence improves. You may be less anxious with a partner you know and trust. If you lose your erection, don't overreact, but simply reassure your partner that it has nothing to do with her (or him). Meanwhile, stay close and intimate – there's plenty you can do to give and receive sexual pleasure without an erection.

Physical causes of erection problems

Until fairly recently it was thought that erection problems were all in the mind. Now it is recognised that, especially among older men, they sometimes have a physical cause. Diseases that affect the blood supply or nerves in the penis can also cause erection problems. So too can some drugs and operations.

Whatever the cause, anxiety about not being able to perform can clearly intensify the problem. If your erection fails frequently, even when you are masturbating, or if you have rarely, or never, had an erection, see your doctor, as there may be a physical cause which can benefit from a range of drugs developed to alleviate erectile disfunction (ED) – see 'Pharmaceutical Treatments'.

Treating a Long-Term Erection Problem

Exercises alone

When performance anxiety has built up over a long period, you may lose all confidence in your ability to keep an erection. This exercise is designed to reassure you that even if you lose an erection, gentle stimulation will bring it back.

- Stimulate your penis by hand until you achieve an erection.

- Before orgasm, stop the stimulation and let the erection subside completely.

- Masturbate again until you have a full erection. Then deliberately lose it again.

- Repeat this a third time, and then ejaculate if you feel like it. Use a lubricant to enhance sensation if it is difficult to regain your erection.

- Repeat this exercise every day until you feel confident that, at least when you don't have to worry about satisfying a partner, you can achieve an erection, lose it, and then regain it.

Exercises with a partner

Stage one: for this stage of treatment you need your partner to be willing to forego intercourse until you have gained more confidence.

- Spend time in bed together simply caressing, without worrying about whether or not you get an erection.

- Let your partner stimulate you manually (or orally) to erection, but not to orgasm.

- Let the erection subside, then have them stimulate you again. Repeat this until you are confident that you can lose and regain an erection in your partner's presence. Then they can bring you to orgasm.

- Practise stage one three or four times a week for three or four weeks, then move on to stage two.

Stage two: the next stage of the exercise is to learn to feel comfortable having intercourse.

- Your partner caresses your penis till you have a full erection.

- Your partner then guides your penis inside them. Begin moving gently, but if you feel you are nearing orgasm, withdraw.

- When you feel you can enjoy just being inside your partner, start to thrust more vigorously. If you lose your erection, or feel anxious, withdraw so that your partner can again stimulate you manually.

- As your confidence grows, experiment with other positions. Slow down and just enjoy being contained any time you feel anxious. Ejaculating inside your partner is the final step.

Pharmaceutical Treatments

Viagra (sildenafil), Cialis (tadalafil), Levitra (vardenafil) and drugs like them are available on prescription for erectile dysfunction (or ED), when a man finds erection difficult, short-lived or impossible. These drugs take about half an hour to work and can produce an erection as long as there is appropriate sexual stimulation.

They work by allowing an increase in blood flow to the sponge-like tissue in the penis (the corpora cavernosa, blood flow into which causes the actual erection, and the corpus spongiosum, which swells and thickens), causing the whole organ to swell and harden. The side effects of ED drugs appear to be minimal and stories about constant erections are rarely true (though medical help should be sought if an erection should persist for more than four hours). When a man is no longer sexually excited, his erection will usually go away as normal.

By contrast to Viagra, Cialis is designed to provide a longer duration during which an erection could occur, usually up to 36 hours, allowing for multiple sexual experiences with one pill. These sets of drugs are not chemically addictive (though they may bring about a degree of psychological dependence), nor are they technically aphrodisiacs, though a renewed ability to achieve an erection may have an effect on desire.

Premature Ejaculation

Men often worry because they feel they come too soon. Maybe their partner doesn't always reach orgasm, maybe they feel they would enjoy sex more if only they could hold off a little longer.

Premature ejaculation (PE) is a condition in which a man ejaculates earlier than he or his partner would like him to. Premature ejaculation is also known as rapid ejaculation, rapid climax, premature climax, or early ejaculation.

Most men experience PE at some point in their life. Premature ejaculation is a common complaint. It is only rarely caused by a physical problem. When it occurs early in a relationship, it is most often caused by anxiety and too much stimulation. Guilt and other psychological factors may also be involved. The condition may improve without treatment.

Learning to last longer

Make sure your partner is fully aroused before you enter them and, during intercourse, try to make less stimulating movements than thrusting. An even simpler approach is for you to ejaculate in intercourse, or by other means, and then try again. This second time around, the edge will have been taken off your excitement and you should be able to last longer.

Practice and relaxation should help you deal with the problem. Some men try to distract themselves by thinking nonsexual thoughts (such as naming sports players or concentrating on utility bills) to avoid getting excited too fast.

There are several helpful techniques you can try:

The "stop and start" method:

This technique involves sexually stimulating the man until he feels like he is about to reach orgasm. Stop the stimulation for about 30 seconds and then start it again. Repeat this pattern until the man wants to ejaculate. The last time, continue stimulation until the man reaches orgasm.

The "squeeze" method:

This technique involves sexually stimulating the man until he recognizes that he is about to ejaculate. At that point, the man or his partner gently squeezes the end of the penis (where the glans meets the shaft) for several seconds. Stop sexual stimulation for about 30 seconds, and then start it again.

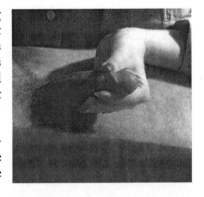

The person or couple may repeat this pattern until the man wants to ejaculate. The last time, continue stimulation until the man reaches orgasm.

In most cases, the man is able to learn how to control ejaculation through education and by practicing the simple techniques outlined. Chronic premature ejaculation may be a sign of anxiety or depression. A psychiatrist or psychologist can help treat these conditions.

Antidepressants, such as Prozac and other selective serotonin reuptake inhibitors (SSRIs), may be helpful because one of their side effects is to prolong the time it takes to reach ejaculation.

Delayed Ejaculation

Delayed ejaculation is the inability to ejaculate or the condition of there being persistent difficulty in achieving orgasm, despite the presence of normal sexual desire and sexual stimulation. It is normal for men to have delayed ejaculation from time to time and it is only considered a problem if it is ongoing or it is the source of stress for you or your partner.

Normally a man can achieve orgasm within a few minutes of active thrusting during sexual intercourse; whereas, a man with delayed ejaculation either does not have orgasms at all or cannot have an orgasm until after prolonged intercourse, which might last for 30–45 minutes or more. In most cases, delayed ejaculation presents the condition in which the man is able to climax and ejaculate during masturbation, but not during sexual intercourse.

Delayed ejaculation can be temporary or permanent. Possible causes of delayed ejaculation include certain chronic health conditions, surgeries and medications. Treatment for delayed ejaculation depends on the underlying cause.

Common psychological causes include:

- A strict religious background causing the person to view sex as sinful
- Lack of attraction for a partner
- Conditioning caused by unique or atypical masturbation patterns
- Traumatic events (such as being discovered in masturbation or illicit sex, or learning one's partner is having an affair)
- Some factors, such as anger toward the partner, may be involved

Physical causes may include:

- Use of certain drugs (such as Prozac, Mellaril, and Guanethidine)
- Neurological disease such as a stroke or nerve damage to the spinal cord or back

Female Sexual Problems

Overcoming Fear Of Penetration

Many women have the expectation that losing their virginity is a painful experience. It need not be. If it is, it is almost certainly because the expectation of fear has made you tighten up and this reaction makes intercourse more difficult. It may even, when a woman's fear is extreme, make it impossible – this is a condition known as vaginismus.

Nearly all of the fears a woman has about penetration are unfounded. Consult your doctor if intercourse really is impossible or feels painful; in the former case you may need counselling and, in the latter, there is nearly always some medical reason for it.

Fears about the hymen

Many women imagine that the hymen forms a complete barrier across their vaginal entrance. In fact, it is a thin membrane with an opening through which the menstrual flow can pass. If a woman uses tampons the opening will stretch, and by the time she has vaginal sex, the hymen has usually virtually disappeared.

Even if it is still intact, it is nearly always thin and elastic enough to rupture easily without causing much pain or bleeding. In older women the hymen may be less elastic, which may be a problem for the woman who first has sex late in life. In rare cases, it may not rupture completely, but leave small strands that can cause pain during vaginal intercourse.

Worries about vaginal size

It is very common to worry that your vagina may be too small. In fact, the vagina is rather like a concertina, with folded, elastic walls lined with ridged and folded skin.

Normally the vaginal walls are collapsed in on themselves, with no space between them, but they can stretch as much as necessary, so that the vagina can distend and shape itself considerably, from taking a penis during intercourse to allowing the passage of a child's head when giving birth.

Fear of pain

Intercourse should not be painful. The inner two-thirds of the vagina are sensitive to pressure, but is so insensitive to pain that a minor operation could be carried out in that area without an anaesthetic. If there is some discomfort when your partner enters you, it is probably either because your vaginal entrance has never been stretched sufficiently - by a finger or a tampon - and is still tight, or there is too little vaginal lubrication because you are not fully aroused.

If you stretch your vaginal opening with first one, then two fingers before intercourse begins, and use a lubricant when you are being penetrated by any object, there should be no discomfort. In some cases, pain may be caused by a medical condition, which may need checking by your doctor or gynaecologist.

Vaginismus

In rare cases, a woman can have such an intense fear of penetration or even of being touched in the genital area, that the muscles around her vaginal entrance tighten up and make intercourse difficult or impossible. This reaction, which is quite beyond the woman's control, may be the result of a sexually repressive upbringing, or it may develop after some painful or traumatic sexual experience. It is natural for someone who has been hurt to tense up against expected pain, and it is easy for this reaction to become a reflex.

The following exercise should help show you that penetration need not be painful and your anxiety should disappear; if not, do see you doctor for counselling:

Overcoming vaginismus
- First, examine your genitals with the aid of a hand mirror.
- Part the outer and then inner lips so that you can see the vaginal entrance. Touch it gently.
- Now lubricate a finger and insert just the tip. Bear down as you do this, as though trying to push something out of your vagina.
- Now push the finger in as far as the first joint, again bearing down. Relax with it inside you. If you feel the urge to tighten up, do so deliberately, tightening around your finger then relaxing again.
- When you are used to this, go on to insert the whole finger, and, finally, two fingers.
- Use plenty of lubrication and progress gradually, pushing the fingers in a little further each time you do the exercise.

SEXUAL CHALLENGES

Achieving Orgasm

Understanding orgasm

Orgasm is a reflex reaction, and like any reflex it can be inhibited, and its intensity can vary according to your psychological state. It is usually triggered by contractions of the clitoris and felt as a series of intense pulsations within the vagina. Nearly every woman can have an orgasm through stimulation of the clitoris alone, and others can reach it without any clitoral stimulation.

Faking orgasm

A great many women find it easier to fake orgasm than to admit that they do not have them. They may feel sexually inadequate if they had to admit it, or they may feel that they are protecting their partner's ego. If you want things to change, you need to develop your own responses through masturbation, or, if you have orgasms only when alone, by involving your partner and working with them to get what you need.

Learning to let go

Orgasm actually depends significantly on your ability to 'let go', to relax and let the sensations over take you. Tiredness, anxiety and tension can all make it more difficult for you to concentrate on your own feelings and reach orgasm. Feelings of resentment or anger towards your partner that make you hold back emotionally and inhibit your sexual responsiveness, can make it almost impossible. There are other emotional obstacles to orgasm, for example negative feelings about sex and, for some women, a fear of losing control. If you are the kind of person who likes to stay in control of yourself and your emotions, the idea of being carried away by orgasm can seem very frightening.

The right mood for orgasm

If you are in the right frame of mind, orgasm can be much easier to reach. Give yourself time and privacy so that you are not rushed or worried about being interrupted. Try not to discuss worries, or topics that usually cause friction, before having sex. If you are feeling tense, relaxation exercises may help.

Avoiding tension

Tension, often quite unconscious, is a common cause of a woman's failure to reach orgasm. Deep breathing exercises can help to overcome this. Practise taking slow, deep breaths, letting each one out slowly as a deep sigh, without forcing it. When you have practised this so often that it begins to feel natural, try doing it during masturbation. It will stop you holding your breath and tensing your muscles, and make you more likely to enjoy your sensations.

Fantasy and masturbation

If erotic fantasies have always helped you reach orgasm when you masturbate, they will probably do so during intercourse. Develop you fantasy library
with erotic literature and films made especially for women. Build up a set of
sexy memories that you can lose yourself in. Fantasy can play a crucial part
in achieving orgasm.

If you wish, and if it helps, you could try making your partner the central figure
in your masturbation fantasies, and then begin to carry these over into intercourse. This may help make you more sexually responsive with your partner.

Experimenting with positions

It is worth experimenting to find a sexual
position in which orgasm is easier – for many
women being on top is effective because it
enables them to have more control over the
movement and bring about a much greater
degree of clitoral stimulation. Try ones that
allow manual stimulation of the clitoris, too.

For some women, stimulation of a small
pressure-sensitive area about half way up the
front wall of the vagina – known as the G-
spot – can produce very intense sensations
which may trigger orgasm.

You may need to experiment with your
partner to find the G-spot and the kind of
stimulation that works best for you – there
are vibrators designed specifically for stimulating this area.

The 'bridge' technique

If you are not having orgasms during intercourse, but you can reach orgasm
when you masturbate, direct stimulation of the clitoris by you or your partner
during intercourse may be enough to tip you over into orgasm.

A variation of this is known as the bridge technique. This method requires that
either you or your partner stimulates your clitoris till you are close to orgasm
while his penis is inside you. The idea then is to try to get to the point where
his penile thrusting can give the final trigger into you achieving your orgasm.

Sex and Ageing

Sexual health is important at any age and the desire for intimacy is timeless. And, while sex may be experienced differently throughout the lifespan, it can still be fulfilling at any age. Studies confirm that no matter what your gender or sexual orientation, you can enjoy sex for as long as you wish. Naturally, sex at 80 may not be like it is at 20, but in some ways it can be better.

As you age, you become more aware of your body and how it responds to pleasure. Over time you get to know, and adapt, to what works best for you when it comes to your sex life.

Older people often have a great deal more self-confidence and self-awareness and feel released from the unrealistic ideals of youth and prejudices of others. With children having grown up and left the nest, and work often having become less demanding, couples may be better able to relax and enjoy one another without these life distractions.

For a number of reasons, many people worry about sex in their later years. Some older adults feel embarrassed, either by their aging bodies or by their body's ability to function, while others are affected by illness or the loss of a

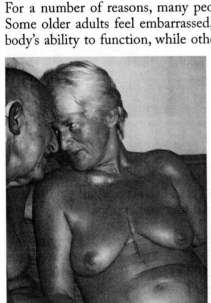

partner. If not attended to, a sexual lifestyle can slip away. You can avoid letting this happen by being proactive.

Whether you are seeking to restart or to improve your sex life, it's important to continue to be sexually active and seek professional help, should there be a problem.

There is much you can do to compensate for the normal changes that come with aging. With proper information and support, your later years can be an exciting time to explore both the emotional and sensual aspects of your sexuality.

Normal Age-related Sexual Changes

Ageing and women's sexual health

As women approach menopause, their estrogen levels decrease and they may notice changes in the vagina. The vagina shortens and narrows and the walls become thinner and stiffer and the ability to lubricate usually decreases, causing vaginal dryness.

Women may experience emotional changes as well. While some women may enjoy sex more without worrying about pregnancy, naturally occurring changes in body shape and size may cause others to feel less sexually desirable. These changes however, do not mean she can't enjoy having sex.

Ageing and men's sexual health

Testosterone plays a critical role in a man's sexual experience. Testosterone levels peak in the late teens and then gradually decline. As men get older, erectile dysfunction becomes more common and it may become difficult to maintain an erection strong enough for sexual intercourse.

By the age of 65, as many as 65% of men are likely to experience problems on at least some occasions. Common erectile issues include finding that it takes longer to get an erection; experiencing erections that are not as firm as they used to be; a smaller amount of ejaculate; losing an erection more quickly after orgasm and taking longer before an erection is again possible.

Extended foreplay may help with some of these problems and there are several medications available to help men achieve or sustain an adequate erection for sexual activity. Ultimately, learning new ways of expressing intimacy will be vital.

Medical conditions and sexual health

Any condition that affects your general health and well-being may also affect your sexual health. Illnesses that involve the cardiovascular system, high blood pressure, diabetes, hormonal problems, depression or anxiety, as well as the medications used to treat these conditions, can pose challenges to being sexually active. In addition, any surgical procedure that affects your pelvis and your central nervous system can have a temporary, but often significant, impact on your sexual response.

The body, however, is resilient. Given time to heal and some loving attention, you can become sexually responsive again. However, even the most serious health problems don't usually have to stop you from having a satisfying sex life.

Some typical conditions that affect intimacy include:

- **Arthritis** - Joint pain due to arthritis can make sexual contact uncomfortable. Joint replacement surgery and drugs may relieve this pain. Exercise, rest, warm baths, and changing the position or timing of sexual activity can be helpful.
- **Chronic pain** - Pain that continues or comes back on and off over time can be caused by other bone and muscle conditions, shingles, poor blood circulation, or blood vessel problems. The discomfort can, in turn, lead to sleep problems, depression, isolation, and difficulty moving around. These can interfere with intimacy between older people. Chronic pain does not have to be a necessary part of growing older and can often be treated.
- **Medications** - Some medications can cause sexual problems. These include some blood pressure medicines, antihistamines, antidepressants, tranquilizers, appetite suppressants, diabetes drugs, and some ulcer drugs like Ranitidine. Some can lead to impotence or make it hard for men to ejaculate. Some drugs can reduce a woman's sexual desire. Check with your doctor. She or he can often prescribe a different drug without this side effect.

Illness and sexuality

If you are ill, your sexuality is likely to take a back seat to other needs, at least temporarily. Pain, discomfort, medications or worry can overshadow your sexual desire. Remember, sexuality can be expressed in a variety of ways, though. Talk with your partner about other ways to be close during this time.

If you are the caregiver, the demands of caring for your partner may take a toll on your sexual desire. Find a way to set aside the caregiver role from time to time, and be a partner instead so that you can relax and feel nurtured by your partner. That way, you can enjoy a mutually satisfying sexual relationship.

Emotions and sexuality

Sexuality is often a delicate balance between emotional states and physical issues. How you feel may affect what you are able to do. For example, men may fear that erectile dysfunction will become a more common problem as they age. Unfortunately, simply being too concerned with that possibility can be self-fulfilling by causing enough stress to trigger the dysfunction. A woman, who is worried about how her changing body may result in her partner no longer finding her attractive, may become too inhibited to fully enjoy sex.

Stress is another factor that can often affect sexual desire and function. Older people experience stress just as younger people do but with the added concerns of age, illness and other lifestyle changes. These worries can cause sexual difficulties. Talking openly with your partner and seeing a counsellor or therapist can help.

Maintaining a healthy and active sexual lifestyle

There are several things you can do to help keep a healthy and active sexual life:

- Make sexual intimacy a priority (at least some of the time).

- Talk about and pay attention to your partner's needs and wants.

- Take time to understand the changes you both are facing as you age.

- Try different positions and new times, like having sex in the morning or afternoon, when you both may have more energy. Remember that sex does not have to include intercourse.

- Don't hurry - you or your partner may need to spend more time touching to become fully aroused. Relish the extra time spent.

- Masturbation is a sexual activity that some older people, especially unmarried, widowed, or divorced people and those whose partners are ill or away, may find satisfying.

Benefits of sex as we age

As a senior, the two things that may have brought the greatest joy, children and career, will likely no longer be providing the same focus in everyday life. Personal relationships often take on a new even greater significance, and sex can be an important way of connecting. Sex has the power to:

- Improve mental and physical health. Sex can burn fat, cause the brain to release endorphins, and drastically reduce anxiety.

- Increase lifespan. Through its health-improving benefits, a good sex life can add years to your life.

- Enhance relationships. Sex is a way to express the closeness of a relationship.

- Offer sanctuary. Sex gives you a chance to escape from the sometimes harsh realities of life.

Though physical and emotional changes can affect the ability to have sex in the same way throughout life, many men and women actually enjoy sex even more as they grow older.

It may not be possible to get back to the sexual activity experienced in your twenties but you can still find ways to optimise your body's responses for very satisfying sexual experiences now.

Sex and Disability

Disability is one of the last remaining taboos about sexuality. Those who have no major disabilities tend to know little about the issues of disability and sexuality; many know nothing at all. However, in most cases disability need not prevent a person from enjoying and expressing sexual feelings.

Historically, the media have emphasised certain aspects of sexual relations, creating the image of an unattainable and unrealistic ideal of attractiveness. The reality is that people are not perfect and everyone has some form of physical, psychological, emotional and/or social limitations or imperfection. Short- or long-sightedness, slight deafness, physical imperfections and personal problems and insecurities are all common, though clearly minor, forms of disability, which can affect people's daily lives and their relationships.

Severe forms of disability, such as visual or hearing impairment, paralysis, multiple sclerosis, muscular dystrophy, cerebral palsy, critical shortness of stature, learning difficulties, and mental illness, are often treated differently by society. However, they are common (severe disabilities affect 10% of the population), they have an enormous impact on the way people live their lives and, like the more minor forms of disability, they do not reduce basic human needs for sex and love, nor for self-confidence, independence and intimate personal relationships.

Learning difficulties

People with learning difficulties are not forever childlike. They mature physically and have sexual drives. Parents, siblings, teachers, carers and society in general sometimes find this difficult to accept and may also fear that the disabled person may be sexually and socially exploited. Sex education for those with learning difficulties and for others about learning difficulties has been shown to improve understanding.

Overcoming limitations

Relationships in general and sex in particular can be more difficult for those who have some form of disability. The difficulties range from the specific limitations imposed by the particular disability to broader issues of the way disability and sexuality are perceived by others. Very often it is these perceptions and attitudes that create the obstacles; although in many cases recognising that obstacles exist can be part of the way to overcome them.

Social factors

Some people find it difficult to recognise those with disabilities as sexual beings. This can be acutely damaging to others' confidence and self-esteem.

Having a relationship with a disabled person can mean taking on all the prejudices that society may have against disability. However, it can still be highly satisfying and exciting for both partners.

The UK's Sex Maniacs' Ball is in fact a charity event to support The Outsiders Club, which provides information and opportunities for integration for people with disabilities. Many people with disabilities attend...

Sex education for disabled children tends to be inadequate or non-existent. Disability also tends to limit opportunities for mixing with peers, which is the other main source of sexual learning among children and teenagers. Even editions of the media designed for the disabled, such as tape recorded newspapers for the blind, are usually edited and tend to take a cautious approach to sexual issues, once more restricting access to information about sex, although more and more organisations are starting to address this matter.

... **even blindness** did not stop this transvestite from attending the ball

Dating agencies too, are often less than welcoming and helpful to people with disabilities, although increasing numbers of organisations now provide a specialised service.

Many homes and institutions for people with disabilities are recognising that their clients have sexual needs and are training staff to address this issue in a realistic way.

Physical factors

Sex is an important and life-enhancing force. It can be a source of health and healing as well as pleasure. If it is practised with due respect for the limitations imposed by a particular disability, it can ease pain, relieve anxiety and preoccupations and build confidence. After an accident that causes disability it can provide reassurance and aid recovery.

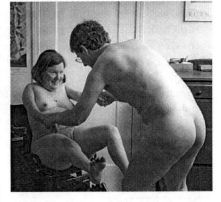

Physical disabilities can interfere with sex, but by being open-minded about sexual alternatives and communicating with partners, sex can become just as varied, sensuous, adventurous and intimate as for people with no form of disability. There is much more to sex than vaginal-penile penetration. Even where this is possible, experimenting with other options – while being realistic about limitations – can be exciting and rewarding.

Loss of feeling in one part of the body can produce heightened sensation in other parts. Erogenous zones can often be transferred and new erotic sensations can be discovered. Where there is some feeling this can be enhanced with the use of sex aids such as vibrators, which produce stronger stimulation.

Adapting to a lack of mobility of strength can involve experimenting with different positions, which do not put strain on weak or painful parts of the body but make other parts accessible and give room for movement. Certain positions also require less energy, to help deal with fatigue or cardiac problems.

Blindness and deafness do not inhibit the other senses, which can provide clear and intimate ways of communicating needs, pleasure or appreciation.

Experimenting with positions can also ease difficulties with muscle spasm. In some cases, muscle-relaxants can help.

SEX AND CULTURE

5

S.J. XII 83   RECREATION #4

Where sex is concerned, there is nothing new under the sun. Every sexual act, every sensation and every emotion has likely been experienced by millions of people time and again since the world began.

Nothing new under the sexual sun...

masturbation

Some 5,000 years ago, disciplining sexual relationships was one of the most fundamental and reliable ways of disciplining people. This was important in the early days of civilization: a stable society could not exist without rules. Initially, the state's interference in sexual matters was limited to areas of public concern – legitimacy, inheritance, and population control – and this was as true in China and India as in the ancient Near East.

Religion brought about a change. In religions that had many gods, those gods were rarely in total agreement about what was right and what was wrong. It was only when the idea of one god emerged that ideas of absolute right and absolute wrong became entrenched, so that religious morality and secular law became inseparable.

69/soixante-neuf

This was what happened to ancient Hebrew society.

anal sex

Like every other tribe of the Near East, the Hebrews needed to increase their numbers for their own security. Since the Lord also required them to '*Be fruitful and multiply*' (*Genesis* 1:22), the laws they passed to help them achieve this end took on the sanctity of Holy Writ. When they banned all forms of unproductive sex, the ban also had the force of religious, as well as social, law. The result was that when Judaism, and later Christianity, developed, the bans imposed for a specifically practical purpose at a specific point in time were carried forward through the centuries as part of a religious package. That is why, until only a few decades ago (and often until today, in the case of the Vatican), contraception was regarded as morally wrong, homosexuality as unnatural, and masturbation as a sin.

homosexual fellatio

It is salutary to remember that even today's most emancipated lovers are still, to some extent, conforming to – or breaking – rules laid down thousands of years ago for reasons that had very little to do with the most intimate and personal of human encounters.

orgy

The Cerne Abbas Giant, Dorset UK

Before Records Existed

Before recorded history, men and women seem to have been more or less equal. In the thousands of years leading up to the Neolithic revolution – between about 10,000 BC and 3,000 BC – man had been the hunter and woman the gatherer of plants and small living edibles such as snails, turtles and crabs. Location and climatic conditions dictated whose contribution to the food supply – and therefore whose tribal status – was superior at any given time.

It was the woman who gave birth to children, of course, but there is no evidence to suggest that prehistoric human beings knew anything about the biological role of the father. This was a role that could not easily be deduced from the communal pattern of everyday cave living, when the only calendar was the moon, and nine months in relation to life expectancy then was almost as long, relatively, as two years would seem today. It was a simple fact of life that the human female, like the wild mare or the reindeer cow, should be either pregnant or nursing for most of her adult years; it was natural for a man and woman, stag and hind, ram and ewe, to enjoy the act of sex without seeing anything but the physical fulfilment of the moment.

Then came the Neolithic revolution, when the sheep and the goat, the cow and then the pig, were tamed and brought into the farmyard; when man no longer had to hunt them but instead watched over them anxiously, waiting for them to drop the lambs or kids that could increase or replenish the flocks, the same animals day after day, all year round.

Now, for the first time in human history, man had the opportunity to sit and observe closely, to think and to make connections.

What must have been traumatic was not only the discovery of the male contribution to procreation, but its potential scale. A single ram could impregnate over 50 ewes.

With comparable power, what could man not achieve?

The men who emerged from the Neolithic era into this period of recorded history were very different from those who had gone before, those who had believed women to be the creative force. There may have been other reasons for this change – archaeology offers no answers to what went on in the prehistoric mind – but these new men had the kind of assurance, arrogance and authority that spring not from useful toil nor knowledge of a good job well done, but from the kind of revelation – beyond argument, beyond questioning – that can make men feel like gods.

It was now possible for a man to look at a child and call him 'my son'; to look at a woman and call her 'my wife'. By Biblical times, when it become necessary for civilization to make laws, write them down and enforce them, those laws made it clear that even the 'free' woman, whether she was Egyptian, Babylonian or Hebrew, had little more status than that of a slave; the property of her father during childhood and then of her husband from adolescence on. It was a situation that was to persist throughout much of the world until the 20th century and, in some societies, still does.

Sex and the Hebrews

Virtually all the Hebrew laws on marital fidelity, legitimacy, incest and prostitution were designed to satisfy the requirements of fertility. By the first century BC, it could be said that: *'The law recognizes no sexual connections except the natural union of husband and wife, and that only for the procreation of children'* (Josephus, quoted in S.W. Baron, *A Social and Religious History of the Jews* (1967) vol. II, p. 219).

Prostitution was practised in the Near East and there were even male cult prostitutes in early Judah but, as time passed, the Jews came to hate prostitutes with a feeling that was at best intemperate, at worst obscene. The problem, of course, was that, when a woman slept with many men, no man could lay claim to her sons.

There were numerous measures designed to reinforce the patriarchal principle, and they were accompanied by thundering denunciations of all kinds of non-productive sex. Where in Babylon homosexuality had been perfectly acceptable, the Lord had told the children of Israel:

'If a man lies with a male as with a woman, both of them have committed an abomination; they shall be put to death, their blood is upon them.'

A Jewish wedding in Portugal, from an 18th century engraving

The Daughters of Judah in Babylon (detail), by Herbert Gustave Schmalz (19th century)

And, without any perceptible change of tone:

'If a man lies with a beast, he shall be put to death; and you shall kill the beast. If a woman approaches any beast and lies with it, you shall kill the woman and the beast.' (*Leviticus* 20:13, 15-16)

Viewed from the perspective of fertility, then, abortion was also considered a crime and contraception a sin against holy writ. To strike a pregnant woman might bring about any punishment from a simple fine to a *'life for life, eye for eye, tooth for tooth'* (*Exodus* 21:22-24).

As in most societies, Hebrew laws had their logical and practical beginnings. But in most societies, the laws are amended to suit changing times. Hebrew law, however, could not be changed since it was believed to be divinely inspired and therefore not open to amendment. As a result, and as the centuries passed and Christianity emerged from Judaism, these ancient taboos were transmitted to the Western world in the form of articles of faith.

'A good wife who can find?' asked the *Book of Proverbs* 3,000 years ago (*Proverbs* 31:10ff) and, given what the men of the Near East expected of a good wife, it was an understandable question.

What they did not require were beauty, charm or sexuality. Beauty was vanity, charm deceitful and sexuality actively dangerous. What they actually wanted was fruitfulness. *'Like arrows in the hand of a warrior are the sons of one's youth, happy is the man who has his quiver full of them!'* (*Psalms* 127:4-5).

In addition to ensuring the succession, a wife's duties included seeking wool and flax and food, rising before dawn to care for her family and instruct her servants, buying fields and planting vineyards, keeping accounts, helping the needy, spinning, weaving and clothing her household in scarlet and herself in linen and purple, making and selling linen garments, and working late into the night when the need arose. In addition, said the Book of Proverbs, she had to look on the future with optimism and to be unfailingly wise, kind and conscientious.

As a reward, she was entitled to share her husband's favour with his secondary wives and concubines. Most Hebrews had several of these, although none approached the record of King Solomon, who ruled from c.955 to 935 BC and was said to have had 700 wives and 300 concubines.

In Babylon, by contrast, a man was not allowed to have more than one fully-accredited wife at a time, though he might have any number of concubines; if his legal wife turned out to be barren, it was up to her to supply him with a substitute child bearer.

Like the good wives of Egypt and Babylon, the Hebrew wife could also look forward to being divorced out of hand if she offended her husband. And she could be stoned to death if she was even suspected of taking a lover. In every way that counted, all wives were unequivocally inferior to their husbands.

Sex and the Greeks

The Athenians, almost contemporaries of the Hebrews, had different problems. Athens was over-, rather than under-, populated, and more concerned with discouraging than encouraging fertility. It did this less by discriminatory legislation than by attitudes of mind.

One of the most noticeable traits of sexual life in Athens from the sixth to the fourth centuries BC was the Athenians' dislike of women, whom they regarded as irrational, oversexed and morally defective. Many Athenians would have preferred not to marry at all but, as the poet Hesiod put it:

'He who evades, by refusing marriage, the miseries that women bring upon us, will have no support [children] in the wretchedness of his old age... On the other hand, he whose fate it is to marry may perhaps find a good and sensible wife. But even then he will see evil outweigh good all his life.' (Hesiod, *Theogeny* 585-612)

Erotic scenes were often depicted on Greek pottery, such as this vase c.500 BC

In such a climate, it was hardly surprising that women had fewer civil or political rights than slaves, having to submit throughout their lives to the absolute authority of their nearest male relative.

A woman received little serious education and spent her days in the women's quarters; she rarely ate with her husband and never when he had guests. If it was necessary to beget an heir in a hurry, she was expected to have intercourse with him at least three times a month until she became pregnant. A husband could repudiate his wife with the greatest of ease, and was legally obliged to do so if, by some miracle of ingenuity, she contrived to commit adultery.

Toward the end of the fourth century BC, however, and with more conviction in the third, Athenian men began to discover a greater interest in women, though not in wives, and turned instead to hetairai, or courtesans.

'We have hetairai for our pleasure,' said one statesman, *'concubines for our daily needs, and wives to give us legitimate children and look after the housekeeping.'* (Demosthenes (attr.) in *Nearam* 122)

One of the special charms of the hetairai was that they excelled in all the things the Athenians had spent centuries in preventing their wives from learning about: not only sex but also culture, literature, art and politics. The hetairai were successful women in a man's world and that was to be true of their successors, worldwide, for most of the next 2,000 years.

Courtesans have usually had a much better time of it than wives.

The well-educated Greek male found the company of adolescent boys much more to his taste. This was a socially-acceptable preference during the two centuries when pederasty flourished, since the Greeks sturdily maintained that it was a branch of higher education, with an older man making himself responsible for his protégé's moral and intellectual development.

Such relationships had three virtues in Greek eyes:

- they helped to channel and control the homosexual phase common in adolescent boys the world over;
- they gave grown men experience of tenderness that they rarely found within the matrimonial home; and
- they delayed the time when younger partners began to think of marriage and making their own contributions to the overpopulated state.

Scholars cannot agree whether this Pure Love was, or was not, wholly spiritual, but all the indications are that, as with the Courtly Love of later times, Greek pederasty was one of those sentimental ideals that are pure in theory but a good deal less so in practice.

Sex in Egypt

To say that men have been dominant in the great majority of societies since written records began may be to ignore the personal relations between the sexes, but by cultivating a way of life that legally and socially favoured the male, the people of the ancient Near East also created a climate in which it was easy for men to dominate. When all social forces conspired to anchor a wife to her home, to limit her acquaintances with her family, and to forbid her to appear before strangers, the result was to imprison her mind as effectively as her body. Concubines, who were servants as much as bedfellows, were little better off.

There were, however, other women who were not so limited. Prostitution, though maybe not 'the oldest profession', as is often claimed – that was likely witch-doctoring – carried no stigma in Sumeria, Babylon or Egypt; there were even sacred prostitutes whose role included that of mediators between worshippers and the gods.

Detail from a 3,000-year-old Egyptian papyrus, depicting a prostitute with her client

Sex and the Romans

Ironically, it was the success of the hetairai in Greece that encouraged wives in Rome to take a hand in their own emancipation. Facing the same generalised dislike on the part of their menfolk as the *hetairai* had overcome in Athens, they had, however, neither the inclination nor the talents to use sex as a means to their own ends. They chose instead to declare war, turning themselves into perhaps the most obstreperous group of women in all history.

Rootless and restless, the women of Rome's upper classes had a freedom rare in the ancient world, but which was also of little use to them. They were permitted to do a great deal as long as they did nothing actually constructive. Legal disabilities and social pressures combined to build around them a kind of intellectual rampart within which they could think and act almost as they wished. But they could not break it, in case they tried to influence others, to trespass on man's preserves, even – unthinkably – to shape the political and imperial policies of Rome itself. They contented themselves, therefore, with spending money, beautifying themselves (usually not for their husbands but for their lovers), taking to one of the new fashionable new religions, or suing for divorce.

'Her score is mounting,' remarked the poet Juvenal sourly of the dashing divorcee of his day. 'She has had eight husbands in five winters. Write that on her tombstone!' (Juvenal, Sixth Satire, 227–8).

The Roman wife's right to part from her husband, unmatched in the ancient world, was not the product of considered legislation but had evolved from the fact that Rome recognised three types of marriage: the grand, ceremonial one; the simpler, civil ceremony; and the marriage by *usus* or simple cohabitation.

Erotic scene from Pompeian mosaic

After a year of living together in continuous association the couple legally became husband and wife, the woman only then ceasing to be a member of her father's family and entering into that of her husband.

There was, however, a loophole that proved large enough for a fair degree of independence to slip through. To the literal Roman mind, 'continuous association' meant precisely that; if a woman absented herself from her common-law husband's house for three successive days and nights the qualifying period had to begin all over again. With careful timing and a little ingenuity, a woman could postpone almost indefinitely the moment when she became legally subject to her husband instead of to her, usually more sympathetic, father. It suited the wife, and it suited her father, too, because for as long as his daughter remained 'in his hand', he also retained control over her assets and was able to reclaim a substantial portion of her dowry if the marriage failed. To the property-conscious Roman, the temptation was irresistible.

There is little doubt that many well-educated, intelligent, bored women did run wild, and the question is why, in a society that was essentially masculine, were they allowed to get away with so much for so long?

Perhaps the main reason was that there were not enough women to go round. Rome, like most of the ancient world, was obsessed with sons. Girls were a burden, and the fate of all too many girl children was infanticide. It was a short-sighted policy, since it meant that the competition for wives was stiff.

A man attracted to marriage by the prospect not only of a son and heir but a useful transfusion of money in the form of the dowry, was forced to recognise that, no matter how he subsequently felt about his wife, if he wanted to keep the dowry, the only sure way of doing so was by keeping her, too.

Where children were concerned, the economical Roman husband had little desire for more than two or at most three. There was plenty of contraceptive advice available for those who sought it, but in view of the general tenor of relationships between husbands and wives, it is possible that the form most widely used was the simplest and most reliable of all – abstention. As the centuries passed, the birth rate continued to fall to such a dangerous level that it became necessary for the Senate to pass laws designed to stabilise family life and fertility.

The laws, though, had no effect. The Romans' failure to raise families had as much to do with involuntary as with voluntary factors. Mortality rates were high and childbearing years correspondingly few.

Most Romans, like the people of the Palaeolithic era, could expect to die before they reached the age of 30. As 10% of the population of Italy was crammed into Rome itself, they were helpless prey for any marauding virus. Even when a woman did conceive, she frequently suffered miscarriage, or suffered difficulties at parturition or from postnatal infections.

There were also other, invisible hazards directly related to sterility and/or impotence that, ironically enough, affected not the poor but the free-living rich, who almost certainly suffered from chronic lead poisoning, which (as well as learning and behavioural disorders, anaemia, seizures and death) can cause sterility in men and bring about miscarriages and stillbirths among women. The Romans absorbed lead from the water that ran through their lead pipes, from cups and cooking pots, from cosmetics such as the white lead women used for face powder, and from their wine, which was often sweetened with a grape syrup boiled down in lead-lined pots.

They drank a lot of wine but almost certainly to no avail since alcohol (in small quantities) may increase sexual desire but detracts from sexual performance in larger ones. Scientists today have shown that excessive alcohol also has a direct toxic effect on the testes, which can bring about a significant decline in production of the male sex hormone, testosterone.

That was not all. Every time a Roman went to the public baths (which he did daily), he further endangered his sex life and his fertility. The water at the baths was sometimes so hot, said Seneca, that one would scarcely condemn an erring slave to be washed alive in it as a punishment.

The normal temperature of the testicles is lower than that of the rest of the body, and modern research has shown that a temperature raised only to normal body temperature (36.9°C or 98.6°F) is enough to inhibit sperm production. (Long cold baths, rather than long hot ones, can significantly increase an otherwise infertile patient's sperm production in a matter of two to three weeks.)

Erotic scene from Pompeian wall painting

Too much wine, too many hot baths, unsatisfactory and unproductive sex... these are not usually considered factors that might bring down an empire.

But it was a shortage of manpower, combined with a devalued currency, that opened the gates of Rome to the barbarians and the destruction of what had once been the most elegant, logical, political and social edifices yet then devised by humankind.

Sex and the Chinese

In Asia, as in the West, society was male dominated. Here, too, humans were concerned with fertility but, instead of discouraging any sexual practices that might interfere with it, they took the more constructive approach of actively encouraging those that might promote it. Sex was part of the pattern of life, and – in its perfected form – made a contribution to the expansion of the spirit.

In China, the philosophy of Taoism held that long life and happiness depended on living in perfect harmony with nature by balancing – in the individual as in the cosmos – the complementary forces of yin (yielding) and yang (thrusting). Taoism held that humanity had been led away from the natural path by its concentration on mind and will, and the disciplines that led back to it were necessarily disciplines of the body.

Sexual intercourse was the human equivalent of interaction between yin and yang, even though the parallels were drawn not in the direct fleshly sense of vagina and penis, but more subtly as yin essence (the moisture lubricating a woman's sexual organs) and yang essence (man's semen). These were interdependent; to absorb yin was to strengthen yang.

The Chinese actively encouraged sexual practices to promote fertility. Here, a young wife or concubine stimulates her lover's penis with a feather to develop or prolong his erection

Since intercourse was one of the main highways to heaven, there was good and valid reason to offer guidance to travellers. The Chinese did so in the world's earliest (dating back from about 200 BC onward), most comprehensive and most detailed sex manuals, which were intended as much for women as men and, indeed, often given to a bride before her wedding. They covered every aspect of the subject and proved that here, as in many other areas of human life and experience, the modern world actually has little to teach the ancients.

A woman's yin essence was believed to be inexhaustible, whereas man's yang essence was limited in quantity and precious: it had to be regularly strengthened by a woman's yin and was on no account to be squandered. The average man was recommended to allow himself a climax not more than once every three days in spring; twice a month in summer; never in winter.

There were special yin-yang rules to be followed when a man wished to father a child. His yang essence had to be at peak potency, built up over a number of sexual encounters without ejaculating until the final, all-important, occasion. The handbooks emphasised that the preliminary yin nourishment should come from several different women. *'If in one night he can have intercourse with more than 10 women it is best.'* (Yu-fang-pi-chueh, *I-shin-po* 28 XIX).

It was essential, though, that he aroused each and every one of them to orgasm, which was when a woman's essence reached maximum potency. To the Chinese, uniquely, a woman's orgasm was as important to her male partner as to herself.

Unsurprisingly, perhaps, in view of all the sexual activity required by a man, aphrodisiacs were much in demand, notably the 'bald chicken drug' and the 'deer horn potion'.

And the brothel trade flourished to service those polygamous husbands who were unable to afford more than half a dozen wives. These 'green bowers', however – havens of calm and relaxation, of good food and entertaining company – served another purpose. The conscientious Chinese husband very often went to them, not for sexual intercourse but to escape from it.

Sex in the Islamic World

The Chinese, until flexible Taoism gave way to straitlaced neo-Confucianism in the later Middle Ages, rejoiced in having as many wives and concubines as they could afford.

In India, too, polygamy was practised, though mainly by the rich. But it was the caliphs and, later, the sultans of the Muslim world who were to supply the West with the most enduringly exotic of the Arabian Nights' dreams – the harem.

In the seventh century AD, the Prophet Muhammad preached a visionary, composite of Arab, Jewish and Christian beliefs, which brought unprecedented unity to the nomadic peoples of the arid peninsula that lies between the Red Sea and the Persian Gulf. Within 30 years, the armies of the Prophet had conquered not only much of the Mediterranean coast of Africa but all of Persia, too.

From desert Arabs to rulers of one of the most sophisticated empires the world had ever seen, this was an enormous step in little more than a generation. From both choice and necessity, the Arabs adopted many of the customs of their predecessors and also of the empire of Byzantium, their cultured (and hated) new neighbour.

The Byzantine habit of keeping women veiled and segregated was imported into polygamous Islam, where it overturned the Prophet's original desire to improve the lot of women, and made them virtual prisoners. Soon, polite society knew only two kinds of women: the courtesan, usually a singer, usually a foreigner, witty, beautiful, talented and inconstant; and the respectable lady, visible in public as no more than a pair of downcast eyes in an all-covering tent of black draperies.

Although such a situation sounded the death knell of romantic love, it had the opposite effect as far as the idea of romantic love was concerned. The Arabs had a strongly poetic streak and there soon developed an idea of 'pure love' that turned segregation into a positive benefit. The real woman within the robes, within the prison of her harem, scarcely mattered. To the poet she was a creature of the imagination, untouchable, unreachable, a dream. Her (enforced) chastity became so important in the idea of pure love that it would have been a betrayal for the lover to satisfy his passion, even if he could.

In truth, if there had been the remotest likelihood of the opportunity arising, the whole concept of pure love would have collapsed. It was, in effect, a masculine game, designed to satisfy intellectualised masculine emotions, but it came to be seen as something ennobling, a love that was a creative, spiritual source of inspiration. By one of the more entertaining quirks of history, it was a dream that was to be imported, though in a somewhat amended form, into the West during the later centuries of the Middle Ages, known as Courtly Love with very odd results.

A vision of the harem was also imported into the West by returning pilgrims and Crusaders. This was another kind of dream, one of perfumed air, tinkling fountains, soft music, seductive and submissive beauties, idyllic sex – and it resembled the real thing not at all. This time, it was a dream that was to remain a dream, wistfully cherished by northern knights bound by the chill fetters of their own lovelessly monogamous marriages.

Humay and Humayan (detail), from the Shahname (1396), a Persian literary text

Sex in India

India, like China but unlike the West, recognized that sensual pleasure was important to human happiness and the human spirit. Indeed, the Hindu ethos identified it as one of the four aims in life, integrally related to the concept of correct behaviour. Success in the first three – morality, material wellbeing and pleasure – was believed to advance the individual toward the fourth and ultimate goal, release from the cycle of rebirth.

Erotic carvings cover the surviving Khajuraho temples built in the 10th century

For Hindus, therefore, as for the Chinese, sex was akin to a religious duty, not one that would put the man immediately in tune with the infinite, but one of the least taxing and most enjoyable ways of improving his spiritual rating. And again like the Chinese, Hindus had sex manuals, the best known of which is the *Kama Sutra* (c. third century AD), but there was one distinct difference. Although early Hinduism was a sophisticated and fatalistic religion that often appeared callous to outsiders, the *Kama Sutra* acknowledged something that had been largely ignored by the Chinese – the possibility of there being more to sex than simply the mechanics of foreplay and intercourse.

Love was a recurring theme. The *Kama Sutra* identified four different varieties of love and the author, Vatsyayana, frequently interrupted himself in the middle of one of his lectures on the nine different ways of moving the *lingam* (penis) inside the *yoni* (vagina), or the steps a man with a small *lingam* could take to satisfy a woman with a large *yoni*, to remind his readers that true lovers needed no rules to govern them, no teacher, that is, but instinct.

Even so, there was little of the poetic or romantic about the *Kama Sutra*; the ruthlessly self-centred nature of the Hindu concept of *karma* (fate) saw to that. Hindus were no more enthusiastic than anyone else about one man seducing another man's wife, but according to the *Kama Sutra* it could be justified by love. It was acceptable for a woman to influence her husband on her lover's behalf. It was acceptable, too, that if the woman could be relied on to help her lover kill her husband, they would both inherit his riches. But lacking motives of self-interest that could be defined in terms of the second of the four aims, mere sexual appetite was no excuse.

The very existence of the eternal triangle in India at this time was almost certainly a product of the marriage system. The law books decreed that a bride should, ideally, be one-third of the age of her husband, because Indians, in common with many other peoples, regarded girls as naturally libidinous and preferred to marry them off at the earliest possible moment. Eight for a girl and 24 for her husband were the ages suggested, although the bride did not go to live with her husband until she reached puberty and was then introduced to the sexual side of a marriage with care.

Even so, a wife was usually still only in her 30s when her sons were grown up and her husband an old man, in relation to life expectancy there at the time. When he died, she would be doomed to the hell of Indian widowhood, forbidden to remarry, forced to sleep on the ground, allowed only one savourless meal a day, and expected to devote all her waking hours to prayer and religious rites. The *Kama Sutra* was probably right to assume that, in the brief intervening spell of relative freedom before this fate overtook her, a woman would be tempted to succumb to the lure of a lover.

A prince taking part in group sex, described by Vatsyayana in his *Kama Sutra*, Bundi Style (that edition c. 1800)

The expulsion of Adam and Eve (detail), by Tommaso Masaccio (15th century)

The Early Christians

Although Christianity, in most senses, was gentler and more tolerant than the Judaism from which it developed, the attitude of the Christian church towards sexuality developed into one of the most repressive in history.

Other societies had condemned, with varying degrees of severity, adultery (usually), contraception (rarely), abortion (sometimes), homosexuality (sometimes), female infanticide (rarely), zoophilia (sometimes), masturbation (never).

The Christian church proscribed them all.

Other societies had suggested suitable frequencies for marital intercourse. 'Three times a month', said the Greeks; 'every day for the unemployed', said the Jews, 'twice a week for labourers, once a week for ass drivers'.

The Christian Church said 'never, unless children were desired'. Other societies had regarded sex as pleasurable, in any position.

To the Christian Church, pleasure was sinful and only the missionary position acceptable.

After the fall of Rome, as reading and writing became the preserve of the monasteries, much in the way of doctrine, that would otherwise have been discussed and argued over, passed straight into the realms of orthodoxy. As a result, the words of the Church Fathers – dedicated but arrogant men who fervently held that what they said was right, because it was they who said it – took on an aura of revealed truth.

Much of what the modern Western world still understands as 'sin' stems not from the teachings of Jesus of Nazareth, nor even from the tablets handed down from Sinai, but from the early sexual vicissitudes of a handful of such men as St Jerome and St Augustine who lived in the twilight days of imperial Rome.

Sex, however hedged by prohibitions, had never actually been held to be sinful until St Paul advanced the theory that celibacy was superior to marriage because, then, no worldly obligations intervened between worshipper and his Lord. For him and his successors – even, or especially, for those whose earlier life had been anything but celibate – sexual abstinence became an indicator of divine grace. Jerome, Tertullian and Ambrose, looking back, viewed the sexual act as being repugnant, degrading, indecent, obscene.

There was an unspoken consensus that God might have found a more seemly way to ensure the perpetuation of the human race and it was St Augustine who, setting his mind to the problem, came up with an explanation.

Sex in the Garden of Eden, if it had ever taken place, would have been cool and rarefied, a matter of utilising the mechanical equipment supplied by the Creator to fulfil the requirements of the reproductive process. But Adam and Eve's fall into the sin of disobedience and lapse from grace was reflected in the sudden and wilful activity on the part of their genitals.

The hypocritical clergy were often the subject of satire, such as is depicted in this 17th century German engraving

Augustine believed that this explained the perversity of the human sexual organs, the intractable nature of the carnal impulse, and the shame aroused by intercourse. Lust and sex were integral to the doctrine of Original Sin, and every act of intercourse performed by Adam and Eve's descendants after the Fall carried the burden of that original evil.

Setting out to validate the Church Fathers' emotional revulsion against sex, Augustine succeeded in justifying it in a way that satisfied both faith and intellect. But by effectively transforming every act of sex into a sin, he had an incalculable effect on the lives of future generations.

Christian Marriage

St Paul and St Augustine made chastity synonymous with virtue. If a priest, therefore, was to have moral authority over his flock, it was necessary for him to be chaste. Or, at least, celibate. The two words often were – and are – used interchangeably, but they do not mean quite the same thing.

The idea of celibacy – the unmarried state – did not, however, go down at all well with the early priesthood; the Germans swore they would rather give up their lives than their wives. It took almost six centuries for the Church to enforce its prohibition on clerical marriage. It never, though, wholly succeeded in enforcing chastity, as endless scandals have continued to show.

Modern churchmen some-times speak of 'the family' as if it were a Christian invention, but their predecessors were more inclined to blame it on the devil. Seeing marriage as a series of concessions to human weakness, to the need for companionship, sex and children, the Church did what it could to undermine all three. One marriage was enough for anyone; second marriages were adultery, third fornication, and fourth nothing short of 'swinish'.

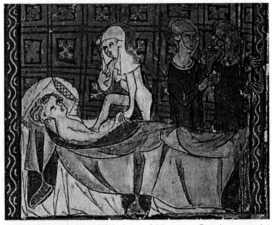

King Arthur's Wedding Night, from a 14th century French manuscript

The Church also refused to consider sex as an integral part of marriage. After arguing about it for 500 years, it finally concluded that what marriage did was confer the *right* (though not the *duty*) to indulge in sexual intercourse, a right that anyway existed only within marriage.

Further, continuing to hanker after chastity even within marriage (though not a total lack of sex; non-consummation could lead to a marriage being annulled), it refused to consider childlessness as a basis for divorce, although it had been acceptable as such in every other society since the beginning of recorded history. However unintentionally, this actually gave unprecedented security of tenure to a large class of women who had previously suffered rejection for something that was as likely to be their husband's problem as their own.

Since sex and marriage had been interdependent since the days of the Hebrews, it might seem as if not very much about sex within marriage has changed. But a number of new factors had been introduced. The Christian calendar included an inordinate number of holy days, and some theologians insisted on abstinence on all of them – on Thursdays in memory of Christ's arrest; on Fridays in memory of his death; on Saturdays, in honour of the Virgin Mary; on Sundays, in honour of the Resurrection; on Mondays in commemoration of the departed. Tuesdays and Wednesdays were largely accounted for by a ban on intercourse during fasts and festivals – the 40 days before Easter, Pentecost, and Christmas; the seven, five or three days before Communion; and so on and so on.

Such rules may regularly have been broken on the principle that no one would find out. But a priest, in his small parish, was perfectly capable of calculating nine months back from a new infant's date of birth, and if conception had taken place during Lent, for example, he was entitled to impose the penance of a year's fast on the child's parents

For sexual, as for other sins, the priest had handbooks to guide him, the 'penitentials', which laid down the penances to be imposed on parishioners who strayed from the path of virtue. Penances included between three and 15 years on bread and water for using contraceptive potions; from two to 10 years for *coitus interruptus*; thirty days' fasting for a monk who masturbated in church; and many more.

The Rise of Women

With Judaism in its ancestry and the women of imperial Rome as an example of what could happen when women got out of hand, the early Church had no great opinion of the female sex. As St Paul pointed out, woman had been created for the benefit of man and ought to defer to him in all things; she was not to teach in church (a prohibition that remained in force in the Church of England until the early 1990s); should cultivate silence; and submit meekly to instruction, as became the daughters of Eve, who was guilty of beguiling Adam into transgression. The Church Fathers added that she should take care to hide her charms, veil herself in church, and permanently abjure cosmetics.

'*What*', inquired St Jerome sarcastically, '*can a woman expect from Heaven when, in supplication, she lifts up a face that its Creator wouldn't recognise?*' (St Jerome quoted in J. Coulson (ed.), *The Saints, A Concise Bibliographical Dictionary* (1958) p.394)

It was 800 years before things began to change. The period between the early 12th and late 16th centuries was notable in the history of women, perhaps the most critical since the Neolithic era. Although, in the end, women were no better off legally, financially or physically than they had been at the beginning, their image had changed. Whereas once they had been despised not only by men but often by themselves, now they were beginning to be respected, sometimes even admired. This reversal of attitude was to make possible all subsequent changes and improvements.

A number of factors were responsible. The departure of thousands of Western knights for the Crusades was perhaps the first; wives were reluctantly entrusted with the management of their husbands' estates and discovered that taxes, tithes

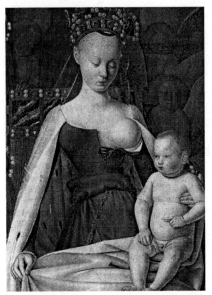

The Cult of the Virgin Mary, as depicted in this 15th century painting by Jean Fouquet

and even politics were not beyond their understanding. When the Crusaders returned, too, they brought with them – among other souvenirs of their travels – the cult of the Virgin Mary, who had long been an object of devotion in Byzantium. Until then, the Western church had equated woman with Eve, the seductress, the architect of man's downfall. When the image of Eve at last began to give way to that of Mary, all women benefited.

But the most unpredictable influence was the strange romantic game that evolved during the first half of the twelfth century, the cult of Courtly Love. It was class-conscious and excruciatingly sentimental; an idealised affair between a highborn beauty and a romantic squire, and it had its origins in the Arab concept of pure love.

Adaptation of this notion to the Western situation was not easy. The whole point of the Muslim original was that the real woman was a mystery to the poet who worshipped her. In Europe, however, the unconsecrated spirituality of such a love was not at all easy to achieve when its object was not only visible and audible but, as far as it is possible to judge, willing and accessible too. In the end, the troubadour-poets were forced to endow their heroines not only with beauty and rank, but (whether the lady liked it or not) with unimpeachable virtue too. Virtue, ironically, became the European interpretation of the harem.

The lady of Courtly Love might ideally be a creature of the imagination, but the notion became so widespread and fashionable that it was enough to help inaugurate a new era. It also had an effect on the fleshly medieval ladies who acted as stand-ins for the image. With their reputations ennobled, they had little choice but to mend their manners. As men became more chivalrous, ladies became, if not necessarily more virtuous or chaste, at least more gracious.

The ideals of courtly love were promoted by medieval romances, as in this story of Sir Lancelot and Guinevere, from a 14th century manuscript

After The Reformation

An improvement in the position of women in the West received something of a setback at the beginning of the 16th century when the men of the Reformation, rebelling against Rome, swept away 1,500 years of Catholic doctrine by going back to the scriptures and rediscovering (among other things) the notion of the 'good wife'.

They also, however, discovered that there was nothing specific in the Bible about celibacy being a virtue, or wedlock a necessary evil, or divorce a sacramental impossibility. Indeed, according to Martin Luther, in Biblical terms, virginity was undesirable, continence abnormal, chastity actively dangerous and marriage as necessary to the nature of man as eating and drinking. The desire to conceive was not the only legitimate justification for sex. Husband and wife might also have intercourse in order to: *'avoid fornication, or to lighten and ease the cares and sadnesses of household affairs, or to endear each other.'* (Jeremy Taylor, *Holy Living* ii 3).

Portrait of the Van Courtland Family,
by an anonymous 19th century artist

The other face of this surprisingly open approach to sex in marriage was, however, an absolute and uncompromising disapproval of any kind of extramarital activity.

The Puritans who emigrated to North America a century later took the patriarchal household values of the Old Testament with them, and also, for good measure, the traditional conviction that all God's creatures, even the Chosen, were born to an inheritance of sin. It was the duty of the strong in faith to help their weaker brethren to fight temptation, and they helped by flogging fornicators and adulterers; condemning the parents of a child born too soon after the wedding day to the pillory; and hanging the occasional adolescent boy for testing his uncertain masculinity on a mare or a goat.

Puritan morality was to have three direct effects on American society that still have echoes there today. It produced a mental state of Victorianism a century before Victoria herself mounted the throne; it taught American women how to control their menfolk by being virtuous to the point of caricature (similar to the untouchably ideal lady of Courtly Love) while yet appearing to submit to them like good Old Testament wives; and it wove the public demonstration of family solidarity into the American ethos.

Although the resurrection of the 'good wife' notion put a temporary damper on the development of women as individuals, in the 18th century a scientific controversy blew up that proved, for the first time, that women had their own independent importance in the general scheme of things. Although even the least observant must have recognised, during the course of 400 generations, that children as often resembled their mothers as their fathers, it had always been thought that woman was merely an incubator for the 'germinal particle' contained in man's seminal fluid; her ovaries were considered to be an unimportant female version of the testicles. But when the microscope was invented, scientists used it to discover, first, that the ovum could itself be mobile and, secondly, that seminal fluid was alive with miniature tadpole-like creatures, thrashing about.

The full truth of how children were generated, though, was not to be resolved until 1854, but long before that it had become accepted that, if God had endowed women with the right to contribute to the creation of their sons, they could not be as inferior as men had always previously thought.

The Age of Imperialism

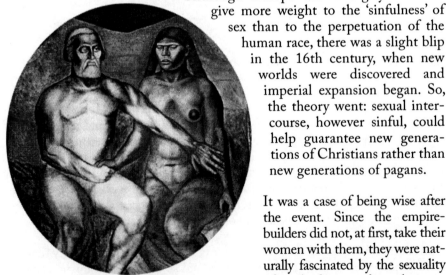

Cortes with his mistress.
Detail from a mural by
Jose Clemente Orozco (16th century)

Although Europe had strangely come to give more weight to the 'sinfulness' of sex than to the perpetuation of the human race, there was a slight blip in the 16th century, when new worlds were discovered and imperial expansion began. So, the theory went: sexual intercourse, however sinful, could help guarantee new generations of Christians rather than new generations of pagans.

It was a case of being wise after the event. Since the empire-builders did not, at first, take their women with them, they were naturally fascinated by the sexuality of newly-discovered peoples, even if the first thing to strike them was something entirely different.

This was what happened with the Spaniards in Mexico, so horrified by ceremonial cannibalism of the Aztecs that they henceforth put the worst possible interpretation on everything else that fell under their gaze.

When they discovered that the Mayans – like the ancient Greeks – saw adolescent homosexuality as a perfectly normal phase of growing up, they promptly inflated it into a continent-wide addiction to sodomy although, in fact, both the Aztecs and the Incas were as dedicated to fertility as the early Hebrews had been and rewarded adult homosexuality with a very nasty death.

The Spanish conquest was to have a dire effect on the native populations of central and southern America. In addition to its own systematic slaughter, Spain had brought European diseases against which the peoples of the New World had no immunity.

In Mexico and the Yukatán peninsula before the conquest, there are believed to have been about 25 million people; little more than a century later only one-and-a-half million pure-blooded indigenes remained.

But the Spaniards had been busy in other directions, too, enforcing the sexual and personal morality of the West while at the same time fathering children who, inherited some of the characteristics of both parents, had a degree of immunity to European diseases.

It was these so-called *mestizos*, part Indian, part Spanish, who were genetically equipped to survive, and it was they who founded the new hybrid races that went on to inherit central and southern America.

It was the Portuguese, however, rather than the Spaniards, who actively saw interbreeding as a politically useful policy. When they captured Goa in the early 16th century – a tiny European foothold on the great land mass of Hindu India – the Portuguese saw no possibility of holding it by strength of arms and, instead, sought to induce loyalty to Portugal by simultaneously imposing Christianity and fostering a *mestiço* population. But, although the Goanese accepted the new religion, the experiment failed and the majority of these people, the *mestiços* (Portugese) or the *mestizos* (in Spanish), were reabsorbed into the Indian – though now Christianised - background.

It was different 200 years later when the British came to rule India. The Eurasians (or Anglo-Indians) were, in terms of Hinduism, outcasts who could not be reabsorbed into the Hindu Indian, caste-based community. They were outsiders, forming an uneasy class of their own, and a class of which the British made calculated use. From the mid-19th until the mid-20th centuries, the railways and the police could scarcely have functioned without them.

The Victorian Era

Good wives, yes. Partners in the creation of sons, yes. But women as independent human beings? Not quite yet.

The frock-coated and increasingly bewhiskered Western gentlemen of the Victorian era, in the grip of acute nostalgia for the medieval period – so much more colourful than their own – cultivated a stilted and excessive courtesy towards 'the ladies' that they fondly believed to reflect the chivalric ideal. By doing so, they reduced them once more to the status of spectators at the tournament of life, giving them indulgence as a substitute for independence. Many women, of course, were happy to be indulged, cherished and treated as pure-minded angels to whom a man could turn for respite from the rough and demanding world of business.

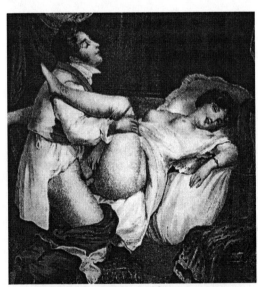

Prostitution flourished in the 19th century as men were encouraged to 'spare' their wives from the demands of their sexual appetites

Though not too often, in the sexual sense at least. There was a general belief that a man should not impose his animal desires upon his wife any more than was absolutely necessary – once a month for preference, once a week if he was desperate, but never during menstrual periods or pregnancy. Men were encouraged, even by doctors, to feel that they were doing their wives a favour by taking their sexual demands elsewhere. Sex with a prostitute, where neither love nor passion was involved, was said to be 'generally attended with less derangement' than sex with a wife.

Prostitution, both amateur and professional, flourished as never before. There was an epidemic spread of venereal disease and a fashion for virgin prostitutes who, because this was their first experience of intercourse, could not be contagious; it took years for their clients to discover that, in some brothels, full-time virgins were patched up several times a week with the aid of a powerful astringent and a scrap of blood soaked sponge.

As the 19th century progressed, the 'angel of the house' went on sitting in her ivory tower while her husband – whom she had been taught to regard as a cross between God and Sir Galahad – sought and was supplied with every conceivable outlet for his needs. Flagellation, boy brothels and masochistic pornography were particularly popular.

There was one surprising and beneficial consequence. In the Christian view, the only respectable form of contraception had always been abstention, which had mean that coitus interruptus, unreliable and unsatisfying for both partners, had always been the most commonly-used method.

By the 1880s, however, every man who had ever visited a prostitute was aware that, in making love to his wife, he ran the risk of infecting her. Condoms, available for over a century, had formerly been intolerably clumsy but recent developments in vulcanisation had led to the development of a greatly improved crepe rubber type and men began using them in increasing numbers.

Middle-class wives, innocently believing that it was to save them not from venereal disease but from unwanted conception, found it more acceptable than coitus interruptus, and gradually began to take a more favourable view of the whole idea of artificial contraception – and also of intercourse itself. Marital relations began to improve. But it was still the man who controlled conception.

The 20th Century

As the 19th century gave way to the 20th, very little seemed to have changed in relations between the sexes. In 1893, New Zealand became the first country in the world to grant women the vote (though, this was actually thanks largely to a miscalculation on the government's part), but elsewhere the real battle had scarcely even been joined. Both sides invoked women's 'special moral qualities'.

The anti-suffrage lobby claimed that women should not have the vote because those qualities would be tarnished by contact with 'the ordinary machinery of political life'.

The reformists argued that they should, that the dangerous experiment had already been tried of *enfranchising the vast proportion of crime, intemperance, immorality and dishonesty [i.e. men], and barring absolutely from the suffrage the great proportion of temperance, morality, religion and conscientiousness [i.e. women]*' (Susan B. Anthony and Ida Husted Harper, *The History of Woman Suffrage* (1902) p xxvi).

It was a long battle, during which the image of the 'angel of the house' gave way to that of the virago, Englishwomen tied themselves to railings and American women opposed racism, prohibition, and self-righteousness. By the period between the wars, however, the battle had effectively been won at least in more Western societies, though even now enfranchisement of women is not worldwide.

Scenes from Woodstock in 1969 demonstrated the extent to which Western attitudes towards sexuality changed during the 20th century

Far more influential in changing women's lives may actually have been the new social freedom of the 1920s that enabled them to take real jobs (in the wake of many taking up war work during the First World War) and earn their own living. As G.K. Chesterton dryly remarked, *'Twenty million young women rose to their feet with the cry, "We will not be dictated to" and promptly became stenographers.'* But still, and with some encouragement from Hollywood, women saw romance as their birthright and marriage as their natural goal. It was a vision that lingered even in the divorce-ridden decades after the Second World War.

Then, at the beginning of the 1960s, a major sexual revolution happened at last, at least, again, in Western societies. Where permission to vote and permission to earn had failed to change women's view of themselves, a single medical development spectacularly succeeded. For thousands of years they had been swallowing powders and potions in the hope of controlling their fertility. For decades they had been struggling with diaphragms and Dutch caps. But the pill, at last, was something that really worked and, since taking it was quite dissociated from the act of intercourse, it aroused none of the moral, political, social or aesthetic unease of other methods. For the first time, reliably and privately, women were in charge of their own reproductive capacity. It was from this transformation in their circumstances that the newly empowered feminists drew much of their strength.

The people of medieval Europe had had 12 generations during which to adjust to the idea that women were worthy of respect and the Victorians had had three generations to accept that they were worthy of the vote.

Many societies in the modern world have had to adapt to the idea of almost complete legal and sexual equality in only a couple of decades – 5,000 years of social and sexual tradition overturned in just a whisker of time. Predictably, some of the results have been chaotic – for women, for men and for moralists.

But it is not, of course, the end of the story. It never is, where life and sex are concerned.

Into The 21st Century

Greater knowledge of and public debate about sexuality during the late 20th century not only brought sexual enjoyment and fulfilment, but also division and confusion. Religious leaders, even within individual religions, remained divided about the acceptability of various sexual and moral behaviours. There was no evolution of a universal consensus on what could be considered 'normal' and 'permissible', even as the world entered the new millenium.

In the 21st century, neighbouring countries – even neighbouring states in the USA – have different laws about abortion, homosexuality, gay marriage, the age of consent and sexual practices. Many regimes worldwide have acted – and continue to act – repressively with regard to sexual issues. Some have been successfully challenged and have made adjustments to their laws and social codes, a good example being the changes that have taken place in post-reunification Germany. Further developments, in the wake of political change, are likely in the future.

The debate on abortion continues both undiminished and unresolved. The pro-choice movement insists on the rights of the women; the pro-life lobby labels abortion as murder – on occasion ironically resorting to violence itself to propound their views. Reconciliation seems unlikely. The reception and legalisation of the abortion drug RU486 in some countries has continued to fuel controversy.

The awareness of HIV and AIDS had forced people to reconsider their attitudes towards sexual behaviour. A consequence of the advent of antiretroviral drugs, (which have to be taken for life) that keep the disease at bay almost indefinitely, is that these fears may be diminishing. The World Health Organisation statistics for the end of the 2010 put the number of people living with HIV to be 33.4 million – more than half of whom were women. In that year, 2.7 million people became newly-infected and there were 1.8 million deaths. Overall, there have been an estimated over 33 million AIDS-related deaths worldwide since the epidemic was first identified 30 years ago (1981).

Other STIs, such as the almost symptom-less Chlamydia, affect significant numbers of people in the USA, western and eastern Europe, Japan and China – and its incidence is still growing.

Population increases of almost a hundred million people a year are unsustainable, forcing governments and individuals to look into measures to limit population growth, such as the one child policy in China. Long-standing views favouring large numbers of offspring are being challenged. Some religions – Roman Catholicism in particular – may need to address the issue of the use of artificial contraception. Many scientists believe that the resolution of the population issue is crucial if the planet is to survive.

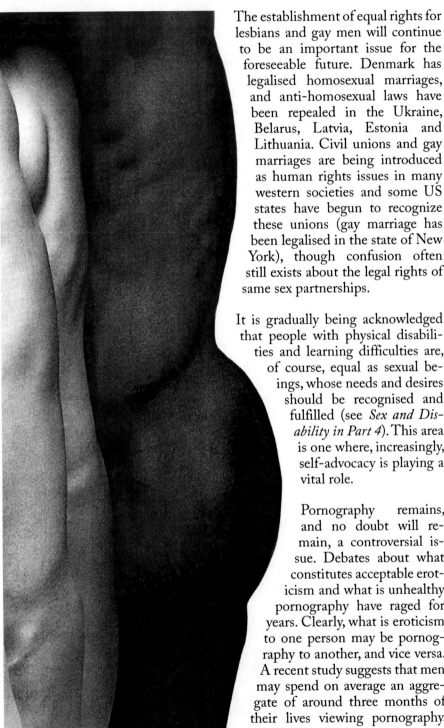

The establishment of equal rights for lesbians and gay men will continue to be an important issue for the foreseeable future. Denmark has legalised homosexual marriages, and anti-homosexual laws have been repealed in the Ukraine, Belarus, Latvia, Estonia and Lithuania. Civil unions and gay marriages are being introduced as human rights issues in many western societies and some US states have begun to recognize these unions (gay marriage has been legalised in the state of New York), though confusion often still exists about the legal rights of same sex partnerships.

It is gradually being acknowledged that people with physical disabilities and learning difficulties are, of course, equal as sexual beings, whose needs and desires should be recognised and fulfilled (see *Sex and Disability in Part 4*). This area is one where, increasingly, self-advocacy is playing a vital role.

Pornography remains, and no doubt will remain, a controversial issue. Debates about what constitutes acceptable eroticism and what is unhealthy pornography have raged for years. Clearly, what is eroticism to one person may be pornography to another, and vice versa. A recent study suggests that men may spend on average an aggregate of around three months of their lives viewing pornography.

Some people see it as a violation, predominantly, of women's sexuality; others support sexual freedom of expression, believing that individuals have a right to express what they do and feel. Some find non-sexist erotic material for women more acceptable.

The spread of pornography - mainly now across the internet but also in literature, films, television and art - causes concern amongst governments around the world. Although laws and attitudes may wax and wane in terms of how liberal or restrictive they are, it seems unlikely that a universal consensus on pornography will be achieved; what is clear from the spread of the internet is that its availability is looking to be unstoppable.

New contraceptive and reproductive technologies will continue to be developed. A male contraceptive pill is already in an early trial phase. Infertility treatments, surrogacy and fertilisation without sexual intercourse (*in vitro fertilisation*, or IVF) are continuing in popularity. Post-menopausal conception is already a reality. The female menopause may now be treated, where necessary, with hormone replacement therapy (HRT) or by natural means, revolutionising the lives of many women.

Some women react negatively to the new reproductive technologies, regarding them as interference with women's physiology and psychology, by a chiefly male establishment. Most, however, welcome the increase in choice as liberating rather than repressive. All aspects of the new hormonal preparations nevertheless require careful monitoring and assessment.

Sex education for young people is likely to remain a source of conflict between those who insist that young people have a right to sexual information and those who see sex education as an encouragement to be promiscuous. There is a clear and apparent need for dialogue and resolution in each society. Thanks to the courage and goodwill of representatives from different religious groups in the UK in discussing sex education, a good deal of mutual respect and agreement has been achieved there.

These debates and concerns will carry on and it is likely that as some problems are resolved, others will emerge. What is clear, however, is that the amount of information about human sexuality can only increase. With the web and the expanding communications industry, this information will become available to an ever-growing world public. The sexual revolution of the sixties – largely brought about by mass access to the contraceptive pill – will be continued in the information revolution of the early 21st century.

Knowledge and understanding, which allow democratic discussion and individual choice, are surely as important goals in sexual matters as in any other area of human activity.

Every religion has its own perspective on sexual issues, drawn from its own beginnings, traditions and specific teachings; these are often set out in written texts.

Buddhism

Buddhists are taught to define their own destiny according to their own understanding and interpretation of the world. They must avoid deliberate harm to living things and pursue acts of kindness (*metta*) and compassion (*karuna*) towards them.

While abortion clearly goes against basic Buddhist principles, other sexual decisions and behaviours, including the use of contraceptives, depend on the attitudes of the individual.

Christianity

The Anglican Church's view is that, ideally, sex should take place within the sacred, and lifelong bond of a marriage. Sexual relations within marriage are encouraged.

The Church acknowledges, but does not condone, homosexuality or masturbation. The predominant view concerning abortion is that a human being, formed in God's image, is created at conception and that, therefore, abortion is not justifiable. However, the Church allows for a wide range of views, and these issues remain controversial.

According to Roman Catholic doctrine, sexuality is part of a loving relationship within marriage. The primary purpose of sexual relationships is to produce children. The alternative is virginity or celibacy. Separation, in the case of marital breakdown, is allowed, but divorce is not recognised. Remarriage is only allowed in the case of annulment (where the marriage is deemed not to have existed), dissolution (where it is considered invalid) or death of spouse. Debates continue around the acceptability of premarital sex and divorce. They also continue around homosexuality and masturbation, in that both are non-procreative sexual acts.

Contraception is seen as part of non-procreative sex and therefore wrong; however, many Catholics in Western societies do use contraception (up to 90% of female practising Catholics in the USA). Natural family planning methods are allowed. Abortion is strictly forbidden as it is seen as counter to human dignity and rights. Life is considered to begin at the moment of conception.

Hinduism

Hinduism is a way of life, a code of values developed from many belief systems in which human sexuality is seen as a symbol of the creation of the universe. Hinduism centres on family life and favours reproduction. Many Hindus see the production of a son as a duty. Contraception is permitted, but not normally practiced until after the birth of a son. Semen is considered the elixir of life and partial sexual abstinence is recommended, particularly during religious festivals.

Arranged marriages are preferred, as the marriage is considered to be between the two families. Divorce is allowed. There are no rules about masturbation or sex that does not have a reproductive purpose. Abortion is not specifically prohibited but neither is it entirely accepted as Hindus believe in the sanctity of life.

Sikhism

Marriage and family are important in Sikh life. Monogamy is seen as essential. Arranged marriages are not obligatory, but common. Divorce is strongly discouraged. Sex must take place within marriage. Girls are protected by the family from premarital sex and a girl who becomes pregnant before marriage brings dishonour to her family. Menstruation is considered an unclean time and women do not take part in religious ceremonies then; likewise they are considered unclean until 40 days after childbirth.

Homosexuality and lesbianism are not allowed, but contraception is. Abortion is only approved under certain extreme circumstances, such as if the pregnancy threatens the health of the mother or if a girl is pregnant outside marriage.

Islam

In Islam, the sexes are notionally seen as equal but different, although men are expected to treat women with respect. Marriage is a civil, rather than a religious, contract. Marriage and the love of husband and wife are 'signs of Allah'. A man is allowed to have four wives, and the woman's right to sexual satisfaction is recognised. A man has a duty to ensure that he does not abstain from sex with his wife for more than three months and a woman must not deny sex to her husband.

Premarital sex is not allowed (though temporary marriages are, with the specific purpose of allowing sex to take place before a 'proper' marriage – this works much better for the men than the women), but sex within marriage is seen as important both for satisfying sexual needs and bearing children.

Contraception is permitted in certain circumstances. Abortion and vasectomy are forbidden. Female sterilisation is only allowed if medical opinion states that the woman's life or mental health would be endangered. The husband is not allowed to practise the withdrawal method of contraception without his wife's permission. Islam disapproves of divorce, but it is allowed in certain circumstances.

Homosexuality and lesbianism are strictly prohibited in Islam and masturbation is discouraged as immoral, views which are erroneously based on these practices believed not to happen in the wider animal world.

Judaism

Marriage is encouraged, and marriages are sometimes arranged, but individual choice is taken into account. Sexual pleasure is seen as an important part of a relationship. Adultery is absolutely forbidden. Marriage breakdown is based on 'no fault' divorce. Premarital sex is not permitted. Sex is not allowed during menstruation. There are rites of passage into adulthood – the Bar Mitzvah for boys and the Bat Mitzvah for girls. Boys are circumcised as soon as possible after birth.

Masturbation is forbidden, as are homosexuality and lesbianism. Contraception is allowed, with the pill being the most acceptable form of contraception, the condom the least, as Jewish law states that a man should not use contraception. Abortion is not generally allowed but if the mother's health is in danger or there is the likelihood of congenital disease, it may be permissible.

Eroticism had manifested itself for centuries in the literature, art and sexual practices of the non-Christian world before studies of sexuality and the promotion of sexual liberation began in the West at the end of the 19th century.

The early pioneers were influenced by new knowledge of the Eastern world as travellers and scholars brought back information on erotica. They were also influenced by the political, legal and medical context in which they lived and worked. Since then, their work has sometimes been challenged as being biased and patriarchal, and often as very dated in outlook. They were, however, the precursors of modern sexology and sex therapy who presented fundamental challenges to the sexual thinking of the time.

More recently, feminist thinkers and sociologists who have been concerned with sexual revolution have pointed to an essential de-medicalizing of sex, and to the need for sexual relationships to be reinterpreted and redefined in the context of differing kinds of sexuality, rather than in the context of the mechanics of sex. Such thinking was not alien to 19th and early 20th century sexual reformers, nor was campaigning for sexual rights. They were often, however, forced to work in isolation.

The world has, since that time, become more of a global village and more challenged and challenging. As the British sociologist, Jeffrey Weeks states, *'The object of sexological study is notoriously shifting and unstable, and sexology is bound by countless delicate strands to the preoccupations of its age'.*

The limitations and methodologies of the early pioneers, the most influential of whom are discussed here (in alphabetical order), need to be seen in this light.

Sir Richard Burton
(British, 1821-90)
Burton was a diplomat, an oriental and Arabic scholar and an explorer, who was interested in sexology. He wrote about the sexual practices of the countries in which he travelled, including India, Arabia and Somalia.

He translated the *Kama Sutra* (1883) and *The Perfumed Garden* (1886), in addition to *The Arabian Nights*, in 17 volumes, between 1884 and 1886. This latter, with its footnotes on sexual practices, encouraged the perceptions of debauchery and unusual sexual licence in the East prevalent in sexually-ambivalent Victorian England and Europe.

On his death his wife destroyed many of his more erotic writings.

Edward Carpenter
(British, 1844-1929)

Carpenter was an upper-class Englishman who influenced British socialism at the end of the 19th century. He was homosexual and lived together with his partner, George Merrill, in Derbyshire for 30 years. He wrote of homosexual and lesbian love as being on the highest plane of love in *The Intermediate Sex* (1908). He also wrote *Love's Coming of Age* (1896).

Michel Foucault
(French, 1926-84)

Foucault is best known for his *History of Sexuality* (1976) in three volumes – volumes four and five were unfinished. He was a radical thinker who challenged the medicalisation of sex and placed it at the centre of 'discourse'. He identified power structures as dominating sexuality and included psychoanalysis as part of these structures.

He has been an important figure in defining sexuality and sexual identity, including that of women, gays and lesbians, as socially – and historically – constructed, rather than a medical phenomenon.

Sigmund Freud
(Austrian, 1856-1939)

Freud left Vienna for London after the annexation of Austria by Germany in 1938. His middle-class Jewish family came from Moravia.

Freud was the founder of psychoanalysis, based on his work with patients suffering from 'hysteria' (literally: 'womb disease') who were encouraged to 'free associate'. His first work on this, co-authored with Josef Breuer, was *Studies in Hysteria* (1895).

His theories on the Oedipus complex postulated that children felt a sexual desire for their parent of the opposite sex and jealousy of their same-sex parent. In boys, this would be destroyed by the castration complex; in girls, the castration complex would make the Oedipus complex reality. His later work explored the concepts of the *id*, *ego* and *super ego* as divisions of the mind.

He had a profound interest in culture and religion, in addition to sexuality. His explorations of the inter-relationships of sexuality, the influences on the developing character and mental life were original and highly influential.

Henry Havelock Ellis
(British, 1859-1939)

Ellis was trained as a doctor, and became a prolific writer and editor of works of science, literature and sociology. He was married to the lesbian writer Edith Lees and pursued a romantic correspondence with Olive Schreiner.

He was an unusual Victorian in that he openly advocated sex as an important element in life. He put forward the notion of sexual practices, including sado-masochism, coprophilia, necrophilia, transvestism and inversion, being on a continuum of behaviour. He also mooted that every child has tendencies which are both heterosexual and homosexual.

Sexual Inversion, the first volume of his *Studies in the Psychology of Sex* (1897-1910), in which he sets out the view that homosexuality is not a disease, but inborn, was prosecuted in England but published in the USA.

He was a supporter of rights for women and strongly advocated their right to the enjoyment of sex, although he felt it would be more passive than in men. He believed, though, that motherhood and menstruation made women dependent on men. In addition, he campaigned for sex education and the right to express one's individual sexuality without fear.

Magnus Hirschfeld
(German, 1868-1935)

Hirschfeld founded the first institute of sexology in Berlin and later became eminent in the World League for Sexual Reform. The Institute of Sexology delivered sex education and marriage guidance. He wrote about transvestism and, more famously, about homosexuality in *Homosexuality of Man and Woman* (1925) and *Sexual Anomalies and Perversions* (1938), the summary of his writings.

He was, as a Jew, persecuted by the Nazis and his books burned in public in 1933. After this, he lived in the USA and later in France.

He rejected the popular view that homosexuality was a disease, insisting that it was another inherent sexual orientation. He pioneered the view that hormones governed sexual behaviour.

He campaigned for the rights of homosexuals and lesbians and, in 1897, founded the Scientific-Humanitarian Committee, which sought to abolish German laws against sodomy. He was also involved in the making of films that were a plea for enlightenment in sexual matters.

Alfred Charles Kinsey
(American, 1894-1956)

Kinsey is best known for his ground-breaking reports, *Sexual Behaviour in the Human Male* (1948), written with Wardell Pomery and Clyde Martin, and *Sexual Behaviour in the Human Female* (1953). The reports were based on thousands of interviews with American men and women across the nation, describing their sexual behaviour.

The interviews were largely with white, middle-class Americans, and spectacularly increased knowledge of actual sexual practices. They revealed an enormous diversity, including premarital and extramarital sex, oral sex, masturbation and homosexuality. This latter (that 37% of American males had had at least one homosexual experience) caused outcry and disbelief. Kinsey suggested a sexual continuum as a six-point scale from exclusively heterosexual activity to exclusively homosexual activity, with bisexuality as the average in the middle.

He also put forward theories of sexuality linked to the different brain functionings of men and women to account for the submissiveness of women and the aggressiveness of men. He also, however, discussed social conditioning and hormonal influences on sexuality.

Heterosexuality, married sex and vaginal intercourse were considered to be the norms for Kinsey. He did, nevertheless, challenge current sexual thinking, and strongly influenced later developments. He founded the Institute for Sex Research at the University of Indiana in 1942, which is still renowned for its research into sexuality.

Richard Freiherr von Krafft-Ebing
(German, 1840-1902)

Krafft-Ebing was a psychiatrist who worked in the courts of Austria and Germany. He was appointed Professor of Psychiatry at the University of Strasbourg in 1869 and was Professor of Psychiatry at the University of Vienna from 1892 until his death.

He attacked Freud's work as fantasy. He saw 'degeneracy' as the vital factor in sexual deviance, and masturbation as a manifestation of degeneracy. He described the dire consequences of masturbation as insanity, disease and hereditary complications. He saw homosexuality as a disease.

In 1886, he published *Psychopathia Sexualis*, a text based on case studies of psychotic behaviour. Although now challenged, and originally written to be read by doctors only, at the time it was an immensely popular and influential work. In 1897 he supported moves to make male homosexuality legal in Germany, but with reservations.

Jacques Lacan
(French, 1901-81)

Lacan was a follower of Freud. He reinterpreted Freud and the theory of the Oedipus complex as being primarily to do with patriarchy and the importance of the *phallus*, which is a linguistic and symbolic term, unlike the word penis which is a biological term.

He put forward the theory of love being not a simple two-way, but a five-way exchange – the subject, the object, the idea that the subject has of the object, the image that the object has of the subject and the Other (the sexual relationship controlled by the law of the Oedipus complex).

William H. Masters and Virginia E. Johnson
(American, 1915-2001 and American, born 1925)

Masters and Johnson researched sexual responses, rather than sexual behaviours. They carried out hundreds of case studies on sexual intercourse, including observing couples, and recorded their findings. They studied the stages and changes during arousal and orgasm and measured the effects on heart rate, breathing and blood pressure.

They found that men and women had similar sexual responses in arousal and orgasm and that the clitoris was the important factor in female orgasm. They also showed that women could have multiple orgasms. The results of this work were published in 1966 in *Human Sexual Response*.

Based on their work, they developed a two-week treatment for sexual problems and published *Human Sexual Inadequacy* in 1970. This created huge interest and encouraged training in sexual therapy.

Their later work has been challenged and criticised – their theories on homosexuality proposed that homosexuality, while not a disease, could be cured and that homosexual and heterosexual sexual responses were similar. These views are recorded in *Homosexuality in Perspective* (1979).

They have also been criticised for writing about AIDS in a sensationalist manner. They married in 1971 and divorced in 1991, the latter event being largely responsible for bringing their research work to an end.

Ivan Petrovich Pavlov
(Russian, 1849-1936)

Just before the turn of the Century, Pavlov, a Russian psychologist, discovered 'conditioned reflexes', and the way they could be manipulated, during his famous experimental work with dogs. One application of his work has been in 'reconditioning' sexual tastes through aversion therapy. Sex therapists, including Masters and Johnson, have also used his work to treat problems such as premature ejaculation, frigidity and impotence.

Margaret Sanger
(American, 1880-1966)

Sanger took up the challenge set out by earlier American campaigners for women's rights to contraception, notably Frances Wright in the 1820s and Elizabeth Cady Stanton in the 1880s.

She worked with Emma Goldman, who also advocated women's rights to enjoy sex. In 1914, Sanger first published *The Woman Rebel*, and the pamphlet on contraceptive usage, *Family Limitation*, for which she was arrested. She then left the USA for Britain. The case against her was dropped and she returned to the USA to open the first birth control clinic in New York. The clinic was popular with women, but closed by the police and its staff jailed.

She founded the American Birth Control League in 1921 to lobby those with power and influence and to monitor and research issues relevant to birth control. Contraception was legalised in the USA in 1965, an event to which Sanger's work had made an enormous contribution.

Marie Stopes
(British, 1880-1958)

Stopes was an important campaigner for sexual and reproductive rights for women. Her first marriage was unconsummated, a fact which encouraged her to research sexuality by reading comprehensively what was available at the time. As a result of this she published the books *Wise Parenthood* and *Married Love*, in 1918. The latter was revolutionary in that it encouraged women to enjoy sex, even during pregnancy, and to take control of their fertility.

Women wrote to her for advice (some of these letters were published in *Dear Dr. Stopes*, edited by Ruth Hall in 1978) in great numbers and she responded with radical suggestions on how to improve their sex lives. She opened the first British birth control clinic, staffed entirely by women, in 1920 in London. This clinic, The Marie Stopes Clinic, still exists.

During her lifetime, she was condemned by the Roman Catholic Church and by the British establishment and fought long battles for her beliefs.

DICTIONARY

6

A

Abortion

Premature termination of pregnancy, either natural and spontaneous, or induced. Deliberately-induced abortion is most commonly by means of a short surgical operation, or by medical means, through the administration of certain drugs and/or prostaglandins. The most common causes of natural abortion (usually known as *miscarriage*) include accident and infection.

Abstinence

Refraining from sexual activity for personal, moral or religious reasons. Abstinence can also be practiced as a contraceptive measure. *See Celibacy.*

Adolescence

The stage of development between childhood and adulthood, beginning with puberty. In the course of adolescence, the young person becomes physically and sexually mature. It is also a time of significant psychological and emotional development, affecting personal and sexual identity.

Adultery

Sexual intercourse where one or both of the partners involved is married to, or in a similarly committed relationship with, another person (also known as *having an affair).*

Adulthood

The stage of development when an individual has reached maturity and is fully physiologically developed.

Afterplay

Term (now rarely used) to refer to intimacies and sexual interactions that take place after the climax of sexual activity. See *Foreplay* and *Outercourse.*

Age of consent

The age at which individuals can legally engage in sexual contact with other people. This varies from one culture to another and by regional laws.

AID (Artificial Insemination by Donor)

Also called *donor insemination*, the procedure by which the semen of an anonymous donor is inserted mechanically into a woman's vagina close to the cervix or ovaries in order to achieve pregnancy.

AIDS (Acquired Immune Deficiency Syndrome)

The syndrome that can represent the last phase of HIV infection, sometimes known as *full-blown AIDS*. It occurs when the immune system has broken down to the point where cancers and opportunistic infections can take hold. The disease is not fully understood but it appears that up to 20 years or more may pass from initial infection to the development of AIDS and, in some cases, AIDS may not develop at all. See *HIV, Kaposi's sarcoma.*

Amenorrhoea

Absence of periods. The term *primary amenorrhoea* is used when menstruation has not started by the age of 16; *secondary amenorrhoea* is when periods stop for six months or longer. Causes of secondary amenorrhoea include pregnancy and rapid weight loss.

Ampallang

Rod inserted horizontally through the glans of the penis as a form of genital piercing. It functions as body decoration and may heighten sexual arousal both for the man and his partner. See *Piercing*.

Anal intercourse

Sexual intercourse in which the man's penis is inserted into his partner's anus. In homosexual intercourse, the man penetrating may be called the 'top' and the one penetrated, the 'bottom'. See *Sodomy*.

Anal stimulators

Devices used to stimulate the anus, such as Thai beads, butt-plugs or anal vibrators.

Androgyne

Person that has both male and female sexual characteristics. Also known as *intersex* or *hermaphrodite*.

Anilingus

Applying the mouth or tongue to a partner's anus to give it erotic stimulation. Also known as *rimming*. See *Rimming, Dental dam*.

Anus

The orifice at the end of the alimentary canal (lower bowel) and base of the rectum controlled by a ring of muscle known as the *anal sphincter*. The anal area is an erogenous zone for many people; the anus itself may be used for penetrative intercourse, between heterosexual or male homosexual couples, or others with the use, typically, of a strap-on dildo, in which the penis (or penile substitute) is inserted into the partner's anus.

Apadravya

Rod inserted vertically into the glans of the penis as a form of genital piercing. It functions as body decoration and may heighten sexual arousal for both the man and his partner. See *Piercing*.

Aphrodisiac

Anything (substance, smell, words, music, etc) believed to increase sexual desire or performance. The word is derived from ancient Greek word *aphrodisios*, meaning belonging to Aphrodite, the Greek goddess of love.

Arab straps

Straps that are fastened around the penis. Like other similar devices – *cock and ball straps, cock rings, Gates of Hell* – they are usually made of rubber or leather, and help produce and maintain a man's erection by trapping blood in the penis. Sometimes they are used therapeutically in cases of erection failure. Some people also find their appearance arousing and they may also provide physical stimulation for both the wearer and the wearer's partner.

ARC (AIDS-Related Complex)

An HIV-related illness; the stage before full-blown AIDS. See *AIDS*.

Areola

Area of pigmented skin surrounding the human nipple that can swell a little and darken during sexual arousal.

Armpits

The armpits are erogenous zones for many people, particularly women. *Axillary intercourse*, in which a man's penis is gripped in his partner's armpit while he thrusts, is a common form of non-penetrative intercourse. The strong body odours produced in this area also give it a fetishistic appeal for many.

Arousal

Physiological and psychological changes that occur to the body in response to sexual stimuli and which prepare it for sexual interaction or intercourse.

Auto-eroticism

A term for masturbation.

Axillary sex

Where the penis is stimulated by rubbing and thrusting it into a partner's armpit. See *Armpit*.

AZT (Azidothymidine)

The first drug authorised by Western governments for use in the treatment of HIV and AIDS.

B

Bacterial vaginosis

Infection caused by an overgrowth of the bacteria that occur naturally within the vagina. Symptoms may include a watery, grey vaginal discharge with a fishy odour.

Balanitis

Inflammation of the glans of the penis or clitoris, usually caused by an infection. Irritation may also occur.

Barrier contraception

Contraceptive methods that act as a physical barrier to prevent the male sperm from coming into contact with the female ovum. Barrier methods, especially the condom and other methods used in conjunction with spermicides, can give some protection against sexually-transmitted diseases. See *Cervical cap, Condom*, and *Diaphragm*.

Bartholin's gland

A gland located near the vaginal opening. During sexual arousal it produces secretions that may provide some lubrication. Some have believed it to be responsible for reported cases of female ejaculation at orgasm but this is more likely to be the Skene glands. See *Ejaculation*.

Bathhouses

Sometimes used as meeting places for sexual encounters for gay men, and sometimes lesbians, since Roman times.

Ben-wa balls

A pair of weighted balls inserted in the vagina. See *Love balls*.

Bestiality

Sexual activity with animals involving intercourse, masturbation or oral stimulation. Pleasure may also be derived from watching animals engage in sexual activity, or a fetishistic attachment to animal skins or furs.

Bigamy

This is the illegal practice of entering into a marriage with another spouse when already married to a first. The practice of having more than one wife is illegal in some cultures or religions, where it is traditional in others.

Birth control

Limiting and/or planning of pregnancies by means of contraception.

Bisexuality

Sexual attraction to and/or intimate activity with people of both sexes.

Blastocyst

A small sphere of cells that enters the uterus from the Fallopian tube and develops a cavity within itself as it implants in the lining of the uterus. The inner cell mass of the blastocyst develops into the embryo, an early stage in the human prenatal development.

Blue movie

A pornographic film or video. The term is derived from the blue pencil originally used to censor material considered unsuitable for general viewing. See *Pornography*.

Body hair dressing

The style in which the body hair is fashioned. Many women shave their underarms and legs; some men shave their chest hair. Hair around the genital area can be dyed, plaited, trimmed, shaved into shapes and patterns, or removed completely. See *Body Decoration*.

Body language

Movements and gestures of the body that convey signals or messages, often at an unconscious level, to other individuals.

Body rubbing

As it suggests, rubbing body parts, usually erogenous zones, against another's body. See *Frottage, Frotteur, Tribadism*.

Bondage

A sexual practice in which pleasure is gained by one partner being physically restrained by being tied up or bound. It can be a way of defining active and passive sexual roles and is also sometimes part of *dominant* or *sadomasochistic* (see also) sexual practices.

Boner

A slang term for an erection of the male penis – though the stiffness comes from the spongy tissue inside the penis being tightly filled with blood; it is a misnomer in that the organ does not contain a bone. See *Erection*.

Bottom

As well as the human posterior or rump, made up of the buttocks, the term is used for the receiving (penetrated) partner in homosexual sex and can refer to the passive partner during dominant/submissive sex play, particularly where sadomasochistic practices are involved.

Breasts

The fleshy female mammary glands that provide milk for offspring. In humans they are associated with being strong sexual signals and are also an erogenous zone, stimulation of which can produce sexual arousal in some women.

Buggery

A common term for anal intercourse. See *Anal intercourse*.

Butch

A type of lesbian identity involving the rejection of conventional femininity for the adoption of masculine characteristics and, in homosexual men, the one (if one does) who takes the traditionally masculine role in the relationship. Its counterpart is *femme* which is used for the one demonstrating feminine traits.

Buttocks

Fleshy muscular tissue, which constitutes the human rump or bottom. The buttocks are a source of attractiveness and/or an erogenous zone for many people.

Butt-plugs

These are usually quite firm or solid tapering blocks, most often made of latex or rubber, though also glass and metal, for use in the anus and rectum. Most are between 15 to 18 cm long and about 25 cm in girth. Many have a wide base to prevent them being drawn too far into the lower bowel. They may be used to dilate the sphincter, or muscles surrounding the anus, prior to anal sex or as anal stimulators in their own right.

C

Calendar method

A so-called 'natural' method for working out which days a woman is most likely to be ovulating by keeping an exact record of the timing of her menstrual cycle. See *Natural methods*.

Camp

An expression used in reference to male homosexual subculture. It is used to describe someone whose demeanour is characterised by exaggeratedly effeminate styles of speech, dress and/or movement.

Candaulism

The practice of a spouse watching their partner having sex with another person.

Candida albicans

An infection, sometimes known as *thrush*, caused by a type of yeast. It is a common organism, occurring naturally in the gut and on the skin, that can cause symptoms if there is excessive growth. These may include irritation and soreness around the genital area and a thick, white, yeasty discharge from the vagina or penis. It can be spread by sexual contact and sexual partners can reinfect one another. Treatment is usually with topically applied *antimycotic* (anti-fungal) creams, though there is also a one-time pill, *flucanazole*, taken orally, which is reported to be 90% effective.

Castration

The surgical removal of the testicles, scrotum, or ovaries and can also include the removal of the penis or clitoris. The procedure would include any other action, for example by chemicals whereby the male would lose all functions of the testicles or the female all functions of the ovaries. Castration is also known as orchiectomy (removal of just the testicles), oophorectomy (removal of the ovaries), gelding (usually referring to horses) or spaying (usually referring to animals, particularly pets).

Cassolette

From the French word for a perfume box, this term can either mean the full scent of a woman as the mix of her perfume, sweat and pheromones or simply the smell of her vagina.

Casual sex

A series of one-off, short-term or expressly-limited sexual relations. It usually involves an emphasis on the physical rather than the emotional side of sex. This can be with a stranger, a friend or even an ex.

Catamite

A boy kept for the purposes of homosexual intercourse usually in a pederastic relationship. The term derives from the name of Catamitus (latinised form of Ganymede), a handsome Trojan youth abducted by Zeus to be his companion.

Celibacy

A commitment to refrain from sexual activity or intercourse; this may be for personal, moral or religious reasons.

Cervical cap

A barrier method of contraception, consisting of a circular dome of thin rubber which is placed over the cervix and is held in place by suction and thereby blocks sperm from entering the uterus. It is best used in conjunction with spermicidal cream for extra protection. See also *Cervix, Diaphragm*

Cervical mucus method

A method for working out which days a woman is most likely to be ovulating by observing the regular changes in vaginal discharge, which becomes more copious, slippery and clear near the time of ovulation. Also known as the *mucus method*. See *Natural methods*.

Cervix

The neck of the uterus, which extends into the top of the vagina. It forms a passageway between the vagina and uterus. See *Vagina, Uterus.*

Chancroid

A bacterial infection that usually occurs only in tropical or sub-tropical regions. The symptoms include ulcers and sometimes abscesses that appear around the genitals.

Change of life

A common term for the *menopause* or *climacteric*, the period in a woman's life during which the menstrual cycle ceases. See *Climacteric, Menopause.*

Chastity

Abstaining from sexual activity, and especially intercourse, at any time for religious purposes or before marriage.

Child sexual abuse

Sexual activity involving children beneath the age of legal consent; it may be against their will or without their understanding, and is usually perpetrated by an older person.

Childhood

The stage of development from birth to the onset of puberty.

Chlamydia

Sexually transmitted disease caused by a bacterial infection. Initially symptoms may include some pain and discharge, or there may be no symptoms at all. However, if untreated, the infection can cause pelvic inflammatory disease in women, which can affect fertility, and urethritis in men.

Chromosomes

Units found in every living cell of the body, responsible for the transmission of hereditary characteristics. Chromosomes are arranged in pairs consisting of two identical parts, except in the case of the pair that determines gender. This consists of two X chromosomes for a female and an X and a Y for a male. Any other combinations of X and Y chromosomes can result in gender anomalies, as in Klinefelter's Syndrome where an XXY combination produces a person with male outward appearance but underdeveloped testes and penis, who will be infertile. See *Genes*.

Cicatrisation

The deliberate scarring of the body, originally practised in certain African tribes as signs of fertility, accomplishment or bravery, and in other cultures for other reasons, such as body decoration, sexual arousal and ritualistic purposes.

Circumcision

For males, the removal of the foreskin (prepuce) of the penis, often performed for religious reasons or for reasons of hygiene. For females it involves an incision into, or complete removal of the tip of the clitoris and sometimes *infibulation* (sewing together) of the outer labia. See *Clitoridectomy*.

Climacteric

The period of time during which there is a gradual decline in the production of sex hormones. In women, it is marked by the end of menstruation, when the ovaries cease to be active, which usually occurs between the ages of 45 and 56. In men it is less pronounced but generally the production of testosterone begins to decline from about the age of 40, with a corresponding drop in sex drive. See *Menopause*.

Climax

The height of arousal during sexual activity, usually the point at which orgasm is reached. It is characterised by involuntary muscle spasms and waves of intense pleasure through the body. See *Orgasm*.

Clitoral stimulator

A rubber, latex or plastic device worn by men, sometimes with a variety of knobs, bumps and soft projections, sometimes even a battery-powered vibrating device, that is placed round the base of the penis and rubs against the clitoris during intercourse. It may also provide extra sensation to the vaginal opening and vaginal wall. See *Sex toys*.

Clitoridectomy

The surgical removal of the tip of the clitoris in female circumcision. In certain cultural groups – including some

African societies and Islamic groups
– it is a male-imposed practice, performed as a social or initiation rite, to
reduce the woman's enjoyment of sex
in order to discourage women from
adultery. It may also be performed to
keep orgasm as a male prerogative. In
more repressive times in Western societies, it has been used as a means of
discouraging juvenile sexual activity. In
some rare cases, it may be performed
for medical reasons. See *Circumcision*.

Clitoris

Female erectile organ, the tip of which is
situated above the vaginal and urethral
openings, where the inner labia meet.
It develops from the same tissue in the
embryo as the penis in the male. The
head or glans of the clitoris is roughly
the size and shape of a pea, although
it can be significantly larger or smaller.
The clitoris is a complex structure, with
both external and internal components.
Following from the head back and up
along the shaft, it is found that this
extends up to several centimeters before reversing direction and branching.
The resulting branched shape forms an
inverted V, extending as a pair of legs
known as the *clitoral crura*.

The clitoris contains muscular tissue
and many nerve endings, as well as
erectile tissue arranged in two columns, the *corpora cavernosa*. In the
course of sexual arousal it thickens
and may lengthen as it becomes engorged with blood, and the glans or
head emerges from beneath the *prepuce* or hood formed by the inner labia,
making it more exposed and sensitive.
Just before orgasm the tip withdraws
beneath the prepuce but remains sensitive. The sole function of the clitoris

is sexual arousal and pleasure, where
it plays a key role in the stimulation
leading up to a woman's orgasm.

Cock and ball straps

Straps that are fastened around the base
of the testicles and penis, usually made
of rubber or leather. See *Arab straps*.

Cock ring

Ring fastened around the base of the
penis to help produce and maintain a
man's erection. It should be an easily
removable device made from rubber
or leather, never metal or hard plastic.
See *Arab straps, Cock and ball straps*.

Coitus

Another term for *sexual intercourse*
(see also). The term is most commonly
used to refer to the penetration of the
vagina with the penis, but also used to
describe other kinds of intercourse:

Coitus analis

Latin term for anal intercourse.

Coitus in axilla

Sexual intercourse in which the man's
penis is inserted into the armpit of his
partner. See Armpit.

Coitus inter femora

Sexual intercourse in which the man's
penis is gripped between his partner's
thighs, without penetrating the vagina or anus.

Coitus interruptus

Also known as withdrawal (see also), it
is a so-called natural method of contraception and involves withdrawing the
penis during intercourse, before ejaculation occurs to avoid sperm entering the
vagina and fertilising the ovum.

Combined pill

A contraceptive pill that contains both oestrogen and progestogen. It is usually taken for 21 consecutive days with a seven-day break before recommencing the cycle.

Come or Cum

Verb meaning to reach orgasm. It is also used as a noun meaning *semen*, when it is more commonly spelt cum.

Come out

An abbreviation of the expression 'to come out of the closet', meaning to openly declare one's homosexual or bisexual orientation. When a third party does this to someone, often against their will, it is known as *outing*.

Computer sex

Sexually-explicit material – text, pictures, videos – accessed by individuals or exchanged between people by means of computer networks and the internet. Bulletin boards may be set up and correspondence may develop. When this is used to tempt a child to have sex this is known as *grooming*.

Conception

Fertilisation of an ovum by a sperm, resulting in the start of a new life. The union of the two cells usually occurs in the Fallopian tubes. About a day later the fertilised cell starts to divide, and the growing ball of cells passes down the Fallopian tubes to the uterus where it continues to develop.

Concubine

In polygamous societies this is a secondary wife, usually of lower social rank. In other societies it simply means a woman who cohabits with a man.

Condom

The male condom is a thin latex sheath, which is placed over an erect penis before intercourse. It functions chiefly as a barrier form of contraception, by preventing sperm from being released into the vagina, and as a means of preventing the spread of sexually-transmissible diseases. Coloured, textured, flavoured and even padded condoms are also available for use as sex aids/toys. The female condom, made of polyurethane, is a tube closed at one end with a flexible ring at each end, one of which is inserted into the vagina, behind the pubic bone, while the other lies flat against the vulva. It has the same function as the male condom. See *Sex aids, Sex toys*.

Contraception

Any means of preventing conception from occurring as a result of sexual intercourse. The range of options include natural, mechanical and hormonal methods.

Coprolalia

The use of sexually-arousing language during sex. Also known as 'talking sexily' or 'talking dirty'.

Coprophilia

Sexual arousal from practices involving faeces and/or the process of defecation. See also *Scat*.

Copulation

Another term for *sexual intercourse* (see also) or *coitus* (see also).

Cowper's gland

Gland located below the prostate gland in the male, possessing ducts which lead into the urethra. It produces a mucus substance that is important in lubricating the penis and that neutralises any acidity caused by urine, which could kill sperm. This substance also forms part of the seminal fluid.

Crabs

Common term for pubic lice. See *Pubic lice*.

Cremaster

One of the two sets of muscles that support the testes and are attached to the testes themselves. See *Dartos*.

Cross-dressing

Dressing in the clothing, under clothing and sometimes make-up associated with the opposite sex. See *Transvestism*.

Crotch

The area between the legs, where the torso ends and the legs begin. The term is often used to refer specifically to the genital area.

Croupade

Any rear-entry position taken during intercourse, in which the man penetrates squarely from behind, that is without either partner having one leg between that of the other's. See *Cuissade*.

Cruise

To actively seek a sexual partner. The term is most commonly used with reference to looking for a homosexual partner.

Cuissade

A half-rear entry position during sexual intercourse in which the woman has one of her legs between those of her partner.

Cunnilingus

Oral sex in which the mouth or tongue is used to stimulate the vulva and clitoris.

Cutting

The activity of cutting the body with razors or knives, which may form part of sadomasochistic practices. Not to be confused with the term being 'cut' referring to men who have been circumcised. See *Circumcision*.

Cum

Slang term for *semen*. See *Semen*.

Cystitis

An inflammation of the bladder. Causes include certain bacterial and non-bacterial infections, allergic reactions to toiletries and friction during intercourse. Symptoms typically include a burning sensation when passing urine, a need to pass urine more often, and cloudy urine or blood in the urine.

D

Daisy Chain

A group sex practice that involves a circle of people, each engaged in sexual interaction with the person in front of them. It can involve oral, vaginal and/or anal sex.

Dartos

One of the two sets of muscles that support the testes, attached to the inside of the scrotum. See *Cremaster*.

Deep-throat

A form of *fellatio* that involves accommodating the whole length of the penis in the mouth and throat. In order to do this the person performing fellatio needs to overcome the gagging reflex.

Dental dam

A square of latex rubber which is placed over the vagina or anus to avoid risk of the transmission of sexually transmissible infections and diseases during *cunnilingus* and/or *anilingus* (see also).

Detumescence

The subsidence of a swelling, in particular the return of the penis to its original flaccid state, following an erection.

Diaphragm

A barrier method of contraception consisting of a circular dome of thin rubber, kept in shape by a pliable circular spring. It should be used in conjunction with a spermicide. The diaphragm is inserted into the vagina and sits behind the pubic bone, covering the entrance to the cervix. Previously known as the *Dutch Cap* (see also).

Dildo

An artificial erect penis – usually made out of plastic or rubber and available in various sizes and shapes – that may be used in masturbation or as a sex-aid for couples.

Dom

Abbreviation of the term dominant, used to refer to an active partner in practices involving bondage and sadomasochism. The term *top* (see also) is similarly used.

Donor insemination

The use of sperm from a donor. See *AID*.

Drag

Women's clothes worn by a man, sometimes with theatrical effect, when he might be called a 'drag artist' or 'drag queen'.

Dutch cap

Common name for a barrier contraceptive method used by women. See *Diaphragm*.

Dydo

A piercing through the edge of the glans of the penis See *Ampallang*.

Dysmenorrhoea

Particularly painful menstruation, typically involving nausea, cramps and headaches.

Ectopic pregnancy

A type of pregnancy in which the fertilised egg becomes embedded and starts to grow outside of the uterus, usually in one of the Fallopian tubes.

Egg or egg cell

The female *ovum* (see also), one of which is released each month.

Ejaculation

1) The release of seminal fluid from a man's penis at orgasm.

2) Ejaculation has also been observed in females where fluids are released, often following stimulation of the G-spot. Sometimes referred to as 'she-jaculation.'

Emergency contraception

Contraceptive measures, including a hormonal pill combining oestrogen and progestogen (effective up to 72 hours after intercourse) or the insertion of an intrauterine device (IUD) within five days of the expected ovulation date. These can be used by women who have had unprotected sexual intercourse or who suspect their method of contraception may have failed.

Endometrium

The lining of the uterus, made up of cells and blood, that is shed once a month in the process of menstruation if no fertilised egg is implanted. If an egg is fertilised it is passed along the Fallopian tube until it reaches the uterus, where it becomes implanted in the endometrium. See *Menstrual cycle.*

Enema

The introduction of liquid into the anus to clean it or to clear out the bowels. It is sometimes performed for sexual stimulation or as a preparation for other sexual practices. See *Anal intercourse, Rimming.*

Eonism

Term for *transvestism* (see also), introduced by Havelock Ellis.

Epididymis

The tube through which sperm is passed from the testes, where sperm cells mature and are stored before being passed into the *vas deferens* (see also) prior to ejaculation.

Erection

The stiffening and swelling of the penis, clitoris or nipples following engorgement with blood as a result of sexual arousal.

Erogenous zone

Any part of the body that is particularly sensitive to sexual stimulation. Erogenous zones vary from one person to another and can include the breasts, mouth, ears, nose and any other part of the body, as well as the genitals.

Erotic

Sexually-arousing and exciting – though not as harsh or exploitative as *pornography* (see also).

Erotophobia

The fear of sex and sexuality.

Eunuch

A man whose testes have been removed in castration.

EveryDay pill

A contraceptive pill, either progestogen-only or combined, that is produced in packs containing – as well as the 21 active pills – seven inactive pills that are taken in the seven-day break. It is often taken by women who find it difficult to remember to start taking the pill again after the seven-day break. See *Combined pill.*

Exhibitionism

Pleasure derived from displaying one-self sexually, especially in public. See *Flasher*.

F

Fallopian tubes

Two tubes, each about 10 cm long, that extend from either side of the uterus. The ends lie near the ovaries and are bell-shaped, with finger-like structures (*fimbriae*) that help to catch the ovum as it is released from the ovary. The tubes are lined with hair-like *cilia* that help to carry the ovum down the tube towards the uterus. Fertilisation of an ovum usually occurs within a Fallopian tube. They are named after the 16th century anatomist, Gabrielle Falloppio (hence the use of the capital 'F').

Family planning

Planning and controlling the timing, frequency and/or number of pregnancies by means of contraceptive measures. See *Birth control, Contraception*.

Family planning clinic

A clinic that provides information and advice about family planning and contraception and provides the contraceptives themselves where necessary.

Fantasy (sexual)

Imagining sexual situations, involving real or imaginary places and people, as a sexual stimulus.

Fellatio

Oral sex, involving the tongue or mouth in the stimulation of the penis.

Female sterilisation

A surgical operation in which the Fallopian tubes are clipped or cut and tied, so that the ovum cannot travel to the uterus or the sperm travel to meet the ovum. Hysterectomy, the removal of the *uterus* (see also) can be a more extreme form of sterilisation though is also indicated in cases of womb prolapse or uterine cancer). See *Sterilisation*.

Femme

Term sometimes used to describe a feminine, as opposed to a butch (overly masculine), lesbian. See also *Butch*.

Fertilisation

The penetration of an ovum by a sperm and the fusion of their genetic material. See *Conception*.

Fetishism

An attachment of a particular object (including apparel and costumes), material or part of the body other than the genitals, which enhances sexual arousal.

Fisting

The insertion of the whole hand into the anus or vagina.

Flaccid

Lacking firmness, therefore limp and soft. In the sexual context this usually refers to a penis that is not erect.

Flagellation

The act of whipping or flogging for sexual arousal. It is usually a sado-masochistic or dominant/submissive sexual practice.

Flanquette

Any of the half-facing group of sexual postures in which the woman lies facing her partner with one of her legs between his.

Flasher

A man who displays his genitals in public places. See *Exhibitionism*.

Foreplay

Term to describe sexual activity that takes place in the early stages of arousal, typically prior to intercourse. The term is becoming less popular as the definition of sex broadens to include all types of sex play that may not include intercourse. See *Afterplay, Outercourse*.

Foreskin

The retractable fold of thin, hairless skin, also called the *prepuce* (see also), that covers the head or *glans* of the penis. This is sometimes removed in part or whole in the practice of circumcision. See *Circumcision*.

Fornication

Archaic term for sexual intercourse between unmarried people.

Fourchette

The delicate area of skin about two to three centimetres in front of the anus, where the inner labia join at the bottom of the vaginal opening in the female also known as the *perineum* (see also) in both sexes.

French kissing

A kiss with one or both partners' tongues inserted into the other's mouth.

Frenulum or frenum

The bridge of particularly sensitive skin at the back of the *glans* (see also) of the penis in the male, between the glans and the skin of the shaft.

Frigidity

A psychological block preventing a person from being able to become completely involved in or to enjoy sexual intercourse

Frottage

Sex play that involves rubbing the penis between the partner's thighs, armpits or chest, without penetration. See *Coitus in axilla, Coitus inter femora, Gluteal sex*.

Frotteur

The practice of rubbing up against another person's clothed body – with or without their consent – for sexual excitement.

Furtling

A rather archaic term for the use of fingers inserted into cut-outs in the genital areas of photographs, for sexual arousal. This was particularly popular in Britain in the Victorian age.

G

Gang bang

Common term for the sexual practice where a woman has vaginal intercourse with several men in succession, which may be consensual or not. When not it is also used to refer to group rape.

Gardnerella

It is a bacterium which lives in the vagina and can cause a mild vaginal infection. See *Bacterial vaginosis*.

Gates of Hell

Rings, usually made of metal or leather, that are placed around the penis. See *Arab straps*.

Gay

Term commonly used to refer to homosexual behaviour, people, culture, etc. The word lesbian is used more commonly to refer to women who prefer sex with women.

Gender

The range of characteristics of being male or female based on sex, social roles and gender identity.

Gender identity

The individual's conscious sense of being male or female, as determined by biological, psychological and social influences.

Gender reassignment

The process undergone by some transsexuals, to bring their physical sex characteristics into line with their gender identity. The process includes living for a period of time as the desired sex, a course of appropriate male or female hormones, surgery to remove or enlarge the breasts, and surgery on the reproductive organs and external genitals.

Gender role

The pattern of behavioural characteristics associated with being male or female in a particular culture. It is the outward expression of gender identity, often related to socially-ascribed roles. See *Chromosomes*.

Genes

The units that make up chromosomes, which are found in each body cell. Genes are made up of DNA, which is responsible for the transmission of inheritable characteristics. See *Chromosomes*.

Genital herpes

See *Herpes*.

Genitals

The external sex organs; in a male, the penis and testicles; in a female, the vagina, clitoris and labia.

Genital warts

Small warts or growths caused by the human papillomavirus (HPV). They are found on or around the genitals and can be transmitted through sexual intercourse.

Gerontophilia

Sexual interest in and attraction to older people.

Gigolo

A man who receives money from women for escorting them and/or having sex with them.

Glans

The rounded, highly sensitive head of the penis or clitoris, which has a high concentration of nerve endings and is therefore very responsive to stimulation. See *Clitoris, Penis, Frenulum*.

Gluteal sex

Sexual practice where a man's penis is stimulated by being moved between the buttocks of his partner.

Gonads

The organs that produce the reproductive cells and the sex hormones: the ovaries of a woman or the testes of a man. Male and female gonads develop from the same tissue in the embryo, before sexual differentiation takes place in the ninth week of pregnancy. Also known as *the sex glands*.

Gonorrhoea

Sexually transmitted disease caused by the bacteria *gonococcus*. It can affect the urethra, cervix, rectum and occasionally the throat if it is passed by oral-genital contact. It attacks the mucous membranes, causing inflammation and the production of pus. Characteristic symptoms include a discharge of white or yellow fluid from the penis or vagina and pain when urinating, but these are usually more obvious in men. If untreated, gonorrhoea can lead to sterility.

Grooming

1) The act of preparing for sexual activity, such as shaving ones legs, armpits, pubic hair, combing hair, putting on make up etc.

2) The act of psychological manipulation of a child (and often the child's family), sometimes via the internet, in order to gain their trust to later engage in sexual relationship or for prostitution.

Grope suit

Tight underwear made for women, to produce sexual excitement and orgasm. Usually consisting of a tight rubber G-string and a bra, each with protuberances on the inside to stimulate the vagina, G-spot, clitoris and nipples.

G-spot

A specific area that is particularly and intensely responsive to sexual stimulation in some men and women. Also known as the Grafenberg spot after Dr. Ernst Grafenberg who first described it. The male G-spot has been identified as the prostate gland: the female as a small area on the front wall of the vagina, although opinions still vary with regard to the nature of the G-spot and – in the case of the female – even its existence. For some people stimulation of the G-spot is the key to reaching orgasm, for others it serves to intensify the sensations of orgasm, while for others it has little or no effect. See *Ejaculation*.

Guiche

A piercing in the ridge of flesh behind the scrotum. See *Ampallang*.

H

Hafada

A piercing made through the scrotal sac. It can be made at the side, so that it is visible from the front, or from underneath and behind, running in a line down the centre seam of the scrotum. See *Ampallang*.

Hard on

Common term for the state of male sexual arousal referring to an erection and hardening of the penis. See *Boner, Erection.*

Hepatitis B

A virus present in the blood and other bodily fluids of an infected person, causing inflammation of the liver. It is passed on through contact with infected body fluids and can therefore be transmitted sexually.

Hermaphrodite

A person that has both male and female sexual characteristics. See *Intersex.*

Herpes

A viral infection, the most common form of which is the herpes simplex virus. Type I affects the mouth and occasionally the genitals and Type II just the genitals and anal areas. It is characterised by the formation of small watery blisters on, in or around the genitals and cold sores on the mouth, although it may be asymptomatic. It can be passed through genital and oral-genital contact.

Heterophobia

The fear and/or hatred of heterosexuality.

Heterosexism

Term for the prejudice from some heterosexual people experienced by lesbians and gay men.

Heterosexuality

Sexual attraction to and/or activity with members of the opposite sex.

Human Immunodeficiency Virus - HIV

The Human Immunodeficiency Virus, which prevents the immune system from working as it normally should by attacking the CD4 cells, which coordinate the fight against infections. This leaves the body defenceless to both infection and disease. HIV can be transmitted through sexual activity, See *AIDS, Kaposi's sarcoma, ARC.*

Homoeroticism

Any material that suggests lesbian or gay sexuality and/or love.

Homophile

A (rarely used) term for homosexual. The Greek root *philos*, to love, means that the word literally means love of the same sex.

Homophobia

Fear and/or hatred of homosexuality.

Homosexuality

Sexual attraction to and/or activity with members of the same sex. Current estimates suggest that between 5% and 10% of men and a smaller percentage of women are exclusively homosexual throughout their lives. However, Kinsey's studies suggested that about 37% of males and 13% of females had had some overt homosexual experience in adult life and more recent estimates are higher than this. It is also known that homoerotic fantasy is common amongst people of all sexual orientations.

Hormonal methods of contraception

Methods of preventing conception involving the use of synthetic hormones similar to those produced naturally by the body. Taken either by pill, injection or implant, they have been one of the most popular female contraceptives since the 1960s. Research and trials continue on hormonal contraceptives for use by men. See *Natural methods, Mechanical methods, Pill (contraceptive)*.

Hormone

One of several types of natural, chemical substances produced by endocrine glands in the body and which regulate bodily processes such as growth, metabolism, and reproduction. The sex hormones, including *oestrogen, progesterone* and *testosterone*, play a major role in the sexual and reproductive functions of the body.

Hormone Replacement Therapy - HRT

The treatment in tablet, patch or gel implant form, for menopausal symptoms in women. It involves the administration of natural oestrogen and/or synthetic progesterone, which the ovaries have ceased to produce.

Hymen

A thin membrane that partially covers the entrance to the vagina in young girls. It may be broken by physical exercise, by using tampons or at first intercourse.

Hysterectomy

The surgical removal of the female uterus, usually because of infection, disease, prolapse or excessive bleeding.

I

Impotence

Sexual dysfunction in males that involves an inability to achieve or maintain an erection sufficient to perform sexual intercourse. The cause may be physiological or psychological: among the most common causes are anxiety, stress and emotional conflict.

Incest

Sexual relations between individuals who are members of the same family.

Inner labia

The inner lips of the vulva, revealed when the outer lips are parted. See *Labia minora*.

Intercourse

Common term for *coitus* (see also) and *copulation* (see also), involving the insertion of the man's erect penis into his partner's vagina or anus, followed by rhythmic thrusting that usually involves climax in orgasm.

Intersex

The presence of intermediate or atypical combinations of physical features that usually distinguish female from male. See *Hermaphrodite*.

Intrafemoral sex

Coitus inter femora, or sexual intercourse in which the man's penis is gripped between his partner's thighs, without penetrating the vagina or anus.

Inversion

A now archaic term for homosexuality used at the turn of the 20th century and employed by sex researchers of that time.

IntraUterine Device - IUD

A method of contraception consisting of a copper or copper and silver device, the first designs of which released progestogen, also known as *intrauterine system* (IUS) or *intrauterine contraceptive* (IUC). The device is professionally inserted into a woman's uterus. It prevents fertilisation and/or implantation of a fertilised ovum. May also be used as emergency contraception. *Mirena* is the name of an intrauterine device that releases progestogen. It can be left in place for five years.

InVitro Fertilisation - IVF

The fertilisation of an ovum, by a sperm, which occurs artificially i.e. outside the body, often in a test-tube under laboratory conditions.

J

Jelqing

Also known as *jikok,* is a supposed penis extension technique which involves stretching a semi-erect penis by wrapping the thumb and index finger around the shaft and repeatedly pulling them away from the body; the idea is to enlarge the amount of soft tissue, or *corpus cavernosum*, and thus create a larger erection.

K

Kakila

Term used in the *Kama Sutra* to describe the sexual practice know known as the *soixante-neuf,* or 69 position, which involves two people simultaneously performing oral sex on one another.

Kama Sutra

Possibly the world's first sex manual, also seen by many as a literary classic. It describes the sensual pleasure to be derived from music and poetry as well as giving a great variety of advice and information on the enjoyment of sex. It was written in India by Vatsyana in the fourth to fifth centuries AD, but was based on earlier sources.

Kaposi's sarcoma (KS)

A form of skin cancer that is particularly associated with HIV infection and the development of AIDS. It causes a growth of the blood vessel walls resulting in red and purple lesions on the skin. The condition is named after Moritz Kohn Kaposi (1837-1902), an Austrian dermatologist who first described the condition. See *HIV, AIDS*.

Kegels

A term for the pelvic floor or *puboccygeal* muscles. It is believed that exercising these muscles can improve the strength of erections in men and increase sexual response and the ability to reach orgasm in women. The original pelvic toning device was the *perineometer* invented by Arnold Kegel.

Kinsey Six

Somewhat archaic slang term for a homosexual. The term refers to a scale of sexual orientation devised by the pioneering sex researcher Alfred Kinsey, where a six was reserved for those who had no interest at all in heterosexual activity. See *Homosexuality*.

Kissing

Touching or caressing with the lips and tongue as an expression of love, friendship, desire or respect. See *French kissing*.

Klinefelter's syndrome

An XXY combination of chromosomes. See *Chromosomes*.

KY Jelly

The brand name of a popular water-based lubricant, used widely to facilitate penetration.

L

Labia majora or outer labia

The two lips that surround the vaginal opening, usually lying close together to protect it. At the front they join at the mons pubis; at the back they join at the perineum. They are plump enough to act as a cushion during intercourse. They contain sweat and odour-producing glands, which keep the smooth inner part moistened and give the vulva its highly individual sexual odour.

Labia minora or inner labia

The smaller, hairless lips or folds of skin within the outer labia, immediately around the vaginal opening. At the front they join to form the hood of the clitoris and at the back they form the fourchette. They contain sebaceous glands on their outer side and sweat glands on the inner parts which help with lubrication. During sexual arousal they become engorged with blood (in a similar manner to the penis), which makes

them darken in colour and swell to two or three times their normal size. See *Fourchette, Perineum*.

Latex love

Term for safer sex practices where condoms (usually made of latex) or dental dams are used. See *Condoms, Dental dams*.

Lesbian

A woman who is sexually and/or romantically attracted to other women. The word is derived from the island of Lesbos, which was the dwelling place of the Greek lesbian poet Sappho (610-580 BC).

Libido

The term coined by Sigmund Freud to refer to human sexual motivation. Now understood as sex drive, sexual desire or urge. See *Sex drive*.

Littre's glands

Small mucus glands that open into the urethra in men and women. In the male they are similar to the Cowper's glands, in that they release a pre-ejaculatory, lubricating liquid.

Lordosis

In the medical sense meaning an abnormal curvature of the lower spine; as this tends to thrust out the rump, in the sexual sense it refers to the rump-thrusting position mammals take up when ready to have sex.

Love balls, love eggs

Two hollow balls, usually containing small weights inside them, joined by a cord. They are placed inside a woman's vagina, where the weights cause them to move around as the woman moves. They may keep her in a state of constant arousal or bring her to climax. They are also useful in exercising the pelvic floor muscles. See *Ben-wa Balls, Kegels.*

Lubricants

Oils, creams, gels or other substances, which are used to add slippery moisture to the genital area or any other part of the body, to reduce uncomfortable friction during sexual activity. See *KY Jelly.*

Lust

Strong sexual desire or drive.

M

Maidenhead

A term sometimes used to refer to the retention of the *hymen* (see also), or to female virginity.

Make/making love

A euphemism for having sexual intercourse and/or engaging in other forms of sexual activity, sometimes used to differentiate sex with emotional involvement from mechanical sex.

Masochism

A form of sexual behaviour in which a person derives sexual pleasure from feeling pain, or having humiliation or domination inflected on them. The word is derived from the name of the author, Leopold von Sacher-Masoch (1836-1886), who wrote several books, including *Venus in Furs*, celebrating his own sexual fantasies involving physical abuse. See *Sadism, Sadomasochism.*

Massage

Rubbing, stroking or kneading a person's body, sometimes with oil, sometimes for sensual or sexual pleasure, or to relieve stress, pain or stiffness.

Masturbation

Sexual stimulation of one's own or another's sexual organs, usually with the hands, but also with other parts of the body or with objects.

Mechanical methods of contraception

Means of preventing conception while allowing full penile-vaginal intercourse to occur, by using a device which functions as a barrier, preventing sperm and ovum from meeting. Mechanical methods include the condom, the diaphragm and the IUS and IUD. See *Natural and Hormonal methods of contraception.*

Men who have sex with men - MSM

Male individuals who engage in sexual activity with members of the same sex regardless of their sexual identity. Some men want to use this term as distinct from *homosexuality (see also).*

Ménage à trois

Three people engaging in sexual activity together, often involving a couple and an outside lover. See *Troilism.*

Menarche

The first occurrence of *menstruation* (see also) in a woman's life, usually in the course of puberty.

Menopause

In its precise sense, the last occurrence of menstruation in a woman's life. However, the term is more commonly used to refer to the whole of the climacteric. See *Climacteric*.

Menstrual cycle

The hormonal cycle, lasting approximately 28 days, by which the female reproductive system is maintained. It ensures that each month an ovum is matured and released (ovulation) and the lining of the uterus is prepared for the possibility of a pregnancy. If conception does not occur, this lining is shed in menstruation, so that a new lining can be prepared during the following cycle.

Menstruation

Commonly called a *period*. See *Menstrual cycle*.

Mini pill

A form of the contraceptive pill. See *Progestogen-only pill*.

Missionary position

A position during sexual intercourse where the man is on top of the woman and lying between her legs.

Monogamy

The state or practice of having only one sexual partner over a specific period of time.

Mons pubis

Fatty cushion-like tissue that covers the upper part of the pubic bone in females. In males it is a layer of fatty tissue found overlaying the front of the pubic bone. Also known as the *mons veneris*.

Mons veneris

Another name for the *mons pubis* (see also).

Morning-after pill

Inaccurate but common term for the emergency contraceptive pill. It is in fact effective up to 72 hours after intercourse. See *Emergency contraception*.

Mucus

Slippery, protective secretion produced from the mucous membranes and glands. Mucus produced in the genital area can provide extra lubrication during intercourse.

Mucus method

A form of natural birth control. See *Cervical mucus method, Natural methods*.

Multiple orgasm

Several orgasms experienced in rapid succession, without any refractory (resting) period between each one. Usually, only women are physically capable of having multiple orgasms, but, by practising and developing ejaculatory control, some men may also be able to have more than one orgasmic peak in quick succession. In most cases not all will involve ejaculation. See *Refractory period*.

N

Natural methods of contraception

Avoiding conception without artificial means and usually by making sure that the man does not ejaculate inside the woman's vagina during the period when she is at her most fertile. This includes *coitus interruptus*, but also various methods – sometimes known as *the rhythm methods* – of judging when ovulation is most likely to occur, such as *the calendar method, the cervical mucus method* and *the temperature method* (see also).

Necrophilia

Sexual attraction to and/or sexual activity with dead bodies.

Nipple

The tip of the breast. It is an important erogenous zone and becomes erect during sexual arousal. In women it contains the outlet of the milk ducts.

Nocturnal emission

Involuntary ejaculation during sleep, in particular during a sexually-arousing dream; also known as a *wet dream* (see also). Studies suggest that nocturnal emissions occur in some 80% of young males. Whilst they are associated more with males, they do occur in females, when the vagina becomes highly lubricated, usually in the course of an erotic dream. They involve spontaneous orgasm and the person involved may be awoken by the experience or sleep on through it. They occur most often in the adolescent and young adult years, though they can occur any time after puberty.

Non-gonococcal urethritis - NGU

Inflammation of a man's urethra caused by a number of different types of bacteria other than the *gonococcus* (the bacterium which causes gonorrhoea). It is usually passed on through sexual contact. Characteris-

tic symptoms include discharge from the penis and pain or difficulty in urinating. If untreated, the inflammation can spread to the prostate and sometimes the testes.

Nonoxynol-9

The chemical present in some spermicides used on condoms and other barrier methods of contraception. Its use has declined due to unproven effectiveness during sexual practices and it has been linked to increased risk of human papillomavirus (HPV).

Non-specific urethritis - NSU

Essentially the same as non-gonococcal urethritis. See *NGU*.

Nymphomania

A (supposedly 'neurotic') condition experienced by women who feel a compulsion to have sex with as many men as possible.

O

Oestrogen

A steroid hormone produced in the ovaries and other glands in the female. The counterpart to testosterone, it is often considered an exclusively female hormone, but is in fact produced in both males and females. It is also produced by the placenta during pregnancy. Oestrogen stimulates changes in a woman's reproductive organs during her monthly cycle and promotes female primary and secondary sexual characteristics at all stages of development. See *Testosterone*.

Onanism

A somewhat archaic term for any sexual activity that does not put sperm to procreative use, for example masturbation. It is derived from the name of Onan, Judah's son (Book of Genesis), who 'sinned' by ejaculating on to the ground rather than impregnate his brother's widow.

Opportunistic infections

A general term for infections or diseases that take hold when the immune system has been damaged by HIV. See *HIV, ARC*.

Oral contraception

Hormonal pills taken by mouth for contraceptive purposes. See *pill (contraceptive)*.

Oral - or Oral-genital - sex

The use of the mouth lips and/or tongue to arouse and stimulate the genitals of another. It includes *fellatio* and *cunnilingus* (see also) and is also known as *oral-genital sex*.

Orchitis

Inflammation of one or both of the testicles.

Orgasm

The climax of sexual excitement, usually involving rhythmic contractions of the pelvic and genital muscles, which produces highly pleasurable sensations throughout the body. In the male it is usually accompanied by *ejaculation* (see also) as well. These contractions occur at intervals of 0.8 seconds in both male and female and usually last for less than one minute. Blood pressure, pulse and breathing rates all increase.

Outercourse

The term used to define non-penetrative sex; sexual activity without vaginal, anal, or oral penetration.

Outer labia

The outer lips of the vulva. See *Labia majora*.

Outing

The term given to the practice of publicly exposing a person's homosexuality usually against their will.

Ovaries

The two female sex glands or gonads, located on either side of the uterus, that produce the female sexual hormones oestrogen and progesterone and the reproductive cells, the ova. Each ovary stores as many as half a million ova. In the mature female, one ovum is matured and released into a Fallopian tube every month, alternating between the two ovaries, in the process of ovulation. The ovaries are equivalent to the testes in the male.

Ovulation

The cyclic release of an ovum from an ovary into one of the Fallopian tubes. See *Menstrual cycle*.

Ovum

The female reproductive cell. Usually, in a mature female, one ovum is produced each month in one of the ovaries. See *Ovaries*.

Oxytocin

This hormone, named after the Greek for 'quick birth' because of its role in uterine contraction in childbirth, plays an important part in orgasm, breast-feeding and other maternal behaviours, and in pair-bonding; because of this range of effects it is known as the *love hormone*.

P

Paedophilia

Sexual attraction to, or sexual activity with, pre-pubescent (or, in some jurisdictions, under legal age of consent) children.

Pederasty

(Rarely) the act of penetration in anal sex, though more usually sexual activity between an adult male and a young boy outside of the family (otherwise *incest* – see also). The term derives from the Greek paiderastia, which literally translates as 'love of boys'. In ancient Athens this was considered an ideal. Today, if the boy is under the age of consent, it is illegal and a form of *child sex abuse* (see also).

Peeping Tom

A person who derives sexual pleasure from watching others undress or engage in sexual activity. Also known as a *voyeur* (see also).

Pelvic Inflammatory Disease - PID

Inflammation of the uterine lining and Fallopian tubes in the female. Causes include bacterial infections including *Chlamydia* and gonorrhoea, and long-term use of IUDs. Symptoms include chronic pain and fever. If untreated, it can lead to infertility. See *Chlamydia, Gonorrhoea*.

Penetration

The insertion of a man's erect penis (or a penile substitute, such as a *dildo* – see also) into the vagina or anus of a partner in sexual activity.

Penile implants

Flexible or inflatable rods inserted by surgical operation into the penis to replace the cavernous tissue and thus create a mechanical form of achieving and maintaining an erection.

Penile injections

Used to treat erectile problems by, usually self-, injecting a drug into the cavernous tissue of the penis to create an erection.

Penis

The primary male sex organ. The penis is akin to the clitoris in the female, developing from the same tissue in the embryo. It is made up of erectile and muscular tissue, supplied with many sensory nerves. The erectile tissue lies in three columns, two on the back forming the *corpora cavernosa*, and one on the front forming the *corpus spongiosum* and extending to form the *glans* or head. This tissue is arranged in a honeycomb structure.

In the course of sexual arousal the muscle fibres that make up the honeycomb relax to allow blood to fill the structures, causing the penis to become erect. The urethra – through which urine is passed out of the body from the bladder and semen is passed on ejaculation – passes along the length of the penis through the *corpus spongiosum*, to its opening in the top of the *glans*. The penis is covered with loosely attached, fatless skin, which folds back on itself at the tip to make up the prepuce or foreskin in an un-circumcised male. At the back of the glans is a highly- sensitive bridge of skin, the *frenulum*. See also *Ejaculation, Erection, Frenulum, Glans.*

Penis/Penile corsets

Lace-up coverings for the penis, made of leather or rubber, used to help achieve and maintain an erection or for show. See *Arab straps.*

Perineum

In men, the area between the scrotum and the anus (commonly known as the *gooch* or *taint*); in women, the area between the vagina and the anus also know as the *fourchette* (see also).

Period

The flushing of the uterus in the female monthly cycle. See *Menstruation.*

Pervert

A person who enjoys certain sexual activities that other people consider offensive.

Pessary

(1) A medical tablet that is inserted into the vagina, where it dissolves and releases medication. Some spermi-cides are in pessary form.

(2) The ring pessary is a device in-serted into the vagina for women who have a prolapse of the vaginal walls and who do not want, or cannot have, an operation to repair the vagina.

Petting

An old-fashioned term for sexual activities such as caressing parts of the body, either as a prelude to, or instead of, intercourse.

Phallus

(1) A word for the erect penis.

(2) A false imitation, or image, of the male sexual organ, especially one as-sociated with symbols of reproductive power.

Pheromones

Chemical substances emitted by the body into the air, some of which are reputed to stimulate sexual attraction or desire in members of the opposite, or same, sex.

Phimosis

Abnormal tightness of the foreskin that can prevent it from being pulled back over the tip of the penis. The condition can often be corrected by gentle stretching, but in more severe cases circumcision may be necessary.

Piercing

Sexual body piercing typically in-volves piercing of the nipples or parts of the genitals such as the foreskin, scrotum, clitoris or labia. See *Ampal-lang, Apadravya, Prince Albert.*

Pill (contraceptive)

A pill, taken daily, which contains synthetic hormones, usually oestro-gen and/or progestogen. It works by modifying the level of these hormones within the female body in order to prevent pregnancy from occurring.

See *Combined pill, Progestogen-only pill, EveryDay pill*. A male equivalent has yet to become available. See *Hormonal methods of contraception*.

Pimp

Person who inducts and manages sex workers (formerly referred to as prostitutes). See *Sex worker, Prostitution*.

Platonic love

Term used to describe the love and admiration for another/others that does not involve sexual feelings or activity. The word is derived from a passage written by Plato in *The Symposium*.

Polyandry

The practice of having more than one husband at the same time.

Polygamy

Is a marriage where there are more than two partners. Where there is more than one husband that is *polyandry* (see also), and where there is more than one wife, *polygyny* (see also). If a marriage includes numerous wives and husbands, it is called *group marriage*. See also *Monogamy*.

Polygyny

The practice of having more than one wife at the same time.

Pornography

Any material, such as writing, books, films and photographs containing explicit sexual material designed to produce sexual arousal. Unlike eroticism, the term pornography has come to be associated with material that is exploitative. It derives from the Greek

pornographia which literally means writing about prostitutes. See *Blue movie, Erotic*.

Posthitis

An inflammation of the foreskin (prepuce). It can have a range of causes, bacterial, fungal or dermatitis and should be properly diagnosed for appropriate treatment to be prescribed. It can lead to the tightening of the foreskin called *phimosis* (see also).

Pre-come or Pre-cum

Fluids produced by certain glands, passed out of the penis prior to ejaculation. It consists mainly of lubricating secretions but may contain some sperm. See *Cowper's Gland and Littre's Gland*.

Premarital sex

Sexual intercourse that takes place before partners are married.

Premature ejaculation

A sexual dysfunction where a man involuntarily ejaculates early in the course of sexual activity.

Prepuce

Retractable fold of thin, hairless skin that covers the *glans* of the penis in the male (also known as the foreskin) and the clitoris in the female (also known as the clitoral hood). It is sometimes removed in the traditional practice of circumcision. See *Foreskin, Circumcision*.

Priapism

Prolonged, painful erection of the penis or clitoris due to obstruction of the blood vessels in the penis – it is deemed to occur when the organ fails to return to its flaccid state, despite the absence of any stimulation, within four hours (when a doctor should be consulted urgently).

Primary sexual characteristics

Related to the sexual organs directly involved in sexual activity and reproduction, namely the ovaries and vagina in the female and testes and penis in the male. These develop in the embryo and mature at puberty.

Prince Albert

A ring used in genital piercing which is passed through the *glans* of the penis into the urethra, just above the *frenulum*. See *Ampallang, Piercing.*

Proctitis

Inflammation of the anus and affecting the lower part of the rectum.

Progestogen

An artificial form of the natural hormone progesterone.

Progestogen-only Pill - POP

A contraceptive pill that contains only progestogen - not widely used.

Progesterone

A natural female hormone that is secreted chiefly from the ovaries. It prepares the uterus to receive and sustain a fertilised ovum.

Promiscuous

Pejorative descriptive term for a person who has several different sexual partners over a relatively short period of time.

Prostate gland

The male gland that surrounds the neck of the bladder and urethra. It produces one of the major constituents of sperm and has also been identified as the male G-spot. Stimulating it (using a finger inserted in the anus) can bring some men to orgasm.

Prostitution

The practice of engaging in sexual activities in exchange for money or favours. A person who engages in such activity is known as a prostitute or, more commonly, a sex worker. See *Pimp, Sex worker.*

Puberty

The stage of development at the beginning of adolescence when the sexual organs mature and secondary sexual characteristics emerge. This usually occurs around the age of 10 in girls and 11 in boys. See *Adolescence, Secondary sexual characteristics.*

Pubic bone

Bone at the front of the pelvis.

Pubic hair

Hair that grows in the region around the external genital organs.

Pubic lice

Small wingless, parasitic insects that infest the hair in the pubic area and occasionally on other parts of the body. They feed on blood by biting into the skin. This may cause irritation. They are usually passed through close bodily contact. See *Crabs.*

Pudendum or Pudenda

A single or collective term used to describe the external genitals, especially those of a woman.

Q

Queef

A term for the expulsion of air from the vulva during or after coitus; otherwise known as a *vaginal* or *fanny fart.*

Queen

A popular slang term used to describe effeminate gay men. It is derived from the Old English word *quaen* meaning a female prostitute.

Queer

A slang term used to describe a lesbian or gay man. Its usage has been documented in Britain since as early as the 1920s.

R

Radical sex

Sexual practices that are considered unconventional.

Rainbow

1960s term for group sex involving people of different skin colours.

Rainbow flag

A symbol of diversity for the lesbian and gay movement that has been used since 1978. The artist Gilbert Baker produced the first prototypes, which consisted of eight strips in pink, red, orange, yellow, green, turquoise, indigo and violet.

Ramayana

An Indian literary classic written by Valmiki, which includes descriptions of lesbian sexual activities.

Rape

To force a person to have sexual intercourse against their will. Victims of rape can be male or female, of any age or social background. Rapists are almost always male, although cases of sexual assault by women have also been reported. The relationship of the rapist to the victim may be as stranger, acquaintance, friend, family member, date, lover or long term partner or spouse. It has been estimated that at least 50% of rapists know their victims.

Rear entry

Various positions for sexual intercourse in which the man penetrates his partner from behind.

Rectum

The lowest, straight portion of the alimentary canal whose opening is the anus. See *Anus.*

Refractory period

The period of time following orgasm, during which the male sexual response to arousal is temporarily impossible. See *Multiple orgasm.*

Rent boy

A male sex worker, often young, who provides gay sexual services.

Reproductive organs

The organs that are involved in the processes of reproduction, including the production of reproductive cells (sperm and ova), sexual intercourse enabling sperm and ovum to meet, and the nurturing of the foetus should conception occur. They include the ovaries, Fallopian tubes, uterus and vagina in the female, and the testes, epididymis and the penis in the male.

Rhythm method

A natural method of contraception. See *Natural methods*.

Rimming

The practice of licking or sucking the anus of the partner. See *Anilingus, Dental dam*.

Row boat

Practice where a woman has intercourse with one man on top of her, while giving fellatio to two other men, one standing on each side of her.

S

Sadism

A form of sexual practice in which a person gains pleasure from inflicting pain on another. The word is derived from the name of the Marquis de Sade (1740-1814), whose writings featured descriptions of such practices. See *Masochism, Sadomasochism*.

Sadomasochism - SM or S&M

A form of sexual practice in which pleasure is gained from a combination of sadism and masochism.

Safe period

The stage of a woman's menstrual cycle when she is least likely to be able to conceive. See *Natural methods*.

Safer sex

Any form of sex that does not involve the exchange of body fluids, including non-penetrative sex, penetrative sex with the use of a condom, or the use of dental dams.

Salpingitis

Inflammation of the Fallopian tubes caused by an infection such as gonorrhoea or tuberculosis, or a reaction to an IUD. Symptoms include pain on one or both sides, fever and increased menstrual flow. See *Gonorrhoea*.

Sapphist

Archaic term for a lesbian. The word is derived from the Greek, lesbian poet Sappho (610-580 BC) who lived on the island of Lesbos, from which came the current term. See *Lesbian*.

Sapphism

Lesbianism. See *Sapphist*.

Scabies

An infestation of parasitic mites, which burrow into the skin where they lay eggs, usually on the hairy parts of the body. Their saliva and droppings cause acute irritation. They are spread by close contact, including sexual contact, and poor hygiene.

Scat

Any sexual practice that involves faeces; it's a shortening of the term scatological. See also *Coprophilia*.

Scissors

(1) Term referring to lesbian sex practice involving manually stimulating a partner's anus and clitoris simultaneously.

(2) Sexual position where the partners' legs are between one another's and their torsos are at right angles.

Scrotal sac

The sac of loose skin containing the testicles. See *Scrotum*.

Scrotum

The sac of loose, wrinkled skin that contains a man's testicles. Also known as the scrotal sac.

Sebum

An oily substance that is first produced at puberty. It is released from the sebaceous glands of the skin and makes the skin and hair greasier.

Secondary sexual characteristics

The physical characteristics, excluding the reproductive organs (which are the *primary sexual characteristics* – see also), that develop during puberty and distinguish male and female. They include men's greater facial hair and women's greater body fat.

Semen

A mixture of seminal fluid and sperm, ejaculated from the penis at the point of orgasm. See *Ejaculation*.

Seminal fluid

One of the two main constituents of semen, produced chiefly in the prostate gland. It functions as the liquid medium in which the sperm is carried and nourished.

Seminal vesicles

Small sacs, at the back of a man's prostate gland, which discharge seminal fluid into the urethra just before ejaculation.

Seminiferous tubules

Tightly coiled tubes in the testes where the sperm are produced. Each testis contains as many as 800 tubules, each of which may be 40 cm or more in length.

Sex aids

Any object used to generate or enhance sexual arousal and/or orgasm. Some of the most common are dildoes, vibrators, clitoral stimulators, extension condoms, vaginal balls and various 'stay longer' creams and lotions. See *Sex toys*.

Sex change

The term often used for gender reassignment therapy, which covers the procedures transgender people can have, though is also sometimes used to refer to the whole process of changing gender role. See *Gender reassignment*.

Sex drive

The urge or desire to have sex which is also known as *libido* (see also); also the amount or frequency of sexual activity which an individual requires in order to be sexually satisfied. Sex drive not only varies widely from one person to another but in the same person at different times. Its strength as a drive can be the result of a mix of factors, biological (levels of hormones such as *testosterone* – see also), social (such as work and family) and psychological (such as personality and stress).

Sex hormone

The hormones that determine the development of the sexual organs and secondary sexual characteristics and that also maintain and regulate the reproductive system and sexual feelings. The extent of their role in psychological and emotional changes is not yet fully understood. The principal sex hormones in women are oestrogen and progesterone; in men it is testosterone. See *Oestrogen, Progesterone, Testosterone.*

Sex toys

Objects used to enhance sexual arousal. See *Sex aids.*

Sexting

The act of sending sexually explicit messages or photographs primarily via mobile phones.

Sexual abuse

Any form of unwanted sexual advance or use of sex to intimidate or threaten. This can range from verbal harassment to sexual assault and rape. See *Child sexual abuse, Rape.*

Sexual arousal

Feelings of sexual excitement, accompanied by mental and physical changes. Physical signs of arousal include erection of the penis and tightening of the scrotal sac in the male, and swelling of the areolae and clitoris together with increased vaginal lubrication in the female. Both men and women experience increased pulse and breathing rates. See *Clitoris, Erection, Penis.*

Sexual harassment

The use of sex to threaten or intimidate; in particular, unwanted, offensive and/or repetitious sexual advances.

Sexual intercourse

Commonly refers to the act of a man inserting his penis into the female vagina and is also know as *copulation* (see also) and *coitus* (see also). It may also refer to a range of other penetrative acts, both heterosexual and homosexual, including oral sex, anal sex, fingering or sex with a dildo. See also *Intercourse.*

Sexual inversion or Inversion

An outdated term used at the beginning of the 20th century to refer to *homosexuality* (see also). It resembles the current definition of *transgender* (see also).

Sexual orientation

An individual's pattern of sexual interest and attraction. This may be towards people of the opposite sex, the same sex, or both sexes and may vary within the same person at different ages and stages of his or her life.

Sexual response

The term for the level of arousal of a person during or in reaction to erotic stimuli (be they external, such as erotica, another person's sexual advances, or internal, such as fantasy). See also *Erotic, Fantasy, Sexual arousal.*

Sexual satisfaction

Deep feelings of contentment and well-being experienced after sexual activity, particularly after *orgasm* (see also).

Sexually transmitted disease – STD, or Sexually transmitted infection - STI

Any illness that can be transmitted through sexual contact.

Sex worker

A term coined in the 1980s as a substitute for the word prostitute.

Shaft

The main part of the length of the penis (from the base to below the glans) or clitoris. See *Penis, Glans, Clitoris*.

Sheath

Another, rather old-fashioned, term for the *condom* (see also), the main male barrier method of contraception (which can also help protect against some sexually transmitted infections).

Shrimping

The practice of sucking the toes in an attempt to trigger *sexual arousal* (see also).

Shudo

Japanese term for *pederasty* (see also).

Sixty-nine

Form of oral sex in which two people perform oral sex on each other at the same time. It is so-called because the positions adopted by the couple while performing this practice resemble the figure 69 when viewed from the side. The French translation, *soixante-neuf*, is also used.

Sleep with someone

Euphemism meaning to have sexual intercourse with someone.

Smegma

Sebum (see also) based substance that has lubricant properties and a cheesy-like consistency. It can accumulate under the foreskin of the penis or the hood of the clitoris.

Sodomy

An alternate term for anal intercourse. The word is derived from the sinful biblical city of Sodom. See *Anal intercourse*.

Soixante-neuf

Double oral sex where the participants are head to tail. See *Sixty-nine*.

Solicit

To offer sexual services in return for money, especially in a public place. See *Pimp, Prostitution*.

Spanish fly

Powder made from dried *Lytta vesicatoria* beetles. It contains an active ingredient, *cantharidin*, which inflames the urethra. It is sometimes taken as an aphrodisiac because of these stimulative properties but, in the doses needed, it can be fatal.

Spanking

The practice of smacking or hitting a partner for sexual excitement.

Sperm

The male reproductive cell, produced constantly in the testes of the mature male, and released through the penis at ejaculation. See *Testes, Semen*.

Spermatic cord

The cord that passes from each of the male testes through the inguinal canal in the groin. It contains the *vas deferens* (see also) which conveys sperm to the ejaculatory duct.

Spermicide

Any substance, usually a gel or cream, designed to kill sperm. It may be injected into the vagina prior to intercourse or used in conjunction with other forms of contraception. See *Contraception*.

Sponge - contraceptive

A barrier form of contraceptive that consists of a small, round sponge soaked in *spermicide* (see also), placed inside the vagina over the cervix. It is less reliable than other forms of contraception.

Squeeze technique

A technique for delaying ejaculation or developing ejaculatory control, in which the head of the penis is squeezed (sometimes repeatedly) just before the point when ejaculation becomes inevitable.

Start/Stop

A technique for delaying ejaculation or developing ejaculatory control, in which stimulation of the penis is temporarily interrupted just before the point when ejaculation becomes inevitable. The process is repeated several times in order to be effective.

'Stay longer' creams and sprays

Products designed to help a man to delay ejaculation, usually by reducing penile sensitivity with small amounts of local anaesthetic. Not typically recommended as they diminish pleasure as well. See *Sex aids*.

STD/STI

See *Sexually transmitted disease/infection*.

Sterilisation

A term to cover a number of medical procedures, including by surgery (including vasectomy and castration in males and Fallopian-tubal ligation ['tying'] and hysterectomy in females) and pharmaceutical means (though it is disputed that a working "sterilisation pill" actually exists) that is intended to render an individual permanently unable to conceive a child (woman) or cause impregnation (man). See *Vasectomy, Female sterilisation*.

Straight

Slang term for heterosexuals. It may also be used as an expression to describe a conservative outlook, while its use in drug-taking circles refers to someone who is either not under the influence of a mind-expanding drug or who does not consume such substances.

Sub

Abbreviation of the term submissive, used to refer to a passive partner in practices involving bondage and sadomasochism. The term bottom is also used. See *Bondage, Bottom, Dom, Sub-dom.*

Sub-dom

Sexual practices in which partners take defined dominant and submissive roles. Sub-dom practices may or may not involve bondage, role-playing and sadomasochism.

Swinging

Partner-swapping and sharing within groups of friends, associates or strangers. Swinging may involve singles or couples having sex play in pairs or groups, in front of each other or in private, with mutual consent and usually at the same venue. It may be arranged through swinging clubs or parties, through friends or through advertisements in specialised magazines or on the internet.

Sympto-thermal method

A natural method of contraception where ovulation is determined by noting a change in the female's basal temperature. See *Temperature method.*

Syphilis

A sexually-transmitted disease caused by the *treponema bacterium*. It enters the body through tiny cracks in the skin and lives and multiplies in the blood and other body fluids of an infected person. It is passed on by the fluid secreted from the characteristic sores and chancres. These develop wherever the bacteria enters the body – usually on or near the penis or vagina, or sometimes in the anus or

mouth. If untreated the bacteria can affect other parts of the body including the brain. In very severe cases disfigurement or death may result. Syphilis can be treated effectively with antibiotics.

T

Temperature method

A method of predicting when ovulation occurs by taking a woman's body temperature at the same time each day. Ovulation has occurred when body temperature has risen slightly for three days. See *Natural methods, Sympto-thermal method.*

Termination

Brining a pregnancy to an end. See *Abortion.*

Testes or testicles

The two male sex glands or *gonads* (see also) located in the scrotum, which produce the male sex hormone *testosterone* (see also) and the reproductive cells, the *sperm* (see also). Sperm are produced, matured and nourished in the long, narrow, tightly coiled *seminiferous tubules* (see also) within each testis, before being released into the epididymis where they are matured further and stored until needed. Sperm production is constant and throughout most of the male's mature life. The testes are equivalent to the ovaries in the female.

Testosterone

A steroid hormone produced in the testes in the male and in other glands. Often described as a male hormone, it is in fact produced by both males and females. In males, it causes the development of the sex organs in the foetus. At puberty it is responsible for the maturation of the sex organs and the development of the second-ary sexual characteristics. In the adult it influences both male and female *sexual desire* (see also) and male sexual performance. See also *Oestrogen*.

Thai Beads

A sex aid consisting of plastic beads threaded on to, or moulded in to, a string or rod, inserted into the anus and moved in and out to enhance sex-ual arousal and can cause very strong sensations when manipulated during orgasm. See *Sex aids, Sex toys*.

Thrush

A yeast infection that can cause ir-ritation and soreness in the male and female genitalia. See *Candida albicans*.

Ticklers

Rubber or latex sheaths (condoms) which have bumps and knobs on them, and are placed over the penis, either down the shaft or at the tip, to stimulate the clitoris, vagina and/ or cervix. Ticklers are produced as sex aids, not contraceptives. See also *Clitoral stimulator*.

Transgender

A broad term used to describe indi-viduals, behaviours or groups involv-ing tendencies to stray from culturally conventional gender roles. It may also be used for a transsexual who is any-where across the continuum of sexual reassignment. See *Gender reassignment*.

Transsexual

A person whose gender identity does not follow biological gender. See *Gender identity, Gender reassignment*.

Transvestism

Desired or habitual dressing in the clothing and/or under clothing as-sociated with the opposite sex, some-times with the appropriate make-up and accessories as well. Transvestites (now more commonly known as cross-dressers) may be male or female and may be heterosexual. In most cases the motivation behind transves-tism is a form of fetishistic attraction to the clothing and accoutrements of the opposite sex, but it may also have to do with an attraction to the gender role of the opposite, sex, symbolised by their clothes.

Tribadism

A primarily lesbian sexual practice in which one partner lies on top of the other and both move together to stimulate each other's clitoris.

Trichomoniasis

A sexually transmitted disease caused by a small parasite that infects the vagina, causing inflammation and ir-ritation. It can also be spread to the cervix. Men are only rarely infected, in the urethra, where it can cause *NGU* (see also).

Tricking

(1) Enjoyment of casual sex; a trick re-fers either to the casual encounter itself or to the partner in such an encounter.

(2) Paid encounter secured by a sex worker (see also).

Troilism

Term used to describe three people having sex together, in any combination of male and female. See *Ménage à trois*.

Turn-on

The common term for sexual arousal or something causing *sexual arousal* (see also).

U

Uncut

Term used to describe an uncircumcised penis or a man with such a penis.

Unprotected sex

Sexual activity that does not involve safer sex practices. These may lead to pregnancy or infection. See also *Condom, Contraception*.

Urethra

The tube through which urine passes from the bladder; in men the urethra also carries semen during ejaculation. See also *Penis*.

Urethritis

Inflammation of the urethra, usually caused by bacterial infection. See *NGU*.

Urolagnia

Also known as golden showers, undinism, urophilia, or water sports, it is a fetish where sexual arousal is associated with the sight, sound or thought of urine or urination by either sex. (It derives from the Greek literally meaning "urine lust") See *Water sports*.

Uterus or womb

The female reproductive organ in which an embryo grows, matures and is nourished. The uterus lies between the bladder and the rectum, where it is held in place by various ligaments. The main part of its wall is made up of muscle. The two Fallopian tubes are attached on either side, linking it with the ovaries, while the cervix or neck of the uterus provides the passageway between the uterus and the vagina. The lining of the uterus is known as the *endometrium*, and is prepared each month for the implantation of a fertilised ovum as part of the menstrual cycle. See also *Menstrual cycle, Cervix, Vagina*.

V

Vacuum device

A sex aid designed to help a man achieve and maintain an erection. It is placed over the penis; air is pumped out and the vacuum created helps to cause an erection by drawing blood into the spongy vessels within the penis. A tight band (cock ring) may then be placed around the base of the penis to maintain the erection and the device is removed.

Vagina

The passage between the *vulva* (see also) and the *cervix* (see also). It is a fibro-muscular structure covered with a thin mucous membrane. The various layers of muscle – together with the numerous folds of skin by which they are covered – give the vagina great capacity for expansion and contraction. The smooth muscle within the vaginal wall is not under voluntary control and relaxes and stretches as necessary during sexual arousal, penile penetration and childbirth without conscious effort, while the muscle fibres surrounding the outer third of the vagina can usually be tensed and relaxed voluntarily. In the course of sexual arousal the vagina dilates and 'sweats' a lubricating substance from its walls. As the woman approaches orgasm the upper part of the vagina balloons and the outer parts swell to form what is sometimes known as *an orgasmic platform*, on which the rhythmic muscle contractions of orgasm are focused.

Vaginismus

Condition in which the muscles around the outer third of the vagina contract involuntarily, very tightly, thus making penetration painful, difficult or impossible. This may apply to all attempts at penetration including tampons, Pap-smear instruments, fingers or a penis. Treatments include a range of approaches: psychological (to overcome a mental fear of penetration), physical (including the use of dilators) and paralytics (using such agents as Botox to prevent the muscle from going into spasm).

Vaginitis

Inflammation of the vagina, caused by infection, injury or atrophy.

Vas deferens

The tube that conveys sperm from the testes to the penis, as part of the *spermatic cord* (see also). See *Testes*.

Vasectomy

Surgical operation in which the vasa deferentia are cut and tied so that sperm cannot be passed along them and are therefore not released in the ejaculate. See *Sterilisation, Vas deferens*.

Vasocongestion

The process of tissue becoming engorged with blood, as when the penis becomes erect. See *Erection*.

Venereal Disease (VD)

Any disease that can be transmitted by sexual contact, now more commonly termed sexually transmitted diseases, STDs, or sexually transmitted infections, STIs, (see also).

Vestibule

Is the chamber inside the vulva and defined by the woman's outer and inner labia and includes the clitoral crown at the top, the vaginal opening and the urethral opening. Its edge is marked by what is known as Hart's Line (named after a Scottish surgeon gynaecologist, David Berry Hart) – where the skin changes in texture at its perimeter.

Vibrator

Sex aid, powered by batteries (though sometimes mains electricity), that vibrates rhythmically to produce sensual pleasure. Vibrators are made in a great variety of shapes but the most common are those shaped as erect penises. Some have attachments for simultaneous stimulation of the clitoris, others are for use in the anus. Vibrators are also made in the shape of vaginas. Vibrating devices are most frequently used for masturbation on or around the genitals but they may be used to stimulate any part of the body. In practice, they appear to work better in building sexual arousal and helping achieve orgasm in females than males. There are now vast ranges of vibrators of all kinds on the market and studies suggest more than 50% of the female population in the West have at least one and over 78% of those use them within a relationship.

Virgin

A person who has never experienced sexual intercourse. The term originally only referred to a sexually inexperienced female, with its loss only through penile-vaginal penetration, though others, particularly those of other sexual orientations, may include other sexual practices, such as oral, anal, or masturbation by another to be included in the notion of losing one's virginity.

Voyeur

A person who enjoys and becomes sexually aroused by watching, or usually spying on, others undress or engage in sexual activities. See *Peeping Tom*.

Vulva

The external female genitalia. It is made up of many anatomical structures including the mons pubis ('mound of Venus'), the labia majora (outer lips), the clitoris and clitoral hood, and some would include the labia minora (inner lips), the vestibule, and the urethral and vaginal openings.

W

Water sports - WS

Sexual acts that involve one partner urinating over (golden shower) or into (golden screw) their partner. See *Urolagnia*.

Wet dream

This is when a male ejaculates involuntarily in his sleep or a female becomes highly lubricated and is usually considered to involve a spontaneous orgasm whilst unconscious. See *Nocturnal emission*.

Wide-on

A slang term for the state of advanced female sexual arousal that results in a relaxation of the vaginal muscles. It is analogous to the male hard-on and derives from the female's labia swelling and opening in sexual arousal.

Withdrawal

A natural method of contraception where the male withdraws his penis from the vagina before he ejaculates. See *Coitus interruptus*.

Womb

The womb or uterus is a major female reproductive organ where the foetus develops prior to birth. See *Uterus*.

Women who have sex with women - WSW

Female individuals who engage in sexual activity with members of the same sex regardless of whether they identify themselves as lesbian or bisexual.

EDITORIAL TEAM

Dr. Chris Fariello PhD MA LMFT

Born in New York City, Dr. Fariello has worked for over 25 years as an educator, trainer, public speaker, writer, and therapist. Dr. Fariello is recognized nationally in the US as a Sex and Relationship expert and has appeared on numerous radio, television news and talk shows.

He has appeared in many newspaper and magazine articles and was a weekly "Good Sex" columnist. He has contributed to several videos and books, including Dr. Ruth's *Sex for Dummies*, and has authored *99 Things Parents Wish They Knew Before Having THE Talk*.

Dr. Chris Fariello is the Founder and Director of the Philadelphia Institute for Individual Relational & Sex Therapy (PhIIRST) in Philadelphia.

With many years as a university Professor, he is a licensed Marriage and Family Therapist, a Clinical Member and Supervisor of the American Association for Marriage and Family Therapists (AAMFT), a Certified Sex Therapist, Educator & Supervisor of the American Association for Sexuality Educators, Counselors and Therapists (AASECT) and certified as a Diplomat in Sex Therapy through the American Board of Sexology.

He received his first master's degree in Human Sexuality, Marriage and Family Life Education from New York University and his second master's in Marriage and Family Therapy from MCP Hahnemann (Drexel) University in Philadelphia. His doctorate is in Human Sexuality Education from the University of Pennsylvania. Dr. Fariello currently resides in the suburbs of Philadelphia with his girlfriend Renata and three children, Julianna, Luca and Selina.

Baroness Doreen E. Massey MA,
Chair, National Treatment Agency (NTA)

Doreen E Massey has a BA (Hons) degree in French and an MA in Health Education. She has been a Labour Peer since 1999.

She has been Chair of the NTA since January 2002. The NTA is a special health authority, created by the Government in 2001, with a remit to increase the availability, capacity and effectiveness of treatment for drug misuse.

She has a strong interest in children and young people, and chairs the All Party Parliamentary Group for Children, and is a trustee of UNICEF UK. She is President of Brook Advisory Centres, a charity specialising in young people and sexual health, Patron of the University of Bedfordshire Child Anti-Trafficking Unit, Women and Children First and the Advisory Centre for Education,

Patron of the Family Planning Association and National Secular Society. She is a health education specialist on a range of issues including drug and alcohol misuse, HIV/AIDS and sexual health in national and international contexts. She is the former Director of the UK Family Planning Association, has published a range of books and training resources on health and sex education and is a qualified teacher. In addition, Doreen is a graduate mentor of students at the University of Birmingham, one of the first schemes of its kind in the UK.

She is an active member of the House of Lords, speaking on Bills and on questions and debates about issues concerned with children, young people, public health, sport, education and women's issues.

She is a member of the All-Party Parliamentary Groups on: alcohol and drugs; AIDS; population and development; trafficking; cricket. She is Secretary to the British Humanist Association, Vice-President of the Royal Society of Public Health, Vice Chair of the All Party Parliamentary Cricket Group. She is also a Lady Taverner, a cricket charity which raises money for disabled children to take part in sport. She is a Fellow of the Royal Society of Arts.

Doreen has a lifelong interest in sport. She played county hockey and cricket, regularly takes part in swimming, gym, pilates and walking. Her outside interests include theatre, opera, film, reading, and travelling. She is married with three children and three grandchildren.

Robert Page MA

Robert Page first created *The Lovers' Guide* in 1991, when it was the first non-fiction title to go to number one in the video charts and sold over a million copies in the UK alone. It was translated into 13 languages and went into 22 countries. He has since supervised its growth into the undisputed leading international brand on sex and relationships. It has been released as over a dozen DVDs, two TV programs, two books, games, the biggest adult sex education website on the internet: www.loversguide.com, and the world's first adult theatrical feature film *The Lovers' Guide 3D - Igniting Desire* (2011).

As Head of Production and Chief Executive of the Lifetime Group, he has also produced many other videos, TV series and films including three series of *Floyd On...*, *Runaway Bay* and the Hollywood Genesis Award-winning, Dr Desmond Morris's *The Animal Contract*.

He has written, lectured and broadcast extensively. He is a member of the American Association of Sexuality Educators, Counselors, and Therapists (AASECT); The World Association for Sexual Health (WAS) and The Society for the Scientific Study of Sexuality (SSSS). He lives in New York with his wife, Rebecca, and has two sons.

Contributing Writers for
The Lovers' Guide Illustrated Encyclopedia

Reay Tannahill MA (1929-2007), was a British historian, non-fiction writer, and novelist best known perhaps for two non-fiction bestsellers: *Food in History* and *Sex in History*. For her 2002 revised edition of *Food in History*, she won the *Premio Letterario Internazionale Chianti Ruffino Antico Fattore*. She also wrote historical romance novels under the pseudonym, Annabel Laine.

Her novel *Passing Glory* won the Romantic Novel of the Year Award by the Romantic Novelists' Association in 1990. Before she started to write, she worked as a probation officer, advertising copywriter, newspaper reporter, historical researcher and graphic designer.

Originally Scottish born and bred, she spent most of her working life in London where she belonged to the Arts Club and the Author's Club, for which she was Chairman from 1997 to 2000.

Elizabeth Fenwick is a professional writer specializing in health and family matter. She has worked as an agony aunt advising on sexual problems on radio and fgor Company magazine, a counsellor for Childline and in sex education in various London schools.

Her writing career began with a regular column for World Medicine about life with her psychiatrist husband and three young children.

Her extensive publications include: *The Baby Book For Fathers, The Truth in the Light* and *Living with Epilepsy* (all with Peter Fernwick); *The Complete Book of Mother and Baby Care, Adolescence* (with Richard Walker) and *Sexual Happiness* (with Maurice Yaffe).

Olivia Preston read Hispanic Studies at Manchester University where she was also a Counsellor for the student helpline. That, being single, a seasoned traveller and her expertise in Chilean love poetry, somehow qualified her to act as senior researcher and writer for the *Lovers' Guide Encyclopedia* and associated CD-ROM.

She has since become an executive at an international printing company and then joined the UK's Foreign and Commonwealth Office.

SEXUAL FACTS

Opener: Simon Jennings
4. (bottom) Ann Summers Ltd
5. Joe Bulaitis
9. Musée d'Orsay, Paris
13. Marshall Cavendish
17. Reproduced with kind permission from *The Collected Drawings of Aubrey Beardsley* by Bruce Harris (ed.), Crown Publishing inc.
18. Hugo Boss Ltd.
19. Science Photo Library
28. Science Photo Library
29. Image Bank
30. Image Bank
31. Science Photo Library
32. Image Bank
33. Joe Bulaitis/Ian Seaton
35. Joe Bulaitis/Ian Seaton
39. Image Bank
41. Image Bank
42. Mark Pennington
44. Mark Pennington
45. (top) Mark Pennington
46. (top) Chartex Ltd.
47. (top) Chartex Ltd.
48. Mark Pennington
49. Mark Pennington
50. Mark Pennington
52. Mark Pennington
56. Image Bank
57. (top) Stapleton Collection (bottom) Mansell Collection
58. Wikipedia (circuncidado89)
59. Liba Tayor/Panos Pictures
60. Mark Pennington
63. Mark Pennington
70. (top) Science Photo Library (bottom) Tim Nunn/Panos Pictures
71. Bill Cooper
73. United Colours of Benetton
75. *The Rape of the Sabines* by Peter Paul Rubens (1557-1640) National Gallery, London/Bridgeman Art Library, London

SEXUAL FEELINGS

79. Simon Jennings
81 (top) Renate Hillermann (bottom) Image Bank
82. Zefa
83. Mark Pennington
84. *Seated Woman with Bent Knee*, 1917 by Egon Schiele (1890-1918) Narodni Galerie, Prague/Bridgeman Art Library, London
86. Reproduced with kind permission from *The Collected Drawings of Aubrey Beardsley* by Bruce Harris (ed.), Crown Publishing inc.
88. Reproduced with kind permission from *The Collected Drawings of Aubrey Beardsley* by Bruce Harris (ed.), Crown Publishing inc.
87. Stapleton Collection
90. Image Bank
91. Rex Features
92. Rex Features
93. (top) Rex Features (bottom) Simon Jennings
94. (top) Mary Evans (bottom) Rex Features
95. 3 Over 1 Design
96. (top) Rex Features (bottom) InterAction Stock/Milton Diamond
97. Marshall Cavendish
98. Marshall Cavendish
99. InterAction Stock/Milton Diamond
100. (top) Zefa (bottom) Rex Features
101. Image Bank
102. Rex Features
103. Image Bank
104. InterAction Stock/Milton Diamond
105. Zefa
108. Rex Features
109. Ann Summers Ltd.
110. Zefa

PICTURE CREDITS

113. *La Belle Dame Sans Merci* by Sir
Frank Dicksee (1853-1928) City of
Bristol Museum and Art Gallery/
Bridgeman Library, London
114. Image Bank
115. (top) Beatriz Reis
(bottom) Image Bank
117. Image Bank
118-119. Marshall Cavendish

SEXUAL BEHAVIOUR

121. Simon Jennings
123. *Lovers*, 1911 by Egon Schiele
(1890-1918) Private Collection/Bridge-
man Art Library, London
125. Marshall Cavendish
128. Image Bank; Marshall Cavendish
129. Image Bank; Marshall Cavendish
131. (top) Reproduced with kind
permission from *The Collected Drawings
of Aubrey Beardsley* by Bruce Harris (ed.),
Crown Publishing inc.
(bottom) Stapleton Collection
134. (top) Stapleton Collection
(bottom) Rainer Wick
136. Inklink
137. (bottom) Rainer Wick
138. Stapleton Collection
140. (middle-bottom) Marshall Cavendish
146. Photograph by Robert Taylor from
Safer Sexy: The Guide to Gay Sex Safely by
Peter Tatchell (Cassell 1994)
147. Laurence Jaugey-Paget
149. Image Bank
151. (left) Laurence Jaugey-Paget
(right) Marshall Cavendish
153. (top) Marshall Cavendish
(middle, bottom) Ann Summers Ltd.
154. (top) Marshall Cavendish
155. (top, middle) Marshall Cavendish
155. (bottom) *Proserpine*, 1874 by Dante
Gabriel Rosetti (1828-82) Tate Gallery,
London/Bridgeman Art Library, London
156. (top) Image Bank
(middle) Tuppy Owens

157. InterAction Stock/Milton Diamond
158. (top) Image Bank
162. Rex Features
163. Rex Features
166. (top) Ann Summers Ltd.
168. Lelo "Yva"
169. (bottom) Fleshlight
170. (top) We-Vibe
(bottom) OhMiBod
171. Andromedical
173. Image Bank
174. Rex Features
175. (top) Tuppy Owens
(bottom) InterAction Stock/Milton
Diamond
176. (top) Rex Features
(bottom) Michele Martinoli
177. (top) InterAction Stock/Milton
Diamond
178. (top) Zefa
(bottom) Rex Features
180. (bottom) Tuppy Owens
181. Tuppy Owens
182. (top) Reproduced with kind
permission from *The Collected Drawings
of Aubrey Beardsley* by Bruce Harris (ed.),
Crown Publishing inc.
(bottom) Ann Summers Ltd.
183. (top) Tuppy Owens
184. (top) Gisbert Bauer
(bottom) Stapleton Collection
185. (top) *The Swing*, 1767 by Jean-Honore
Fragonard (1732-1806) Wallace Collection,
London/Bridgeman Art Library, London
(bottom) Marshall Cavendish
186. (top) Tuppy Owens
187. Rex Features
188. Rex Features
190. Reginald Grant Archive/Allied
Entertainment
191. (top) Image Bank
192. Marshall Cavendish
194. Marshall Cavendish
195. Marshall Cavendish

SEX AND YOU
199. Simon Jennings
201. iStockPhoto/David Falk
202. iStockPhoto/Nicolas Monu
205. iStockPhoto/studiovespa
215. iStockPhoto/Diego Cervo
216. iStockPhoto/Ericsphotography
218. iStockPhoto/Vetta
223. iStockPhoto/Niko Guido
226. (top) iStockPhoto/Niko Guido
229. iStockPhoto/000005575695
236. (top) iStockPhoto/bowdenimages
(bottom) Image Bank
240. David Steinberg
241. Tuppy Owens
242. David Steinberg

SEX AND CULTURE
245. Simon Jennings
247. (top to bottom) Werner Forman Archive; InterAction Stock/Milton Diamond; Private Collection, New York Private Collection, New York; Gisbert Bauer
248. Dorset County Council Archaeology Service
249. Mansell Collection
250. *The Daughters of Judah in Babylon* by Schmaltz, Herbert Gustave (1856-1935) Christie's, London/Bridgeman Art Library, London
251. Musée du Louvre, Paris: copyright photo RMN – Chuzeville
253. Werner Forman Archive
254. AKG/Erich Lessing
256. AKG/Erich Lessing
257. Reproduced from *Erotic Art of the Masters, 18th, 19th and 20th Centuries* by Bradley Smith (Gemini-Smith)
259. *Humay and Murayun,* lovers surrounded by attendants, from the 'Shahnama', 1396 Persian Literary Texts, British Library, London/Bridgeman Art Library, London
260. Gisbert Bauer

261. A Prince involved in united intercourse, described by Vatsyayana in his 'Kama Sutra', Bundi, Rajasthan, Rajput School, c.1800 Private Collection/ Bridgeman Art Library, London
262. *Adam and Even banished from Paradise* by Tommaso Masaccio (1401-28) Brancacci Chapel, Santa Maris del Carmine, Florence/Bridgeman Art Library, London
264. *King Arthur's Wedding Night,* French, 14th century (manuscript) Bibliotheque Inguimbertine, Carpentras/ Bridgeman Art Library, London
266. (top) *Virgin and Child* by Jean Fouquet (c. 1425-80) Koninklijk Museum voor Schone Kunsten, Antwerp/Bridgeman Art Library, London
(bottom) *Lancelot proves his love of Guinevere,* Roman de Lancelot du Lac (1344) Pierpont Morgan Library, New York/Bridgeman Art Library, London
267. Portrait of the Van Cortland Family, c.1830 by Anonymous, American Museum, Bath/Bridgeman Art Library, London
268. Mary Evans
270. Stapleton Collection
272. Rex Features
274. Eikoh Hosoe
279. Wikipedia (prior to 1923)
280. (top) Wikipedia (prior to 1923) (middle) Unknown (claiming fair use for educational purposes) (bottom) Mary Evans (Sigmund Freud) copyright courtesy of W.E. Freud
281. (top) Smithsonian Institution
282. (top) Corbis – Bettman/UPI (bottom) Wikipedia (prior to 1923)
283. (top) Wikipedia (claiming fair use for educational purposes) (bottom) Topham
284. (top) Wikipedia (prior to 1923) (middle) Underwood & Underwood (public domain) (bottom) Marie Stopes International

A

B

bacterial vaginosis 64, 291
balanitis 63, 291
bald chicken drug 258
barbiturates 160
barrier contraception 291
Bartholin's glands 10, 291
bathhouses 291
Ben-wa balls 291
bestiality 194, 291
bigamy 291
biology and evolution
  female 84
  male 87
  physical attraction and 106
birth control 292
bisexuality 89, 107, 292
bladder, inflamation of. *See* cystitis
blastocyst 292
blue movie 292
body hair 174. *See also* pubic hair
  changes in puberty 33, 36
  shaving 175
body hair dressing 174, 292
body language 114–119
  exhibitionism 185
  forming relationships and 209
body, liking your own 202. *See also* self-
    image
body odour 56
body painting 174
body piercing 175, 176–177
body rubbing. *See* frottage; *See* tribadism
bondage 179, 292–293
  domination and 181
boredom, sexual 220–221
bottom 146, 292
branding 178
bras 4, 153, 172
breast developers 172
breasts 4–5, 128, 292
  anatomy 4
  changes in puberty 34
  milk production 4
  shape and size 5

breast self-examination (BSE) 6–7
Bridal Roll, The 162
bridge technique 235
brothel 189
brothels 188
Buddhism, attitudes to sex 276
buggery 292
Burton, Sir Richard 279
butch 91, 93, 293. *See also* femme
'butterfly' 168
buttocks 128, 129, 293
butt-plugs 167, 293

C

calendar method (contraception) 44,
    293
camp 93, 293
cancer
  breast 6
  circumcision and 58
  testicular 19–20
candaulism 293
candida albicans 64
candida albicans (fungal infection) 293
cannabis, and sex 159
cap, cervical 48, 294. *See also* diaphragm
  early form 42
Carpenter, Edward 280
castration 293
  cure for masturbation 134
casual sex 87, 294
casual zone (personal territory) 116
catamite 294
celibacy 294
  early Christian teachings 263–264,
    267
Cerne Abbas Giant 248
cervical mucus method (contraception)
    45, 294
cervix 2, 8
chancroid 68, 294
change of life 294. *See also* menopause
chastity 264, 294
child abuse 74–75, 294

D

daisy chain 184, 298
dartos muscles 16, 18–19
  and testes position 19
dates, first 209
  minimal programme 210
dating
  online 190–191
dating agencies, and disabilities 241
deep-throat 299
deer horn potion 258
defilement 181
degradation. *See* humiliation and
    degradation
dental dams 61, 299
detumescence 299
diaphragm 299
  early 42
dildo. *See also* sex toys
dildos 165, 299
  precautions 164
disabilities
  recognition of sexual needs 240, 274
  sex and 240
  social and physical factors 241–242
diseases, sexually transmitted 62–73,
    321. *See also* specific diseases
  19th century attitudes 270–271
divorce
  religious attitudes to 251, 254, 264,
    267, 276–278
dogging 152, 186
domination (dom) 179, 181, 323
donor insemination. *See* AID
drag 95, 299
drag queens 95, 299
dressing for sex 153–154
  undressing 154
dress, symbolic 181
drugs, and sex 158–161
dydo 177, 299
dysmenorrhoea 38, 299

E

ecstasy, and sex 160
ectopic pregnancy 299
  with IUD 49
edible plants, aphrodisiac 156
egg/egg cell 299. *See also* ovum
ejaculation 25, 149, 300. *See also* wet
    dreams
  delayed 231
  masturbation and 132–133
  number of sperm 19
  premature 229–230, 315
Electra complex 113
emotional independence, giving up 204
emotion, eyes and 114–115. *See
    also* body language
endometrium 300
enema 300
eonism 300
epididymis 15, 18, 20, 39, 300
erectile dysfunction. *See* erection
    problems
erection 300
  pre-birth and infancy 99
  prolonging 160, 257
erection problems 227–229
  pharmaceutical treatments for 161,
    229
  treating long-term 228
erogenous zones 128, 300
  breasts as 4–5
  disabilities and 242
  female 128
  male 129
erotic 300
erotica. *See* pornography
erotic touch 125
erotophobia 300
eunuch 300
everyday (ED) pill (contraception) 51,
    300
exhibitionism 185–186, 301

pill, the (contraceptive) 42–43, 50–51,
      314. *See also* progeston-only pill
      (POP)
   effects of development of 272
   male 315
pimps 188, 315
plateau 26
   climacteric and 41
   clitoris during 12
   during menopause 40
   female 22
   male 24
platonic love 315
pleasure, learning to enjoy 224
polyandry 315
polygamy 258, 315
polygyny 315
pornography 315
   acceptability 163
   debates on 274–275
   exhibitionism/voyeurism of 186
   hair in 174
   internet 190
   use of 162
positions, and achieving orgasm 235.
      See also specific positions
posthitis 63, 315
posture, sexual attraction and 117–118
pre-come/pre-cum 315
preening 119
pregnancy, unplanned
   poor sex education and 104
premarital sex 315
   religious attitudes to 276–278
premature ejaculation. *See* ejaculation,
      premature
pre-menstrual syndrome (PMS) 38
prepuce (foreskin) 14, 16, 58, 315
   inflammation of. *See* posthitis
   removal of. *See* circumcision
priapism 315–316
primer pheromones. *See* pheromones
Prince Albert 177, 316. *See also* piercing
problems 223–226
   female 232–235

male 227–231
pro-choice movement 273
proctitis 63, 316
production 18–19
progesterone 316
   effects of 38
progestogen 316
progestogen-only pill (POP) 52, 316
promiscuous 187, 275, 316
prostate gland 15, 316
   female equivalent. *See* G-spot
prostitution/prostitutes 187–189, 316.
      See also courtesans; hetarai; sex
      worker
   19th century 270
   ancient Chinese 160
   ancient Egyptian 253
   Hebrew 249
   law and 189
   professional relationship 187
   recent changes 189
   society and 188
puberty 31, 316
   female 32–34
   male 34–36
   physical changes during 32–36
   sex education during 103–104
pubic bone 316
pubic hair 33, 36, 174, 316
pubic lice 63, 316
public zone (personal territory) 116
pudendum/pudenda 1, 317
'pure love', concept of 252, 259, 266

Q

queen 95, 317. *See also* drag queens
queer 317

R

radical sex 317
rainbow 184, 317
rainbow flag 317
Ramayana 317
rape 75–76, 317

temperature method (contraception) 45, 323

termination. *See* abortion

testes 16, 323
  physiology 18

testicles. *See* testes

testicular self-examination (TSE) 19–20

testosterone 323–324
  effects of 39
  masturbation and 132
  on sex drive 130

Thai beads 167, 324

thrush. *See* candida albicans

ticklers 165, 324

touch/touching 123–125
  in loving relationship 124–125
  sexual 125
  types of 124

transsexualism 94, 96–98, 324

transvestism 94–95, 324
  prostitutes 189

tribadism 147, 324

trichomoniasis 67, 324

tricking 324

troilism 325

Ts (contraception) 49

twins 29
  sexual orientation in 90

U

uncut 325

unprotected sex 55, 72, 325

unresponsiveness 223–224
  long-term 224
  occasional 223

urethra 325
  female 2
  inflammation of. *See* urethritis
  male 14–15

urethritis 63, 325
  non-gonococcal. *See* non-gonococcal
    urethritis

urolagnia 325. *See also* water sports

uterus (womb) 325

V

vacuum device 171, 325

vagina 1–3
  hygiene 56
  inflammation of. *See* vaginitis
  penis size and 9
  physiology 8
  self-care system 10
  substitute 169
  worries about size 232

vaginal fluid 9–10, 137
  taste 137

vaginal intercourse 85

vaginal opening 2–3

vaginal orgasms 13, 149

vaginal self-examination 13

vaginismus 8, 326
  masturbation and 132
  overcoming 233

vaginitis 63, 326

vaginosis, bacterial (gardnerella) 64, 291

vas deferens 15, 326

vasectomy 54, 326
  Islamic attitudes to 278

vasocongestion 326

veneral disease (VD) 62, 326

vestibule 1–2, 326

Viagra. *See* erection problems,
    pharmaceutical treatments for

vibrators 168–170, 326. *See also* penis
    vibrators
  anal 167, 290

virgin 9, 211, 232, 327

virginity, evidence of. *See* hymen

Virgin Mary, cult of 266

virtual reality sex 191

voice, changes in puberty 34, 36

voyeur/voyeurism 185–186, 327
  fantasies 196

vulva 1–3, 327
  anatomy 3
  removal of 59

W

Y

Lightning Source UK Ltd.
Milton Keynes UK
UKOW040638060713

213348UK00005B/62/P